The Dreams
of a
Master

Also by Jesus Garcia:

The Love of a Master

The Dreams
of a
Master

By Rev. Jesus Garcia, D.S.S.
Scott J-R Publishing

The Dreams of a Master
© 2019, 2020
Scott J-R Productions. ® All rights reserved.

Library of Congress Control Number: 2018902972

Cover and Interior Design by Ana Arango
© 2019 Scott J-R Productions

The Mystical Traveler Cover Art © 1985 Lawrence Whittaker.
All rights to reproduction reserved.

The Priestess of the Light art by Larry Whitaker
© 1988 Lawrence Whittaker. All rights to reproduction reserved.

Scott J-R Productions c/o Jesus Garcia, D.S.S.
http://www.soultranscendence.com
utah7@mac.com – (213) 500-2700

Dream Voyages by John-Roger, D.S.S., revised edition
© 1992 Mandeville Press

Fulfilling Your Spiritual Promise by John-Roger, D.S.S.
© 2006 Mandeville Press

Gestalt Therapy Verbatim by Frederick S. Perls
© 1969 Real People Press

Getting Things Done® (GTD®): *The Art of Stress-Free Productivity*,
revised edition by David Allen © 2015 Penguin Books

Leap of Perception: The Transforming Power of Your Attention by Penney Peirce
© 2013 Atria Books/Beyond Words.

Power vs. Force: The Hidden Determinants of Human Behavior
by Dr. David Hawkins © 2012 Hay House.

Excerpts from recorded seminars by John-Roger, D.S.S.
© 1968–2019 Movement of Spiritual Inner Awareness
and Peace Theological Seminary & College of Philosophy

Excerpts from *Spiritual Gems* and *Spiritual Letters* of Hazur Maharaj Sawan Singh (English translation) © 1965 by Radhasoami Satsang Beas

"Ithaka" poem by C.P Cavafy, 1911

Photos by Laurie Lerner, © 1988 Laurie Lerner

Photos by Betty Bennett and David Sand
© 2019 Movement of Spiritual Inner Awareness

Photos by Jesus Garcia, © 2019 Scott J-R Productions. ®

Printed in the United States of America

ISBN 978-0-9996010-2-0

Books by Dr. John-Roger

Blessings of Light

The Consciousness of Soul

Divine Essence

Dream Voyages

Forgiveness–The Key to the Kingdom

God Is Your Partner

Inner Worlds of Meditation

The Journey of a Soul

Living Love from the Spiritual Heart

Living the Spiritual Principles of Health and Well-Being (with Paul Kaye)

Loving Each Day

Loving Each Day for Moms & Dads

Loving Each Day for Peacemakers

Manual on Using the Light

Momentum: Letting Love Lead (with Paul Kaye)

Passage Into Spirit

The Path to Mastership

The Power Within You

Psychic Protection

Relationships: Love, Marriage and Spirit

Service & Giving (with Paul Kaye)

Sex, Spirit and You

The Spiritual Family

Spiritual High (with Michael McBay)

The Spiritual Promise

Spiritual Warrior: The Art of Spiritual Living

The Tao of Spirit

Walking with the Lord

Wayshower

The Way Out Book

Wealth & Higher Consciousness

What's It Like Being You? (with Paul Kaye)

When Are You Coming Home? (with Pauli Sanderson)

Wisdoms of the Spiritual Heart

Dr. John Morton Books

The Blessings Already Are
You Are the Blessings

*Dedicated to the two Mystical Travelers for whom I've had
the privilege of serving:*

*John-Roger, always my Sound Current Master,
Wayshower, and friend;*

*and John Morton, my brother the Traveler who inspired
me to serve my Traveler, J-R.*

"It's important to know that there are many levels of illusion and temptation that you may encounter in the dream state. The teachings of this world are not separate from your dreams. What you learn here also applies to those other levels, just as the teachings you learn there apply to this level."

– JOHN-ROGER, D.S.S.

Table of Contents

Foreword . . . . *xiii*
Prologue . . . . *xxi*
1. Addictions, Aliens, and Crop Circles *1*
2. Overcoming Fear and Fixations *11*
3. No Business Like Show Business *21*
4. Facilitating Dream Guidance *27*
5. Recording Dreams *37*
6. David Bowie and Elton John *45*
7. About Spiritual Exercises *51*
8. A Week with Ishwar Puri *59*
9. Running Away or Running Home? *67*
10. There Is No Separation *73*
11. Yo No Se Contar *79*
12. Discernment in the Unconscious *95*
13. My Etheric Experiment *101*
14. Experience or Information? *109*
15. Consciousness, Health, and Healing Prayer *145*
16. Manifesting Abundance *151*
17. Influence and Assumption *161*
18. Superheroes and Soul Transcendence *193*
19. Loyal Forces of the Opposition *199*

20. Premonitions	*211*
21. My Needs Are Met	*217*
Epilogue: Operation Beautify Mandeville	*223*
Appendix A—Travel Journal	*239*
Appendix B—Glossary of Terms	*281*
Appendix C—Resources	*295*
Ithaka	*301*
Acknowledgments	*305*
About the Author	*315*

Q: How can I discern the Traveler in my dreams?

John-Roger: "*There are several ways to do this. First, there is usually a special loving feeling that is present. Also, the Traveler will usually give you information in an uplifting way and will be very supportive and loving. The Traveler will not tell you anything inwardly or in a dream that he wouldn't tell you on the physical level, so you can always check out the information against what is in the Discourses and the MSIA tapes and books. Another way to know if it is the Traveler is that he will generally (but not always) come to you from your right side or from directly in front of you. If a form looking like me or John Morton comes from the left, it could be from the negative forces, so it's best to 'challenge' this form. You can do that by chanting your initiatory tone or the Hu. If it is of the negative power, it cannot stay in the presence of the tone. You can also ask it directly if it is of the Traveler; if it does not reply that it is, it is not the Traveler.*"

– JOHN-ROGER, D.S.S., *DREAM VOYAGES*
AND *FULFILLING YOUR SPIRITUAL PROMISE*

Q: Is there a way that I can become more attuned to the Christ consciousness through my dreams?

John-Roger: "Ask. As you go to sleep at night, you can ask that you be more attuned to that consciousness of the Christ. You can also ask that the Traveler work with you in whatever way is for your highest good and that you remember that which is beneficial for you to remember, in a way that you can understand. Then, when you wake up, you write down your dreams, or your sense of what went on in the dream state. Use all of this for your advancement. You can really set yourself up for success in having greater and greater awareness of the inner realms, and all of it can lead you to awareness of your Soul and the Soul realm if that is what you want and where you want to go. Baruch Bashan (The blessings already are.)"

– JOHN-ROGER, D.S.S., DREAM VOYAGES
AND FULFILLING YOUR SPIRITUAL PROMISE

Foreword

ह्यू

For most people involved in the Movement of Spiritual Inner Awareness (MSIA), it's hard to believe that it's been five years since our Wayshower, Mystical Traveler, and Preceptor John-Roger ("J-R") physically left the planet. Although much has changed since his transition in 2014, much has, thankfully, remained the same.

Even as we've mourned his loss, many Sound Current initiates have been able to strengthen—or awaken to—our inner connection to Spirit and the Traveler, which is even purer than any physical-level experience we may have had while J-R was alive. In fact, with thousands of ministers, initiates, and Discourse subscribers in dozens of MSIA communities around the globe, numerous students of the Traveler never had the opportunity to meet him personally; so in a way, they've had a head start on people who had regular contact with J-R.

The Dreams of a Master

J-R also lives on in his countless videos, audio seminars, meditations, books, and spiritual practices that he shared in his 50+ years as the Sound Current Master. And, of course, the current Mystical Traveler and Spiritual Director of MSIA, John Morton, continues to build on the foundation of loving that J-R created in his teachings of Soul Transcendence.

Rev. Jesus Garcia (Jsu or "Zeus," as J-R called him) was fortunate to spend more than a quarter century faithfully serving John-Roger on his personal staff, from 1988 until his transition in 2014. By his account, from the moment Jsu first laid eyes on J-R in person, he heard the inner call and honored it for half of his lifetime. Beyond recognizing J-R as his spiritual teacher, Jsu also considered him to be his surrogate father, a dynamic that was explored in depth throughout his first book, *The Love of a Master*. Seeing them together, joking and playing around or riding horses at Windermere Ranch in the mountains above Santa Barbara, California, was to see unconditional love in action.

Throughout their years together, while Jsu supported J-R on staff and in his travels, he also pursued a successful acting career, graduated from the Master and Doctor of Spiritual Science programs (M.S.S./D.S.S.) of Peace Theological Seminary and College of Philosophy (PTS), and co-produced several short films and three full-length feature movies with J-R. *Spiritual Warriors* was based on his teachings, *The Wayshower* was essentially a biopic of John-Roger's youth, and *Mystical Traveler* was a thoroughly researched documentary of his role as spiritual teacher and Sound Current master for thousands of followers around the world.

I would venture to say that only very few people were allowed to know the authentic Jesus Garcia back then. By his own admission in these pages, Jsu discouraged people from approaching him—as

Foreword

a bodyguard, his main concern was protecting J-R; as an actor, his default mode was performance. This made him seem remote and inaccessible at times.

In my observation, the loss of J-R affected Jsu deeply, and still does. During the months immediately following his transition, nearly everyone in our bereaved spiritual family was in need of consolation, comfort, and a sense of belonging. This was a time of tempering, softening, and maturing for Jsu. Today, not only is he far more approachable, but connecting with fellow ministers and initiates has become his primary focus and life purpose.

No doubt Jsu's fiancée Nicole—and their participation in the University of Santa Monica's Spiritual Psychology Master's program together just after J-R's passage into spirit—positively influenced his engagement with the world. Perhaps grief is like a river over time, wearing down the immutable stones until they dissolve, leaving only tenderness and compassion behind. Maybe J-R's transition bestowed us all with a legacy of infinite Grace that continues to bless each of us on our Souls' journeys.

Regardless of the reasons, I am grateful to have gotten to know Jsu as a friend over the past three years, through his MSIA seminars, book events, J-R video marathons, and spiritual counseling. Beyond the personality level, J-R's energy has been tangible in all my interactions with Jsu and in his writings, because of their special bond, which is still as present as ever. In my experience, he remains profoundly connected to the wisdom of the Traveler on the inner levels—and who's to say that 26 years of proximity to the Master might not be absorbed by osmosis over time?

Jsu continues to reach out to our MSIA family around the world. Since launching *The Love of a Master* in late 2017, he has done numerous book tours across the U.S. and overseas. In support of his ministry of *Satsang*, or fellowship, he connects with people who love John-Roger, whether they knew him personally or not. Acknowledging that we are all brothers and sisters in Spirit, he shares his experiences, answers questions, and gives everyone a voice to tell their own meaningful stories. He does this all on a volunteer basis, through his own personal ministry.

Now, with *The Dreams of a Master*, Jsu has an opportunity to expand the legacy of John-Roger's abiding love for all of us and to deepen the fellowship of our global spiritual family. Along with many others, I look forward to experiencing *Satsang* with Zeus often in the months and years ahead.

Rev. Teri Breier
June 30, 2019
Los Angeles, California

"In the beginning was the Word, and the word was with God, and the Word was God. The same was in the beginning with God. All things were made by him; and without him was not any thing made that was made. In him was life; and the life was the light of men."

– JOHN 1:1-4, KJV

"All of you being Ministers have equal access to the power of the line of Melchizedek and Christ and the Traveler Consciousness and the Preceptor Consciousness. You only have the Preceptor Consciousness as long as I'm physically alive, and if I die that goes off your ministry. But the Melchizedek one stays, as well as the Christ and the Traveler.

"I'm going to make my ministry count on this planet, because my ministry is a silent ministry. My ministry is you. Your ministry is out in the world."

– JOHN-ROGER, D.S.S.

"You never will make a mistake, so long as you keep in mind to act simply as the Master's agent. Then let Him take care of all results which may follow."

– HUZUR MAHARAJ SAWAN SINGH, *SPIRITUAL GEMS*

*"'Satsang' has more than one meaning: First, it means the meeting of the Master and a disciple. Second, it means the meeting of all Satsangis who may attend, whether the Guru is present in body or not. There is no formality about it, none at all. It is a simple meeting of all disciples who can attend. We avoid formality and anything that may have the appearance of a rigid organization. The less organization, the better. And there must be no idea of leadership.
The only leader in Sant Mat is the Guru.
Just the Master and His disciples meeting together is the only organization we have."*

– Huzur Maharaj Sawan Singh, *Spiritual Gems*

*"Spiritual path is to discover your true identity
... which is The Ocean and not the drop."*

– Ishwar Puri

(**Ishwar Puri** is the initiate of His beloved Satguru Hazur Baba Sawan Singh Ji, the Great Master.)

Prologue

It's been more than five years since my friend, father figure, teacher, and Mystical Traveler John-Roger passed into Spirit on October 22, 2014. Picking up where my first book, *The Love of a Master*, left off, *The Dreams of a Master* relates my experiences of navigating life since his transition.

The primary theme of this book is the discernment of dreams, and how the inner world is far more important than the material plane. I'm diving deep into the divine unknown. I've traveled the world and talked to many people who are also in the divine unknown, with their comfort zones being challenged. I suggest that as you read, look past the word level and use my book to tap into John-Roger's energy and the Christ Consciousness, which I have continually asked to be present in these pages. Let this book be, not a stumbling block, but a boost for finding the Traveler inside of you so you can follow that into the heart of God.

The Dreams of a Master

Initially, I wrote *The Love of a Master* for myself, then at some point it became about sharing the book widely so more people would hear my story. This was the catalyst for me to travel and join in Satsang (fellowship) with other disciples of the Traveler around U.S. and the world. Connecting in this way reflected back to me over and over that "Where two or more are gathered, there Jesus is"… and there J-R is also. During community sharings, I realized that something special happens when we get together in Satsang with a focus on the Loving—our world, our consciousness, and our inner awareness can change dramatically.

In particular, my consciousness began to transform when my fiancée Nicole and I started the University of Santa Monica (USM) Master's in Spiritual Psychology program, right after J-R passed into Spirit. She, along with Founding Faculty Drs. Ron and Mary Hulnick, were my go-to "Master ministers" during that time. We were among the final cohort to earn a degree, and the whole two-year process was fantastic. For the second-year Mastery Project requirement, I chose to write *The Love of a Master*.

One year after graduating USM in August 2016, I launched my book at the Mystic Journey metaphysical bookstore in Venice, California, on September 24, 2017. This was my first experience sharing with MSIA ministers and initiates and also dramatically deepened my intuitive contact with the direct knowing of the divine. It was a process of stepping into the divine unknown and taking chances to go to those places that I normally wouldn't go—inwardly as well as out in the world. My intuitively guided travels have taken me to over a dozen MSIA communities, literally around the globe.

Prologue

From fall 2017 to fall 2019 (as of this writing), I have visited 19 countries (some more than once) on all six inhabited continents during my Love of a Master World Tour, including:

North America – multiple U.S. states and Mexico
South America – Argentina, Brazil, Chile, and Colombia
Asia – China and Russia (as well as the eastern European side)
Europe – Bulgaria, France, Germany, Greece, Netherlands, Switzerland, Spain, and U.K.
Africa/Middle East – Israel and Nigeria
Australia

Due to the extent of my travels, the organization of *The Dreams of a Master* is far from linear. It is a direct reflection of my time "on the road" while I was giving book talks, presenting John-Roger video marathons, conducting Question and Answer sessions, shooting Facebook Live videos, and audio journaling. Where possible, I have indicated the location and source of these edited transcriptions. Some material from the original audio or video recordings has been moved and combined with similarly themed sections. You may find some of the text to be repetitious, since I responded to similar questions at various events. See Appendix A for reprinted articles about these trips that originally appeared in MSIA's online blog, *New Day Herald* and are now hosted on my website at www.soultranscendence.com/our-impact.

I have also included descriptions of numerous practices that I have incorporated into my personal spiritual regimen over the past three decades, which may be supportive for you. I'd like to be clear up front that everything in these pages, including quotes, meditations, spiritual processes, J-R's guidance, and so on, are all coming from my direct experience, interpretation, and recollections, colored by the lens of my perception and the passing of time.

Consequently, my memories may not be 100% accurate; so before embarking on any exercises I discuss here, please be sure to check out John-Roger's specific instructions first. To learn more about John-Roger, visit www.msia.org. References to specific MSIA materials are provided within the text; stock numbers are listed near the back of the book in **Appendix C–Resources**. Most items cited are available for purchase at www.msia.org/store and some can be found on Amazon.

J-R often suggested spending two or three years to truly understand something, whether it is a relationship, new job, or other major life change—yet even by fall 2017, his absence was still new to me. Recently, under the guidance of Revs. Robert Waterman and Karey Thorne, I discovered why it was so important for me to spend time away from Los Angeles during that period, up until now. I realized that I had been viewing my three decades living at the Mandeville Canyon house through the lens of sentimentality, which greatly distorted my perception. I'll talk more about that in the following pages.

Having spent 26 years with J-R, my perception has been colored by some very unique shades. Although there are people who were with him longer, I was present with him every single day during those years, unless I was shooting a film. A few others were there day to day, but I am choosing to write about my experiences as part of my ministry.

As time passes, more information is coming in from Spirit through me, to include in other books and writings. Perhaps it's all just really "ham and eggs," as J-R used to say; only words on a piece of paper. But in between those words on that piece of paper is space and between the black and the white is space, and in that space, is Spirit. It is that energy you are actually picking up as you read or listen to the audio book. I deeply appreciate your support of Jesus Garcia Ministries, as a reader of this book.

Globally, there are more than 5,000 Movement of Spiritual Inner Awareness (MSIA) ministers and initiates, who each can write their own book and share their story. I lovingly invite you all to do so if you feel called by Spirit.

From my point of view, the state of MSIA is doing very well all over the world. The Traveler is connected everywhere, there is no border, there is no limit except what's in the mind and what people want to believe. In my experience, the Traveler as J-R is powerful everywhere, and this line has continuity with John Morton, the current Traveler, who is working everywhere.

"...the greatest similarity we have of all of these groups that are out of the Sound Current would be the Surat Shabd Yoga out of India, out of Hazur Sawan Singh, who is the great Master that brought it forward through the line of the Sikhs. I have the same spiritual lineage as that."

– John-Roger, D.S.S.
(May 30, 1982, Q&A in Gustavus, Alaska)

Chapter 1

Addictions, Aliens, and Crop Circles

May 19, 2017

Nearly three years following John-Roger's transition, I recognized that a constant sense of depression had become my new "normal." Whether I was traveling or at home in L.A., I felt depressed, and still do sometimes. That's OK ... I appreciate my depression and don't take any pills for it. (There's nothing wrong with medication for people who need it; prescriptions can be very helpful under a doctor's supervision.)

It's not that I wanted to hurt myself in any way, but I missed J-R deeply and felt low all the time—which was understandable, considering that I had spent 26 years with this extraordinary man who had been my teacher, friend, and father figure.

In that realization, I identified addiction patterns I had taken on; not to any substances, thank God. But I was definitely hooked on coffee—and pizza. I love both of these things. Pizza handles my depression in a very cool way. It's not pharmaceutical, but it's right down the street, and so is Starbucks.

My food addictions went back a long way, and J-R had helped me to identify and release them several times. For instance, we often went to the movies with the guys on staff. I loved popcorn and J-R liked Red Vines. One night, he looked at me and said, "You know, you're having a bit too much of that. So how about staying away from popcorn for six months?" I responded, "Oh man! Six whole months?" That's how I first learned to be disciplined about not allowing something external, such as my addiction to popcorn, to get a hold of me.

This can apply to alcohol and other consciousness-altering substances, too. Personally, though, I was never much of a wine or beer drinker. My dependence issues tended to be around food and caffeine.

My coffee obsession started when Laura and John invited J-R up to the Seattle Goodwill Games in 1990. We brought one of Laura's kids up to Washington, and they took us out for coffee at this upstart spot called Starbucks. The guy there was talking about coffee beans. I tried one and couldn't put it down. So that was that ... I was officially a coffee bean addict.

And then Starbucks stores opened up everywhere; there was no place you couldn't find one. Their green logo was seared into my brain, so every day when I would drive J-R somewhere, I'd say, "I want to stop at Starbucks." I think I was up to seven or eight espressos a day. That's the artificial energy I used to power through life, rather than cultivating my inner vitality from Spirit. Even when we attended Peace Awareness Trainings, Living in Grace retreats, Conference, and other MSIA events, I was constantly buzzed on coffee beans.

Eventually, J-R started working on me. Whenever I'd ask, "Can I pull over to get a Starbucks?" He would respond, "No." So then I pushed back. "What does that mean?" What that meant was, Starbucks had a hold of me. With J-R's support, I switched up my coffee habit so it didn't feel like I was addicted. I started to go to Coffee Bean and Tea Leaf, along with other non-mainstream coffee shops instead, to break the pattern of surrendering my will to Starbucks' hypnotizing green logo.

In the end, this approach broke my addiction to coffee. Today, even though I still drink the stuff, it is no longer eight espressos a day. I certainly don't go to Starbucks as often as I did back then. So much of that was J-R working with me, breaking those habitual patterns, and talking about the addiction in a way that loosened its power over me.

However, on May 18, 2017, I was back in the throes of my coffee (and pizza) habit, still depressed about losing J-R three years earlier. I asked a friend, who is a holistic practitioner, to administer a NAD+ (*nicotinamide adenine dinucleotide*) solution IV, which is supposed to help with addictive behavior and mental focus. It lasted four hours; we started on Thursday night at 7 p.m. and I left around 12:30 a.m. Receiving the actual infusion was miserable, but I had fun spending time with my buddies. Being in fellowship together brought back many wonderful memories of J-R.

I awoke the next morning with more optimism and clarity than I had experienced in a long time. Looking out the window from

The Dreams of a Master

John-Roger, D.S.S. and John Morton, D.S.S.
leading crop circle tour group
in United Kingdom, 1998

the Mandeville house, I enjoyed its scenery, the same way I always had when I used to sleep in my bedroom loft there. I could hear the birds chirping and see the beautiful environment outside. It was very inspiring and a lot of things opened up for me then. I called the practitioner and shared my impression of the whole experience.

J-R said that things get crystallized in the body, whether it's food or substance abuse patterns, when you're trying to alleviate pain or trauma. I was consciously aware that my mind, emotions, and body at a cellular level had been traumatically inflicted on, which the NAD+ treatment had alleviated. I think this would be very supportive for soldiers coming from the war with PTSD, since it totally resets the brain without losing any cognitive abilities. That day I was very sharp in my thinking, my memory came back, and I could think of J-R without feeling down energetically. Two key memories came to mind that day that illustrate what I learned from the Master about seeing beyond the physical reality.

A while ago, we took a group on a crop circles tour to England. For several years, extraterrestrials supposedly were visiting the U.K. during the summer, where they created intricate, beautiful crop circles. Seeing them close-up, the phenomenon is something that is believable on a metaphysical level. However, from a physical point of view, it would take a lot of intensive work; it seems next to impossible for humans to create those intricate designs, as the hoax debunkers claim. I wrote about this in *The Love of a Master* book.

You can't see the overall patterns when you're standing in the fields on these circles. But the stems of the crops (typically wheat, barley, canola, or other grains) are quite thick and fibrous, similar to strong elephant grass or hay. They are never broken, only bent about an inch from the ground, laid out in one direction or another, and sometimes even layered like a braid. There is no physical instrument that could do that, and certainly any vehicles like a truck would leave tracks behind. Our tour guide explained that some kind of radiant heat combined with weight created the patterns. Some were more circular and laid out in either direction. Others would start out clockwise, but ended up counter-clockwise for a portion of the arc; it was never predictable or fully explained.

The "manmade" explanation involves cutting pieces of plywood symmetrically, then laying them down or spinning them on an axis with a lot of pressure—which would end up breaking, not bending, the stems. Perhaps some of the rudimentary hoax crop circles were created that way, but the genuine ones clearly involve far more than that.

After a full day of touring crop circles, a lot of people left the bus that evening, but J-R, Nat, and I stayed on board. We were out in the countryside without city lights to diffuse the stars and constellations, and we noticed odd movements up in the sky. Then J-R started pointing out unidentified flying objects (UFOs), as differentiated from the blinking lights of a plane. It was incredible! I bring this up because J-R was always teaching us and demonstrating the subtle energies that are out in the world. So it's more than just this dense manifestation called Earth and the physical body; there are many levels, and J-R was in touch with all of them.

We also traveled to Medjugorje, in what used to be Yugoslavia before the war. There were young kids having visions of the Mother Mary talking to them, which intrigued J-R and something I never would forget, which would allow me to be open to all things. For the *Mystical Traveler* film, I interviewed a long-time MSIA minister, Ashtar Athena SherAn (an avatar formerly known as SaiVahni), who said a lot of pretty far-out things about

UFOs and geodesic domes. When I repeated this to J-R, he said it was all accurate. I would have loved to include it in the movie, mainly because J-R loved scientific stuff like that, but we just didn't have room. (You can watch all the full interviews on YouTube's "Mystical Traveler" channel.)

Interestingly, I heard from Ishwar Puri about the Space Brothers who are looking for a Guru or to connect with humans. This matches up with J-R's explanation that aliens actually exist in other dimensions, yet they're still part of the realms below Soul. So if the Traveler is working on all those levels, then it's a good bet they want to connect in some ways and end up becoming partners and friendlies. This is not some kind of Star Wars phenomenon or Independence Day, where they emerge as hostile and want to blow up the White House. We're talking about something very multi-dimensional.

In 1997, I traveled to Switzerland with J-R for some business. John, Laura, Claire, and baby Zane came along, too, which was really nice. We all did some sightseeing together, but when the family had to head back for school, J-R and I stayed behind. We went to Zermatt near the Matterhorn and drove through other areas of the Swiss and Italian Alps.

J-R was constantly aware of the dimensions beyond the physical level and encouraged me to be open to seeing other realms. As I was driving him through the Alps, he pointed to the mountaintops, saying, "Look at those etheric temples." I tried to look directly but couldn't really see anything. He said not to look at them straight on but to relax my vision and look from the side. J-R explained the first thing we usually notice is the floaters in our eyes; but if you don't push yourself, these sort of etheric, normally invisible things like the temples show up obliquely in our peripheral vision.

Eventually, I was able to see them in a pattern that followed along the upper peaks of the Alps.

That was a spectacular experience. I still cannot describe what it was like to drive with the Master for all those years, just the two of us. We didn't always do a Q and A session in the car! It was mostly all about taking care of him; driving smoothly enough to allow him to leave his body and do the spiritual work. J-R would send the Light ahead of us to create a clear, safe path to drive through.

"You stop fixations of the past by not entering into reverie and memory of the past. You stop fixations of the future by not moving into fantasy and wishful thinking about what's coming up. You live now, entirely present and participating in each moment of your life, and your life just unfolds to you in the way that is right and proper for you."

– JOHN-ROGER, D.S.S., *THE WAY OUT BOOK*

"When you do not maintain your awareness of and your responsibility to the now, the present moment, you separate yourself from your reality. And in that separation, you can create your own hell. Then you know your Soul only by the reflection of those who know the Soul, rather than through your own direct experience of the Soul."

– JOHN-ROGER, D.S.S., *LOVING EACH DAY*

Chapter 2

Overcoming Fear and Fixations

हू

July 3, 2018

Much of the relationship between me and J-R was through dreams. I love dreams and have been aware of mine almost since birth. Since I was very young, I've had a recurring dream of a beautiful, Tudor-style home surrounded by a wrought iron fence, somewhere in the English countryside. The weather is wintry, the occupants have passed into Spirit, and I seem to be "gone" somehow; perhaps I was part of the family or had loved one of them. In the dream, I can see myself looking out the window, wanting but unable to leave the house.

After J-R passed into spirit, my strong attachment to the Mandeville house where we lived was triggering some unconscious, sentimental thoughts that made me feel like a distant kind of ghost. I repeatedly had thoughts like, "Oh, it's not the same anymore. I wish he was still here." Of course, I was missing him on both the conscious and basic self levels.

This fixation distorted my perception of reality. The same thing happened whenever I was at PRANA (where MSIA is headquartered) or 2101 Wilshire Boulevard, the Santa Monica campus owned by MSIA—everything started there for me inside that building: USM, Insight, J-R seminars, M.S.S./D.S.S. classes, and so much more.

That experience brings to mind the "inner objects" technique taught by renowned acting coach Uta Hagen, which I learned during my long-ago acting studies. Often there is a traumatic or significant memory associated with certain objects, which sets off a series of emotional reactions, that actors can tap into and draw upon. In her fantastic book, *A Challenge for the Actor*, Hagen relates the example of being outside her apartment as it was burning down; she noticed a hose running from the fire truck to the building, with water everywhere. After that event, whenever she wanted to tap into the feeling of loss, focusing on that fire hose in the gutter would bring up the associated emotions.

Similarly, in the Stanislavsky System, there are sensory exercises where you think of a memory and tap into its related sensations. Even something simple, like pretending to hold a hot cup of coffee; you sense the warmth within your hands and see the steam rising from the top. Such an experience can be so vivid, you feel like it's really happening. Psychologically, this is similar to a Gestalt technique developed by Fritz Perls, which we studied at USM. However, after J-R's transition I was doing this process in reverse; I was not acting but living through a movie called "Sentimentality."

I sensed that this overwhelming nostalgia was related to my basic self level. I loved J-R's basic self and both of our basics were inseparable. The basic self is a subconscious part of us, similar to a young five-year-old inner child, that likes routine and supports habitual behavior. However, if this part senses that it is being abandoned, lied to, or betrayed with broken agreements by the high self and conscious self, it can sabotage and undermine through a lack of cooperation.

For instance, there was a period when I was rebelling, fighting inside myself, and not cooperating at all with what was going on. So J-R sent my basic self to missionary school and gave me a new, more cooperative basic self. Another time, during my baptism in Israel, the guardian angel I received from J-R was the Archangel Raphael. Those were both very supportive actions for my spiritual progression that really helped me a lot.

The sentimentality about Los Angeles and the Mandeville house after his transition dropped me into the reptilian or "lizard" brain that expresses self-preservation. My interpretation of this is that, during prehistorical times, when our caveman ancestors would encounter a predator such as a sabretooth tiger, an automatic "freeze, fight, or flight" response would kick in. Nowadays, that instinct still gets triggered when something occurs that we perceive as a threat to our survival. We go right into the reptilian brain, fear sets in, and a series of events takes place, known as the stress response.

Many people have said that there are only two ways to live your life: with love or fear. Love is connected to the right brain. Fear and worry come from the left brain, the negative aspects. The most important thing is to be aware when you flip to the left side, which is very linear. It can happen when we worry about being able to pay our bills or max out our credit card. Or it can happen when we hit a traffic jam while running late for an appointment, or if we get pulled over by a policeman flashing his lights into the rear view mirror. Our heart skips a beat, then races. Our mind starts chattering on auto-pilot: "Oh no! I messed up. What's going to happen? I'm not safe!" That is where the L.A. sentimentality took me for many months.

Now that I have some altitude, I can see where I was then and count my blessings. Moving into my right brain brings me into balance: "Everything looks good. I trust God and we'll figure this out together. I'll leave this in His hands and heart. Meanwhile, I'm going to go meditate, run, paint, create beauty."

There are other supportive methods that have helped me along the way, which I recommend. For instance, my friend David Allen developed the world-renowned Getting Things Done (GTD) organizational system. As a martial artist, he advocates the goal of having a "mind like water," referring to a pebble being absorbed by the pond it is tossed into. Essentially, the GTD method supports making the mind a servant; it is designed to get everything out of your head and into a trusted tracking system (digitally or written in a notebook). The way I experience this is that the system frees up my left brain so it isn't preoccupied with remembering details that put the mind into sequential self-preservation, which allows me to flow into the right brain. That's the whole key and it works that way for me, although others may use it differently. I know many wealthy businesspeople who use this system as a way to give themselves the freedom to follow a creative passion such as music, painting, and traveling, or actually use music and art to pull them into their right-brain creativity.

Overcoming Fear and Fixations

The session I mentioned in the Prologue with Robert Waterman and Karey Thorne revealed to me that this plane, the material level, is all a distortion, like a funhouse, where everything appears to be something it is not. It is similar to *The Matrix* movie, where the protagonist, Neo, is faced with the choice of taking a blue pill and remaining oblivious, or a red pill, which opens him up to the truth of reality, changing his consciousness for the better. Like Neo, I was plugged into the paradigm until I chose the red pill, then became conscious of what was really going on beneath the apparent reality of our world.

Through direct knowing and intuition, I learned that leaving town was important for me; by traveling all over the world, I would see there is actually no distortion or sentimentality. This allows me to bring John-Roger forward in the moment and not get stuck in nostalgia for the past.

As a result of this understanding, a transformational shift occurred inside of me. I was finally able to let go of my obsession with the Mandeville house, and on October 22, 2017, three years to the day that J-R transitioned, I moved out willingly and amicably. My current apartment in Santa Monica has an altar for J-R, and there are photos of him everywhere, reflecting the ongoing connection we have in the true reality, which is beyond what my senses can perceive.

I've concluded that nothing has really changed since J-R's transition, except his body is no longer on the planet. We, his initiates and ministers, are the living testament. However, I truly miss all those years that I sat in Satsang with the Master (the Sanskrit term for "sacred gathering with a teacher" or "getting together and speaking truth"). My present ministry of going out into the world and holding these meetings is now creating an environment where

The Dreams of a Master

Early days with J-R in Kenya, 1989

we all gather to create Satsang with each other, in sacred, honest communion with God, the Christ, the Preceptor, the Mystical Traveler, and John-Roger's energy.

During the University of Santa Monica's Consciousness, Health, and Healing curriculum, which functioned as the third year of its Master's in Spiritual Psychology program, we studied something called "entelechy." This refers to each person's innate calling, or Soul's purpose, using the metaphor of an acorn with potential that exists inside every one of us. Once we become aware of our entelechy and nurture the acorn, we begin to mature into a mighty oak tree.

In that class, I discovered that my "acorn" has always been related to travel. I love hanging out in airports, watching the people and planes come and go. In the old days (before 9/11), my mother used to bring us straight to the gate to wait for the arrival of relatives who were flying in. As a little boy holding my mom's hand, I was fascinated to look out the big window and see the huge Pan Am 747s and Continental DC-10s as they landed. Traveling in a car was another favorite childhood activity; sitting in the back seat and feeling the vibrations as we hit different grooves on the road. I would also play with square strawberry containers and other objects, using my imagination to make them into cars. All these activities naturally connected me with my right-brain creativity. What activity does that for you?

Intuitive counselor and author Penney Peirce suggests that if you immediately want to get right into your right brain, get down on all fours and start barking like a dog or meowing like a cat. What works best for me these days is singing karaoke, acting like a fool, and just being in the expansion. J-R used to say, at the moment of contraction, move into expansion. During a recent spiritual counseling, my client told me he felt like that things were coming down on him, which I identified as a left-brain issue. To shift that, he decided to go up on stage and perform a few minutes of standup comedy. He said he loved it and felt much freer afterwards. It's not about being famous—it's about expansion.

Circling back to inner objects and dreams, when I was a 17-year-old high school student in 1980, I dreamt vividly that President Ronald Reagan was going to be shot. I couldn't believe it; I'd wanted to be a psychic since I was little kid. I wondered, "Who do I tell? What will happen?" The next thing I knew, John Hinckley, Jr., shot Reagan in an assassination attempt. Since then, I have read many books on premonitions and déjà vu, as well as talking to J-R about it. There are several different dream states that you can experience. Déjà vu moments have usually been benchmarks about my own life, to show how I am doing. Sometimes they can be warnings. J-R used to say, it's either a warning or you're on track. I recommend journaling about such experiences to provide perspective; I've been keeping journals since I was a teenager.

Later, when I was a serious acting student, all the leading teachers—such as Howard Fine, Peggy Fury, and Stella Adler—told us to start journaling. Then when I moved into J-R's home and started working on his staff, journal writing was highly encouraged. God speaks to us in many forms and you better believe that when we're down and out of the body, there will be some images and information that appear. Life keeps us busy and sometimes we don't find the time to be open and receptive. But once you lay down, it's a perfect time to do Astral Travel or Soul Travel—on the other side, we do all sorts of traveling in many realms. "There are many rooms in my mansion." That's in the Bible and has been what J-R, God, and the Christ said. When you travel, you get information. Unlike many people, I love those crazy, chaotic, mixed-up dreams that seem so real, like falling from a long distance, car accidents, or getting killed or shot.

However, there may be some confusion involved in those kind of dreams, because they can be a combination of different levels. You might get caught up between the astral and causal realms, or maybe you're in the etheric level, about to burst into the Soul realm. You don't need to panic during those dreams. Many times I've experienced Soul Traveling in the chaotic crazies of the etheric realm—whoever invented that was genius, because they really want to scare you before you get to the Soul. It's like, the jig is up, time to get serious. But at that moment you've got to hang tight and follow through. That's something you start learning in dreams. A really accurate movie about what goes on in the inner levels is *Inception* by Christopher Nolan. It's a dream within a dream, just a fantastic film. I remember J-R saying that this movie is right on target and an accurate depiction of some of the realms of dreaming.

"Use your energy to go inside where you have developed your inner sight. Look with the eyes of the Beloved. The Beloved isn't just the Christ or the Mystical Traveler or God. The Beloved is You."

– JOHN-ROGER, D.S.S.

Chapter 3

No Business Like Show Business

घू

My career in show business was often a catalyst to learn many fascinating things from J-R. He worked with me quite a bit in relation to my acting, but it wasn't about getting famous. It could have been anything, like a job at McDonald's. He would support my intention to work, improve my acting skills, and audition for the roles that I wanted. If I was going after something for the wrong reasons, he would reflect that back to me and help me turn it around so I could get the job.

For instance, we worked a lot with the process of seeding to support my acting goals. [For more details on Seeding, see **Chapter 16, Manifesting Abundance**.] J-R instructed me on how to seed correctly. Ultimately, the best approach is giving it over to God, who always knows best what is for your highest good. Also, when you have a vision, it's not a bad idea to let the right-brain imagination go wild, because the imagination, via the astral level, will create a vivid and much more limitless picture than the mind; the mental level, or left brain, may be more apt to tear your vision apart with objections and judgments.

Another tool J-R used with me was remote viewing and ranging. For instance, let's say I wanted to work with someone like Andy Garcia, Benicio Del Toro, or John Travolta. In my imagination, I would fly into their production offices and visualize specifics, such as: "What would the office look like?" "How would it feel like to be there?"

Similarly, acting coach Stella Adler originated the "What if?" technique, which opens up the possibilities for everything that your mind won't consider. You put yourself in the character's shoes, then create a journal of your character's personality, emotions, behavior, motivations, and so on, always asking "What if…?" or "What would they do if…?" Through doing this, there is no limit to the possibility of what an actor can strive for with character development and in their career.

So I would combine this technique with the ranging practice that J-R taught me. At one point, I was ranging to Andy Garcia and had incredibly vivid, realistic dreams that we were working together. In a seminar, I heard J-R talk about dreams as a "dream reality" experience when you're on the other side. And if it's real there, then this physical existence is not actually real. So you can go back and forth, doing multi-dimensional things, from the astral, causal, physical, etheric, and Soul realms. As initiates, we use the Soul unit, or Soul energy, to traverse all those realms and clear karma on those levels because we have over-created here on the physical.

Soon after those dreams, I actually ended up working with Andy Garcia in *Lost City*; I also collaborated with Benicio Del Toro twice, in *Traffic* and *Che: Part One*, as a result of using this practice. These are great examples of things that I wanted that I put my intention toward creating. A clear, strong intention has so much power in it. Then messages can come to you through dreams, which you need to learn to interpret.

Dreams have been recognized for their spiritual wisdom since Biblical times. For instance, after Joseph interpreted the Egyptian Pharaoh's dreams accurately, he was promoted to an influential position. This indicates that the Pharaoh was aware of Spirit, even though he didn't know how to translate the messages he received.

The Dreams of a Master

J-R sitting in as a Director of Spiritual Warriors film while shooting at PRANA, 2004

"Allow your unconditional loving to expand into the unconsciousness. It may try to pull you over to make you drop into its sleep. What we do is an inner statement that says, 'My unconsciousness is being flooded with the unconditional loving of my Soul. And it is awakening. I am getting more of it every breath.'"

– JOHN-ROGER, D.S.S., *LOVING EACH DAY*

"To die, to sleep—No more—and by a sleep to say we end the heartache, and the thousand natural shocks that flesh is heir to. 'Tis a consummation devoutly to be wished. To die, to sleep—To sleep, perchance to dream: ay, there's the rub, for in that sleep of death what dreams may come when we have shuffled off this mortal coil, must give us pause."

– WILLIAM SHAKESPEARE, *HAMLET*

Chapter 4

Facilitating Dream Guidance

ॐ

*W*riting *The Love of a Master* book several years ago set the tone for me to move into *The Dreams of a Master*. Many times over the years, J-R called me a "dream prophet" or "dream master," because I was able to bring back my dreams in detail, and many things I dreamed about actually ended up coming true. For a long time, I've tracked this process using manuals and journals, which demonstrate that my prescient dreams have about a six-month window of predictability. I first became aware of this gift in 1980 at age 16 or 17, when I dreamed that then-President Reagan was going to be shot, several months before it happened (as described earlier in **Chapter 2**). That was the start of my intuitive ability to tap into universal knowing.

To connect more consciously to your dreams, in his book, *Dream Voyages*, J-R recommended keeping a journal next to your bed, drinking water before falling asleep, and asking for Spirit's assistance in the dream state. For instance, you can ask the Travelers, John-Roger, John Morton, the Christ or all, "Please give me some answers. I'd love to look into this situation. Can you show me more about such-and-such?" And then go to bed.

Sometimes, I have found it valuable to do the Flame Meditation exercise as a ritual before bedtime, which J-R described in *Dream Voyages* as well as in the *Inner Worlds of Meditation* book and audio packet. Basically, this involves lighting a candle, gazing into the flame, and sending any negativity, desires, needs, unhealthy preoccupations, etc., from your day into the flame. The fire burns it up. It's important not to go into a trance state during this process or to do it longer than five or ten minutes when you first start. Afterwards, drink a glass of water. Ask God from within, the Traveler, to be your guide—then let the dreams take you where they may.

Upon awakening in the morning, drink more water and record your dreams as best as you can, or even just a few recollections that come forward, in your dream journal. You can also ask Spirit throughout the day, "Please show me something that would elicit a response to remember my dreams." When I do this, nine times out of ten it comes through.

There are many great books by numerous authors that address the ability to predict events. In *One Mind* and *The Power of Premonitions*, Larry Dossey discusses how every person is capable of connecting to their inner knowing; thus, anyone can develop the talent of accessing foreknowledge, whether of a positive or negative nature.

What's important is that you can have this relationship with God not only during the day but also overnight as you sleep! The best thing about the sleep state is that it is actually quite similar to meditation; you are not really shutting everything down, but just setting aside the ego and body temporarily. Meanwhile, the Soul and higher consciousness are traveling and learning within the inner realms, as directed by your Spirit guide. My guide, of course, is the Mystical Traveler John-Roger. You may have many experiences of traveling on all different levels: the physical, astral, causal, mental, etheric, Soul and above—even if you don't consciously remember these experiences.

In her best-selling book, *Sacred Contracts: Awakening Your Divine Potential*, Carolyn Myss evokes the wisdom of many Eastern philosophers in suggesting that we each agree to our life lessons before we are born. Essentially, in our Soul form, we meet with a committee of etheric beings (which may include J-R, John Morton and/or the Christ) who explain what we will be doing and learning. Upon agreeing, we embody onto the planet again. I once had an exceptionally vivid dream that showed me how this process went prior to my current lifetime.

So is the course of our lives predestined? Or is it more like a premonition, tapping into the thread of our lifespan in advance? Many of the great Masters have implied that linear time is only an illusion, and J-R often said that, from a higher perspective, all experiences in everyone's lifetimes are occurring simultaneously. Basically, time is an artificial construct to keep everything from happening at once in our limited perceptions here on earth.

Have you ever had a strong sense of déjà vu—an awareness or "memory" that you have already lived through your current experience? This can be a sign that things are going well in your life. I love these moments, because I have personally found that instances of déjà vu serve as a benchmark, sign, beacon, or light beam that confirms that I am making progress on my path and am doing all

The Dreams of a Master

THE PRIESTESS OF LIGHT
© 1985 Lawrence Whittaker
All rights to reproduction reserved

right. On your path, in between marker one and marker two, you may stray a bit–wander over there, do that other thing, become a little distracted. When you hit marker two and experience déjà vu, you realize you're still on track and continue on. Do you see that it might be a confirmation that you did agree to your learnings before this lifetime?

Sometimes, however, dèjá vu can be a warning signal. Everything has to be checked out, you need to stay alert, be aware, and never drop your guard. All sorts of things might happen. In particular, whenever I'm driving, as John-Roger taught me, I remember to send the Light to the road ahead or envision an eight-square-foot cube of Light around me.

Intuitive counselor Penney Peirce discusses the concept of holographic perception and multiple centerpoints in her book, *Leap of Perception: The Transforming Power of Your Attention*. She suggests imagining a small diamond light radiating and expanding in your head, then your heart, and finally your tailbone; when the light in these three areas merge, you can "suddenly feel yourself in the center—as the center—of everything and anything… the entire unified field of consciousness-and-energy."

Similarly, J-R has shared about the purple flame lit in your heart. Purple is the sign of the Traveler, so I would recommend always visualizing a purple flame, or purple or white light, which can be a valuable imaginary process to enhance your Soul awareness. Or, if you have taken PTS's "Walking in the Light" workshop, you can do those processes. As J-R says, "If you don't know what the Soul realm is like, mock it up. What would it be like?"

Peirce also addresses the left-side and right-side brain influence. I myself am exceptionally right-brained, very intuitive; my preference is to stay there and stick to what I am good at. However, you need to balance both sides. I believe the analytical left brain can be a good support when "you use the mind as a servant," as both Peirce and J-R have said, which applies in particular to the left brain. Whereas, her statement, "the right brain is the Master," refers to intuition, creativity, and non-linear thought processes. In other words, I would say the Master represents the Soul.

So it is helpful to use the mind as a servant to assist you logistically, be a scientist; this is where spiritual science comes into play. With the left brain as a scientist, you can track sequentially, use deductive reasoning, and "check things out for yourself," as J-R always advised. Tracking is fantastic for spiritual warriors who want to know what's going on. Remember, it's important to use the left brain as a servant for the right brain, which is intuitive, artistic, imaginary, tapping into the cosmos, connecting to God, dreaming, and receiving messages from Spirit.

The Soul and above are realms that are non-verbal. I cannot explain it, and even J-R repeated often that there is no verbal or mental way to describe what takes place there. So whatever I am thinking, writing, and telling you, and that you are reading or listening to, is most accurately identified as the Universal Mind. Perhaps through my words (or J-R's words), you pick up the impulse of the Soul, then try to put words on it and this is what comes out. Ultimately, it is all a lie anyway. Because the truth is in your heart, in the loving, connecting to the Soul, traveling with the Traveler into the heart of God. That's the truth. The rest is what you think about it, how you feel about it, what you imagine or even fear about it.

In my experience, traversing through the Etheric, or unconscious, realm has seemed quite frightening—but that is almost always a precursor to having a fabulous Soul Traveling experience! There is an "angel at the gate" attempting to scare off anyone who doesn't belong there. But as an Initiate, the Traveler holds there, supports you, and gets you across.

Related to this are other ways to broaden your horizon on the inner levels. For instance, the variety of sounds that are a part of the Sound Current are something that many people have heard—the whooshing sound of blood flowing past your inner ear, bells tinkling, or a bubbling brook. You may experience a sense of profound quietness in the midst of the wilderness, yet simultaneously hear a lot of noise inside your mind. I call this "cosmic noise."

Your inner, spiritual ears represent a deeper level of awareness than what you hear with your outer, physical ears. By developing your spiritual ears and keeping them open, you may begin hearing messages from Spirit or the Mystical Traveler. This can be in the form of actual words you hear inwardly, pictures in your mind's eye, or even just a sense of inner knowing.

To become more aware of your spiritual hearing, focus on the area of your head midway between the ears, behind your eyes. This is where the seat of the Soul resides, also known as the "third eye." Once you shift your attention to that spot, simply sit in observation. That's the part of you who is the listener, the watcher. Then you may begin to hear those cosmic sounds or messages. It's important to know that the Traveler's energy is represented by purple Light and always comes from the right side. All of the Sound Current Masters, including John-Roger, have talked about this. So if you hear something from the left side, don't pay attention.

Personally, I don't just let anybody come up and start a conversation with me, to be clear on the inner. But J-R would always know how to tap into my inner hearing and communicate with me. Sometimes, this was in response to calling out for his assistance. We can call out for J-R by asking, "Oh, help!" and there is the Traveler, because he received your inner voice through his inner ear.

J-R helped me develop my inner hearing. Often, I would be in my room when he called my name inwardly. I would hear it in my inner ear and say, "That's J-R, wow! He's calling me exactly." Many times, I heard him say, "Zeus" in my right inner ear and walked to his bedroom, asking, "What's up?" He'd respond, "What?" and I'd say, "You called me." And he'd go, "Oh, I just want to make sure you're listening." So he knew what he was doing.

Many times since his transition, J-R has called me that way, and it's been 100% real. Recently, Nicole was in that same frequency. Some part of her would say my name inwardly, my inner ear would hear it, and I would ask, "What's going on?" And sure enough, she had called out for me. It was quite amazing.

Service

*"If you don't listen to the inner voice,
it shuts off.
The inner voice is noninflictive,
And to awaken it again
Takes a lot of prayer, a lot of devotion,
A lot of spiritual exercises,
And I'll tell you a way it opens
In a hurry:
Be of selfless service
To the people around you
That opens the heart.
The spirit heart opens,
And the communication of the Lord
Starts to come with you."*

-JOHN-ROGER, D.S.S.

"Our dream is the dream of God, the dream of our own divinity."

– JOHN-ROGER, D.S.S.

Chapter 5

Recording Dreams

घू

When we go to sleep at night, we lay the body down and put the mind to rest, which allows the Soul to travel within its consciousness to different realms. If you're fortunate enough to be an initiate of the Mystical Traveler and chant your *Simran*, you may be taken to the Soul realm and beyond. For more information, I highly recommend John-Roger's book, *Dream Voyages*, for an excellent discussion of *sleeping*, dreaming, night travels, and the levels of consciousness.

From day one of working on J-R's staff, I've done a process of "forgiving the day" before going to bed every night, which he spoke about many times. Basically, you watch the movie in your mind of all the things you did and interactions you had that day. Some of it might make you cringe or judge yourself, but the more neutral you remain, the faster you can come into balance. Just observe, send Light and love to it all, and ask for the clearing to take place, perhaps in the dream state. You may also pray for God to replenish and rejuvenate your body as you sleep. Use the manna from heaven to fill up your cup, so when you chant your tone, the energy of the *Simran* may come in. Ask Spirit to reveal the truth through your dreams and keep a journal and pen or mobile device on your nightstand to record any memories, awarenesses, or learnings that are present upon waking.

As I mentioned earlier, J-R used to call me a "dream prophet" because I would remember my dreams and bring them back so clearly. I feel this has dissipated lately, so I get up to audio record them on my phone while they are still fresh. Typing them takes too much time because I forget the details as I write. I love using OmniFocus, DEVONthink, Voice Record, or the EVERNOTE® applications as a way of capturing my thoughts and clearing my mind so I am not holding anything in there. *Mind like water.*

In general, writing things down, whether you are journaling, recording dreams, or scheduling appointments in a calendar, can be very supportive to keep your mind clear. From listening to tons of J-R videos and reading many books written by him and others, particularly David Allen's *Getting Things Done*, I've learned that the mind can be a huge problem if you don't make it your servant. If you give your mind mastery over you, you can create a lot of issues through your uncontrolled thoughts and feelings.

Another valuable technique that I suggest is regular journaling. There are numerous ways to keep a journal—handwritten in a blank book, typed online, or using any of various mobile apps that capture your voice. The method is up to you. You may choose to journal about your feelings, awarenesses, interactions, daily appreciation and gratitude, and/or record your dreams.

Over the years, I have identified four main categories of dreams. The first is what J-R calls *clairvoyant dreaming*. If I have a strong belief that what I dreamed is going to happen in real life, I'll write it down and watch for how long it takes to come through. Most of the time, premonitions are not designed to scare you, but as a warning to prepare a soft landing when it happens. It could also be about something good—your attitude determines how you see it.

When I have what seems to be a precognitive dream, or premonition, I write the date and subject in my online journal. I've heard J-R say that some dreams are dream reality experiences, so I'll write, "I had a dream reality experience" or if it's a premonition, I'll highlight that. I also track déjà vu or karmic dreams. Then I can go back to that date and check whether that premonition ended up coming true. I encourage you to create your own system that works for you.

Next, there's the karmic dream. This may appear as a very vivid experience of being in a car accident or other event, and it can feel extremely real. J-R often said that Grace allows us to clear such karma through our dreams instead of experiencing it physically. Writing it down can help to ground any learning you get from clearing the karma. Maybe it's an awareness to drive more safely or a prompt to apologize to someone.

Even after 34 years clean, I would sometimes have vivid dreams of falling off the wagon into substance abuse and addictions, losing myself. I'd be asking, "Is this real?" when all of a sudden I woke up and realized, "Thank God, I was dreaming!" In my journal, I wrote the date, then the category of "Karma, discernment" and a simple description: "Clearing karma. Thank God I'm awake. Drugs." The day following this dream, I had a great time.

The third kind of dream is a Sound Current or Mystical Traveler dream; what J-R calls *Soul dreaming* or *night travels*. This can be very similar to Soul Traveling, and often such dreams are a prelude to Soul Travel during the night. For instance, once I saw myself flying. It was very eerie. I went through a door and then "whoosh," I felt a breeze on my face.

When recording a Soul Travel experience or Sound Current dream, it's important to honor its sacredness by not sharing it with others; so I won't be writing about my own examples here. I use an app called "Voice Record," to capture the dream as quickly as I can, before I move fully into the awake state. As usual, I would date and title my journal entry with "Sound Current." You can go into detail, describing the level you were on, the sights and colors you saw, what sounds or smells were present. Did you hear anything from the chart of the realms: a breeze, thunder, running water, a flute? All these things illustrating where you were may assist when you are ready to write to John Morton for your next initiation.

The last type is what I call discernment dreams, which include déjà vu. J-R used to say this kind of dream is either a warning or a confirmation that all is well, so don't worry about it. As an example, just before I moved out of the Mandeville house, I dreamed of cobwebs. I didn't know how to interpret that; I just figured it was about things getting neglected, so I cleaned the house. For months after leaving, I went through the process of detaching from my ego attachment to memories and sentimentality. But when I was up at Mandeville recently, I saw the actual cobweb that I had seen in my dream nearly a year before, which was a déjà vu moment for me. So under my "Discernment" category, I wrote, "This is to remind me that things are good, and they are."

Some convoluted dreams are simply a compilation of the last things you did before bed: you fought with your partner, watched Narcos on Netflix, then started reading a book. Once asleep, you have a crazy dream that your boyfriend or girlfriend shoots you, then you are flying on a plane and end up in a dark place, but you don't know where that is, and then you wake up. This might be what J-R calls a *twilight dream*, which is resolving the day's activities. However, the airplane flight might indicate Soul Travel, or Soul flight. As you write down or record all the details, the type of dream often becomes clearer, and you can interpret the different aspects.

Going into detail about interpreting your dreams is beyond the scope of this book, but there is plenty of material available. Again, you might want to start with J-R's book, *Dream Voyages*, or his out-of-print book, *The Master Chohans of the Color Rays*. Another approach is the Gestalt method. Renowned psychotherapist Fritz Perls, whom we studied at University of Santa Monica, wrote, "In Gestalt therapy, we don't interpret dreams ... Instead of analyzing and further cutting up the dream, we want to bring it back to life."

In USM, they say, "How you relate to the issue IS the issue." If I have an issue with my mom, how I relate to it is my problem. There's not really an issue; my mom is just my mom. So I sit down with her and talk it out, then it's gone. When you have personal karma, how do you deal with that? The best approach is loving. That's why I do my best to get rid of everything possible from the mind, so I can move right into my loving and neutral observation. Loving doesn't mean to emotionalize or get caught up in emotional flooding. But that sometimes happens anyways. I find that journaling statements of gratitude every day keep things clear and moving in my consciousness. "I'm really grateful to be alive. I'm grateful to be breathing. I'm grateful for friends like you. I'm super grateful to have spent 26 years with J-R." Once I move into that place, I can overcome what I don't have.

The mind, with its correlating emotions, often convinces many people that they are lacking, that they've been abandoned or forsaken … but the truth is that not one Soul will be lost. The comforter is Spirit. Don't worry, it will all be taken care of. To be realistic, the mind is probably going to keep on worrying. Movement is the best way to dispel worry, concern, and negative thinking. Whenever there were problems with staff up at Mandeville, four miles up the canyon from Sunset Boulevard, J-R would tell that person to run down to Sunset and back up. That's about eight miles. When they returned, he'd ask, "How are you feeling?"

"Oh, I feel great, sweating."

"Go take a shower, then let's have dinner."

I've said earlier that healing practitioners can also help to clear things, because when two or more are gathered, you can bring in the energy of Spirit. Another point of view is, if you feel depressed or melancholy, that's an opportunity for you to spend time with yourself. We all have the ability to enter this kingdom inside and be with everyone from within. It's hard to feel alone, though. One part may be kicking and screaming, yet there's another part saying, "This is awesome because we get to go deal with stuff." It's a good time to ask those inner voices a bunch of questions. J-R did a great SAT seminar, "Which Voice Do You Follow?" that discussed how important it is to listen to only one voice: the voice of your heart. Everything else is mind chatter. Another seminar along those same lines is "Inner Voices: Diabolical or Heavenly?"

Lastly, with everything going on the world today, this is the time for spiritual warriors to hold firm in loving and send Light to those places that need it, without contributing to the negativity of againstness. Those of us who have studied J-R's teachings know how to do this. Regardless of your beliefs, universal truths found in religions like Christianity, such as: "Judge not least ye be judged"; "Love your neighbor as yourself"; "Love God with all your body, mind, and Soul"; and "If you do it to the least one, you do it to me," can be helpful precepts to follow as well.

Golden Spiral From the Deep
© 2017 Timothea Stewart

"Instead of cursing the darkness, light a candle."

– BENJAMIN FRANKLIN

Chapter 6

David Bowie and Elton John

हू

January 2019, New York City

New York City has always been a touchstone for me. It is the place where I can reboot, restructure, regroup and get my bearings; to check in on my path, my purpose, and where I'm going. Every time I come to NYC, I'm renewed. It's like a lighthouse in the vast ocean that helps me to navigate. J-R has always said after two years you'll know what to do. I do know what to do. I'm checking it and I continue forward with that.

Many of the flashbacks included in this book come from nocturnal dreams that I've had since John-Roger passed. It's important to remember that only the person who is dreaming can interpret their own dreams, although bouncing it off someone else can provide a different perspective to consider.

The Dreams of a Master

For instance, in early March 2018, I had a dream about David Bowie and Elton John. The way I approached it was to ask, "What do David Bowie and Elton John mean to me?" I recalled that when I was young and living in San Juan Capistrano, California, I really liked Elton John's music. At that time, I had a dog that I loved, who was my constant companion. We would have long, imagined talks; much later, I realized those were actually the same kind of dialogues I have today with my inner self.

Sadly, it happened that my dog's parents died, and their owners wanted their puppy back. When they came to take my dog away, I was devastated. That was one of the first really big losses in my life and represents an opportunity to heal, clear, and release another layer of the grief that has been so present since J-R's passing. It's a domino effect; losing J-R surfaced the old pain of losing my dog—so clearing that grief from many years ago helped me to heal the fresher grief of J-R's loss.

What's more, writing about this experience has helped me to see that I have been able to continue my inner dialogue even without an outer source, like my dog. In the same way, although J-R has passed physically, I still can—and do—continue my inner conversations with him.

The other person in my dream was David Bowie. When I was very young in Miami, Florida, each evening, my grandmother would walk me and my brother to the restaurant where our grandfather worked as a chef. As we walked down the street, I noticed posters of some strange, androgynous guy laying down. Looking back now, I realize that they were the album cover for David Bowie's *Diamond Dogs*. So I didn't understand then what I know now.

What did that mean to me? It was a metaphor or inner object that reminded me of a wonderful time in my life. I had my grandma and family. I was nurtured. There were no problems. We had our daily routine: my brother and I would play all day and eat mangos, then get called in by our granny. She would clean us up, feed us milk with sugar, put us down for a nap, and then take an early evening walk to see our grandpa and have dinner in his restaurant. Those were great, innocent times.

Perhaps David Bowie's presence in my dream represented nurturing, and Elton John was a confirmation that the true dialogue is an inner conversation, which helped me to adapt during the loss of both my childhood dog and my friend and teacher, J-R.

During my spiritual counseling, I do a lot of listening and observing as my client expresses what is going on for them, whether it's emotional, mental, or karmic issues. (Well, actually, everything is karmic.) I am able to see the various behavioral matrixes that J-R has talked about, such as how the physical, astral, causal, etheric, and Soul levels connect with those situations that the person is dealing with here on Earth, in this lifetime.

With this awareness, I am clear that it is not my role to fix anybody—they need to heal their own unresolved issues. Often I am able to see certain things where there is nothing for me to do but offer love. Ultimately, love is really all that anyone can offer someone else.

The Elton John dream was a great indication of the way Spirit talks to me in particular. It might be a similar process for some and different for others. All I can share is my own experience. Just keep in mind that you may not necessarily hear a voice but perhaps see images, or experience feelings or sensations.

The Dreams of a Master

Personally, I relate to objects and their meanings, which is perfect for my brain structure. Having studied acting for so many years, I learned that the meaning behind the props and scenery of a play or movie provided a lot of insight about my character. So this comes naturally to me.

Upon recognizing Elton John in the dream, I asked, "What does he mean to me?" As I explained earlier, Elton John represents both loss and comfort. His music comforted me during a time of loss when my dog was taken away, and it reminds me of the conversations I had with that dog inside of myself.

Today, in my mid-50s, I still spend a lot of time talking inwardly, which is the way that I nurture myself since losing J-R physically five years ago. Dreams have been a significant part of my life for as long as I can remember. After reading Penney Peirce's *Leap of Perception* in USM's Consciousness, Health, and Healing program, I was able to identify much of my process. J-R would say, when you name something, you take dominion over it, rather than it having dominion over you.

It's important to seek and go after whatever is bothering or attacking you. I was overrun by sentimentality that distorted my perception of what was actually happening in the inner level. Elton John's music nurtured me, so that's what I used to get through that difficult time. More recently, the sentimentality of losing J-R physically hit me quite hard. Through the help of others reflecting back to me, I was able to get into my right-side brain and see how my consciousness was distorting the situation.

David Hawkins said, "Perception is edited observation," which is so true—we observe something, then edit what we see through our own filters. I've come to realize that, while J-R's physical body may have passed, his inner consciousness has actually grown larger. We cannot understand or access that knowing with our minds. The brain takes us only so far; it is love that lifts us above to a higher perspective. We must rely upon the development of our higher consciousness, like an orb that surrounds the mind and the brain.

In *Leap of Perception*, Peirce says that human consciousness continues on, even after the brain is dead or has been damaged due to injury or illness. That's something we can all look forward to when our time comes. If we develop as much consciousness as possible here through practices like spiritual exercises (a foundation of J-R's teachings through the Movement of Spiritual Inner Awareness), then we can lift into the Soul Realm as much as we are allowed to enter while still embodied. I'm not sure that any part of our consciousness except the Soul itself is permitted there. And if the Soul has gathered experiences during that incarnation, then it brings those with it. See, this is a perfect example of how my brain is trying to make sense of something that it can't, because it's not made for those levels.

J-R once said that the reason books keep getting written is because no one's gotten it yet; it's not over. People continue to write (and read) books to appeal to the endless questioning of the mind. That's why it is vital to meditate, chant your mantra or tone, and take off to the higher planes. One sacred tone that is an open mantra for anyone to chant is "Hu" (Sanskrit for "God"), pronounced like the first syllable in "human" or as individual letters ("H…U…"). You can also chant "Ani-Hu" (ON–I–HU), which brings empathy, unity, and the love you have for all things.

"Practice spiritual exercises. Practice seeing the Light. Practice hearing the Sound. Practice seeing yourself through the eyes of the Master. Practice the Mystical Traveler consciousness."

– JOHN-ROGER, D.S.S.

Chapter 7

About Spiritual Exercises

हु

Spiritual exercises (often abbreviated s.e.'s), are the foundational practice of those who study Soul Transcendence in the Movement of Spiritual Inner Awareness (MSIA), including ministers, initiates, and Soul Awareness Discourse subscribers. Spiritual exercises are similar to, but different than, meditation or contemplation. Also referred to as *Simran* in Sanskrit, the practice involves " … joining the mind and attention to the Sound Current through [silently] chanting a spiritual tone such as 'Hu,' 'Ani-Hu,' or one's initiation tone." This assists you "in breaking through the illusions of the lower levels and eventually moving into Soul consciousness." (See **Appendix B–Glossary** for full definition.)

Active students in MSIA agree to work with the Mystical Travelers, John-Roger and John Morton, in order to connect the Soul to the Sound Current, Soul Travel, and once ordained, we minister to ourselves and the world through our divine connection to the ancient line of the Melchizedek Priesthood.

The Dreams of a Master

In *Fulfilling the Spiritual Promise*, Discourses, and many of his recorded seminars, J-R often said that devotional s.e.'s are better than mechanistic chanting or time-based sessions. Of course, I never heard J-R chant aloud, but I observed him "going out" thousands of times while I was driving him somewhere. My perception is that each time, he would leave his body and come back different, like a reboot. Essentially, going in and out of the body through the vehicle of chanting allows you to return with a new outlook on life. So whenever things seem "funky," do your *Simran*, chant your tone, get out of your body, and come back with a higher perspective.

I've found that most of the people I share with agree that we have fallen short in our devotional meditation and spiritual exercises—including myself. It's important to nurture that discipline of getting up to do them early in the morning, or routinely at nighttime, or whenever works best for you. J-R always said, "there's no wrong way to do s.e.'s, except not to do them." So just do them, whether it's five minutes or two hours—but do them devotionally.

However, J-R did say that the most optimal time to do s.e.'s was before dawn: 3:00 or 4:00 until 5:00 or 6:00 in the morning, while the rest of the world is still asleep. This has been my own preference for many years. Those of us on J-R's personal staff would typically be on the go all day, working, driving him to appointments, and other activities. Then we'd eat dinner and watch TV to wind down until everyone settled in for the evening; most went to bed, but one of us would stay with J-R to watch over him all night until morning.

Sometime very early in the morning, well before dawn, around 4 to 6 a.m., there is a "sweet spot" when the world is completely quiet. In that silence, you may start listening to the universe and the noise inside you, and the universe in you, then you start touching on that golden thread of divinity and away you go. It's a place that feels like an "inner twilight"—going in and out of consciousness, floating through the astral level, then POP! You hear a sound, take off, and ask J-R or John Morton to be with you as you Soul Travel.

Because J-R has always been my physical Traveler, I insist on traveling with him in the radiant form that I tap into. While I may see John in the dream state, I can sense J-R taking me often; his presence is bigger than ever on the inner levels.

Hands down, the quietest time for s.e.'s is between 4 and 6 a.m., or 5 and 7 a.m. After that, the leaf blowers start to power up or your neighbor's construction project gets underway, cars start driving by, and other daily noise begins. So if you can, I encourage you to do s.e.'s during that special time for the deepest experiences.

It's also very important to keep yourself clear. What I share here is something I learned from J-R, as well as Ishwar Puri and others; I also recommend reading *Spiritual Gems* by Sawan Singh or *The Path of the Masters* by Julian Johnson.

Basically, the idea is that you want to get rid of any negativity in your mind. So you chant your *Simran* and kick it out. J-R has said something to the effect that—I'm paraphrasing—the mind is a representative for the negative Kal power in your head. So how do you get out of your head and dissolve negativity? Chant your tone and kick it out.

If you're trying to make a decision, going inside and chanting your tone can be even more effective than kinesiology (also called muscle testing) or biofeedback. You'll get much clearer information through a direct connection with your intuition that way. Otherwise, you may be influenced by internal voices or your own mind talking to you, which you may mistakenly think is the Master, so you need to be very careful and check it out.

J-R used to say that muscle testing is a guideline or direction, not the final word. In other words, it is possible for you to direct it, even unconsciously, to get the result you want. While I'm a fan of muscle testing, I don't agree with doing it for every minor ten-percent-level choice in your life, which your basic self can handle—such as what food to eat, where to go to the bathroom, and which clothes to wear. By trivial muscle testing, you may allow a force field or negativity to come in and work with you.

In that case, you've already given yourself over to the mind or opinion, letting one Kal power after another decide what it wants to decide on. This can all be a good thing because it makes you stronger. The loyal forces of the opposition are there to help you grow and be strong.

However, by chanting my tone, I can be clear inside of myself, and then I know what my day will bring. There's no need to make it into a big production.

Spiritual exercises are a key part of Peace Awareness Trainings (PATs), the Spiritual Science programs (M.S.S. and D.S.S.), some Conference workshops, and other MSIA/PTS retreats. Often, following s.e.'s or a particularly sacred process, the facilitators send participants on a silent break. Time and time again over the years, I have observed myself talking, whispering, or otherwise communicating with friends during these breaks, which disperses the Traveler's energy from within. I'd like to encourage myself and others to honor silent breaks as a time to walk and commune with the Inner Master and the Sound Current. Maybe we can do a self-counseling inside or sit and listen to the Sound Current inside, behind the eyes, between the ears, and flow with that force and that source. I know it's hard not to talk when we see an old friend that we haven't seen in years, but we can save that for the meal breaks. To support our inner spiritual awareness, observe the Silence signs by remaining quiet so you can hear your Inner Master.

The Dreams of a Master

Japan, 1998

"A dead Master is not dead to his Initiates. The disciples on earth have lost the benefit of His physical form, no doubt, and for that they must go to His Successor. His Astral Form remains with them and if they have access to their own eye center they make contact with that Form and get guidance from it on the inner planes. In case they have not entered the eye center, and their attention is confined to the physical plane, their efforts should be to reach the eye center, while receiving encouragement and guidance from the Successor. Dead Masters are not dead for their Initiates, but they can not make new Initiates. This is done by the living Master."

– Huzur Maharaj Sawan Singh, Spiritual Gems

"You never will make a mistake, so long as you keep in mind to act simply as the Master's agent. Then let Him take care of all results which may follow.

"He who is born as human and by good luck is connected with the Sound Current and practices it, is great. He is the monarch of monarchs, for he will be one with the Creator."

– HUZUR MAHARAJ SAWAN SINGH, SPIRITUAL GEMS

"Spiritual path is to discover your true identity ... which is the ocean and not the drop."

– ISHWAR PURI

(**Ishwar Puri** is the initiate of His beloved Satguru Hazur Baba Sawan Singh Ji, the Great Master.)

Chapter 8

A Week with Ishwar Puri

धू

Wisconsin, April 2018

From March 31 through April 5, 2018, I spent a week at Ishwar Puri's retreat in Wisconsin for the annual Bhandara Celebration, which commemorates the anniversary of the passing into Spirit of Master Huzur Maharaj Sawan Singh on April 2, 1948. During this celebration, Ishwar shares stories about his life as an initiate of his Master—much as I do now about my time with John-Roger. Ishwar's stories moved me and resonated inside, so I began to share my own stories about J-R.

At one point, I noticed Ishwar being pushed out of the meeting center in a wheelchair. There was nothing wrong with him, it was just faster and easier than walking to get him to the car; felt a disturbance in my awareness and asked myself, "What am I doing here?" The intuitive part of my Soul responded, "Relax."

I recognized that the 26 years I had spent with J-R were primarily on the outer physical level … and now I was observing another "outer" master in action. I became very aware that in the three-and-a-half years since J-R passed into Spirit, he had been growing stronger and stronger inside me, deepening the true connection. All those times that J-R referenced Jesus by saying, "Go inside, the kingdom of God is inside" is all true. At that moment, I realized I didn't need to seek an outer recognition or acknowledgment of any sort, and I felt very elevated in that awareness.

The comfort I had experienced with J-R for all those years was amazing; he was really like a father to me. So when I lost J-R physically on October 22, 2014, at 2:49 in the morning, my basic self, as an inner five-year-old, freaked out. It triggered old memories and unresolved issues of not having a father present throughout much of my childhood. To overcome that missing piece, I often sought out elder people who could provide that sense of comfort, in school and in my community.

Along those lines, Ishwar seemed familiar to me, because he demonstrated mastership and had been an initiate of Sawan Singh, who was the Traveler before J-R. At first, it felt like, "this is it," and I got pulled in. As the week progressed, I almost felt like his staff was deliberately putting me off, or making me wait in the back. I didn't feel rejected, although it did cross my mind. Finally, I realized that I had waited six days to sit down and really talk with him and thought, "There I go again." It was the Law of Reversibility in action. "Do you really want to do this again? Will you step outside yourself once more and forget that inner connection?"

I was reminded that my true master is John-Roger. During the time I was there, it almost appeared that Ishwar's people were conspiring for (not against) me. The care and devotion they had for Ishwar, which I really loved, was reflected back to me. Similarly, when I look back at no longer being with J-R physically and moving out of the Mandeville house, it's as if there is nothing left there anymore. I recognize that the necessity to leave was all designed FOR me, so I could get up and go look for work. I also realized that trying to get the answers from anyone else meant undoing everything that J-R helped me to become. Rather, I need to let go of attachment to others' opinions, honor myself, and seek my own answers inside.

It was very clear to me that the inner energy was phenomenal. I experienced it and as I'm recording here, it's fleeing away. As I'm writing or speaking this, the problem is that my awareness is like a fragrance I am trying to articulate, but ruining it by attempting to put the experience into words and make sense of it grammatically. It reminds me of all those times J-R would say something like, "Everything I am telling you is a lie, but it's as close as I can get to explaining spiritual phenomena on the physical level. Always check everything out for yourself through your own experience."

My last full day at the Bhandara, celebrating the great master Sawan Singh and Ishwar Puri, was April 5, 2018; I would be leaving for home the next day. While waiting to see Ishwar in person, I reflected on the dreams I'd been having. In particular, early that morning, I had a phenomenal vision that reflected back to me this other side, while witnessing other devotees or *Satsangis*, as they are called here. I realized, "That's me and I'm seeing it from another perspective." The answer is not to run to the next person, but to experience freedom in cooperation with my basic self, to seek the inner awareness, to seek the kingdom.

I used to accept truisms like, "Seek the Kingdom of Heaven," "The Kingdom of Heaven is inside," and "I'm in the Kingdom," as Christ and others have said, on an intellectual level. I would think, "Oh yeah, of course, close your eyes and there it is," but not really get it inside. Now, however, I understand what that means as a direct knowing by first-hand experience—not by being told or repeating it or trying to figure it out in my left brain. Rather, this comes from my right brain: "I know it—I experienced it." It's flow … a oneness with God … integrated with my own experience.

Many times, J-R said something to the effect that what you are seeking is actually your own self; I've been having a direct experience of that. Looking for something outside of yourself is designed to make you go into the inner. The passing of J-R's body was the catalyst to get me to turn inward, not to seek and to close the door. It was genius the way J-R set this up—no longer living in his house, etc. At first, my viewpoint was a misinterpretation or misperception that I'm abandoned, alone, not valued, and other misinterpretation that were coming from a personal, hurt place within.

The further I've moved away from anything out there that pulls me with sentimentality, the less direct attachment I've felt. Now, I am no longer attached to the outside pull of the external world. Instead, I go within, and it's almost like it was all done for me; as if everyone and the universe conspired for me, not against me. Yet, it can be very easy to go into the negative perception and use it against yourself. In Wisconsin, I experienced the positive perception. I had to get away in order to really see this. By fooling my eyes and my perception of the world out there, I was able to go inside and it was beautiful.

Tracking dreams is a very important part of this spiritual progression for me. So I continue to record my dreams through the process that I explained earlier. Sometimes I do J-R's candle meditation before going to sleep. [See *Dream Voyages* or *Inner Worlds of Meditation* in **Appendix C—Resources**.] Start by calling in the Light, always for the highest good. Essentially, you focus on the burning flame and dump your negativity into it; I call this "negative dumping!" Don't allow yourself to go into a trance-like state, which J-R warns against. And keep it short when you are first attempting this process, because it can be pretty powerful. Afterwards, drink some water, then set an intention at bedtime that you are going to remember your dreams.

Also be aware of what you let into your mind before you go to sleep. Perhaps there is a television show you are hooked on or a book you are reading. I try to complete all my TV watching by 9 or 10 p.m. Sometimes I watch CNN as food for my brain; I'm not really interested in it, but it distracts my mind so I can do Soul Traveling on the other side. I'm not aware of the Soul Travel; I just know that I'm being used. And I always read just before bed, even just a few paragraphs of a Discourse; only enough to get me tapped into J-R's energy. Sometimes I play the Ani-Hu or Luxor Meditation audio or listen to the Soul Awareness Teachings, which are recorded seminars released by MSIA as a monthly subscription. If you are a Discourse subscriber, you should gauge for yourself what works best for you.

I have experienced nights when too much activity before bed over-stimulates me so I can't get to sleep. J-R actually suggested drinking a cup of coffee, tea, or juice when you are unable to sleep, once you have passed that threshold of naturally nodding off. It's kind of bizarre, but it works to lift your energy high enough for you to go back down and then get out of the body where you can really go traveling. So when you find yourself wide awake, in an agitated state after the midnight Soul Train has left the station, and you're left there staring at the wall, it means that you missed the wave, that frequency for you to leave. You're in a different state with jumpy legs, being run by your body—maybe even nervous and a little anxious. Get up, go for a walk, or drink something to raise the energy; then when you go back to bed and lay down, you will take off.

Ishwar and Toshi, 2016

*"We're in the flesh, and this is where we're going to work out much of our karma. We'll work out a good percentage of it here and the rest of it in the negative or psychic worlds while the body is sleeping.
If you don't get hung up on the physical world, you can feel yourself lifting."*

– JOHN-ROGER, D.S.S.

Chapter 9

Running Away or Running Home?

May/June 2018, Latin America

Once my first book was translated into both Spanish and Portuguese, new avenues opened up. In May and June 2018, I traveled to South America and Mexico to share *The Love of a Master* with many of the MSIA communities there. During that trip, I gained new awareness about traveling and dreams, which I share here in my journal entry from June 1:

> It has been quite a blessing to walk alongside the Traveler and Preceptor, John-Roger, and to have had that experience physically for 26 years. Inwardly, it is developing even more and more; I feel protected and guided. There are times where I'm left to my own karma, my own experience, so I can sit in it and then develop this love. Ultimately, we're all connected, so whether I'm pulling from my Soul or I'm pulling from J-R or God or Christ, it is true—not on a word level, but as

an experience—that the Kingdom of Heaven is inside and you can go in. And the Kingdom of Heaven is at hand.

I used to hear this, listen to it, but it never really landed. And now it's landing. So traveling has been quite a blessing for me. In particular, being in China in April allowed me to get physically far away from those worldly things that I identify with, assisting me to develop the inner familiarities, the inner paths, the inner guidance, the realness, the reality.

So much traveling far from home may look like a form of running away, but I realize it's actually something else. The smart part of me travels to gain greater awareness within myself and tap into the Traveler and Christ that is inside of all of us; these are not separate, but not quite the same either. From my viewpoint, the Christ energy is the cessation of againstness, which was J-R's definition of "peace"—letting go of anything you hold against a situation, another person, or even yourself. Simply, you cannot move into the flow of Love or Christ consciousness when you are against something. If the external is a reflection of inner reality, and you are experiencing againstness in your life, you most likely have againstness inside. This can look like judgment, conflict, resistance, anger, stubbornness, resentment, etc. Once I let go of my againstness (of which I had quite a bit), I moved into the Christ energy, which was absolutely amazing and purifying.

J-R said that dreaming should more accurately be called "dream reality experiences." For me, the most satisfying type of dream is Soul Traveling, where I can hear and even feel the Sound Current. Just before taking off, it can feel etheric and kind of scary, but it really isn't. At that moment, you let go and tremble like thunder. When you start to see colors or have different body sensations, you're breaking through. Upon waking, you may shudder or feel a breeze.

Occasionally, a Soul Travel experience has felt like someone pouring warm, soothing milk all over my body, giving me the best relief—when I wake up, nothing hurts! It's like going to a doctor on the other side and being fixed by Spirit. Now I understand better what J-R was doing whenever I drove him after giving a seminar or going through a hard time. He would leave his body and was able to reenergize, recharge, and bring in that Soulic energy there, so that he could be healed upon returning. Other times, we need to see a physical practitioner.

The Dreams of a Master

Wadi Rum walking into the desert, 2004

"The sacred scripture said that the 'seat of the Soul is in the third eye area.' The third eye area is usually represented as a pineal gland. So, if we're putting eyes in here some place we're saying something here. Also, we're saying, 'Often the mind is found to be associated within that same sphere.' We're talking about mind as being found in this area. <u>The mind is actually found outside the physical body. The brain is found inside the body and becomes just a thing that [has] relationships and associates things through the body out into the world for manifestation</u>. If it didn't, every time you thought, a thing would take place in and around your body immediately. Do you people understand that? Because thinking is very powerful and it produces energy and energy produces movement. So as you said, 'Oh I think I'll go outside' you would be starting to walk out. Sometimes people who aren't too intelligent are caught in that. So they haven't integrated the mind function down into the brain to have it distributed through the body. And that can be done. A person can be taught that. Autism–often found in this area. The mind (coming under the jurisdiction of the Kal power) has deputized the mind to keep the Soul imprisoned into this area as long as possible, and has given it all the legal authority to do so."

– JOHN-ROGER, D.S.S.

"At least once a day, allow yourself the freedom to think and dream for yourself."

– Albert Einstein

Chapter 10

There Is No Separation

हूं

June 2018, Mexico City

While visiting Mexico City, I spent a lot of time walking around the streets. When I walk, I'm one with the Spirit, one with God. I feel stifled if I'm shut up in a house or apartment. My friend David Allen says in his book, *Getting Things Done*, that great ideas and projects usually get created outside the office or workplace. So I like to go outside. Then I'm surrounded by new things to see, which facilitates a greater connection with God and Spirit.

This chapter was transcribed and edited from a live video that was broadcast on my Facebook page during one of my daily walks in Mexico City. As I usually do, I started by calling myself forward into the Light: "Lord God of the universe. Father-Mother God, we ask the Light of the Holy Spirit to surround, fill, and protect us. We ask for the Traveler and for John-Roger´s energy, as the

Preceptor, to clear any negativity and to bring me into greater alignment. Amen."

I've been calling in the Light for a long time but only using J-R's name in the last seven or so years. I think it might have been 2012, two years before J-R's transition, that Paul Kaye asked him, "Is it all right for ministers, initiates, and students of the Traveler to call forward the Light specifically in your name and energy?" J-R replied, "Sure," and that's how it started. I loved that. Since that was confirmed by J-R personally, I don't mind hearing people calling in J-R, or calling in his energy, or calling John-Roger's Light, because I'm all about that now. I lived with the man, and I lived with the energy. I'm fine with it. I've had amazing experiences that are just undeniable and inexplicable.

I've heard J-R say that you can tell a lot about someone by which book they last read or what movie they watched. He also told me a book can be absorbed by osmosis if you leave it next to your bed. I remember him saying that we are the living testament, which I interpret to mean finding your answers within, not from a book. You can read all sorts of books, but who is it reading the book? If there wasn't a person to read it, what would the book be? It would be only pages made from trees and binding, and thread, and some fonts and words that mean nothing, if it weren't for the reader, the watcher, the observer. On the one hand, I agree ... then again, I like selling my books! Recording my awarenesses on paper is a way to remember them and maybe even help somebody in the future who reads them.

This is a time when I don't feel any separation at all. It's a time of the disciples. We—the students of the Traveler—are all John-Roger's disciples now. Much like the Christ's disciples did two thousand years ago, we are going off to different places in the world to share his teachings. And that doesn't mean, "Here's a pamphlet—sign up." It means walking the path of the Masters as a minister ordained into the Melchizedek priesthood, as we do in the Movement of Spiritual Inner Awareness, as was taught by John-Roger, the founder. We walk with tremendous authority. We are initiates into the Sound Current of God and above all, we are Living Love. Simply walking in that focus brings the Light to those places, to ourselves, to our family, not like some kind of crusade, but as something we are called to do. I don't ask questions about this; I've had enough of a connection with J-R over the years that I can now easily distinguish between the counterfeit and the real Masters when I encounter them in the inner realms.

Earlier on this 2018 *Love of a Master* South America tour, I spent time in Bogotá, Colombia. During my spiritual exercises sessions one day, I tapped into what J-R calls the *Golden Thread*, which acts like a kind of elevator or hyperloop taking you right into the Sound Current. I'm sure that happened to me during my 26-plus years with J-R, but I wasn't as courageous.

As this was occurring, I saw many bright colors inwardly, which reminded me of the Peter Max poster near John Morton's office by the back staircase of the University of Santa Monica building. Then, from right to left, a man appeared with a beard who seemed to be a friend; but as he gazed at me, I got chills. In that moment, I realized that it was the negative power trying to pull me and many other people off their path. The disagreements and against-ness were actually a distraction from what we are about in MSIA: moving into the Spirit, studying Soul Transcendence, and doing s.e.'s. Above all, Love is the key. J-R used to say, "Love is how this thing works."

Although beautiful in some ways, that experience was really disturbing. I was told by an inner spiritual master that basically, "for every good thing you get, you're going to get a negative thing." It's all part of the process here, not in the wrong way, and you aren't going to hell. So along with this great experience I had was a lesson about the negative. If you don't have that awareness, then you're stuck in the karmic flow. It's like lava pouring downhill or a river. You have to be careful that you don't get burned and get pulled down.

However, when you're above Soul, you have no duality—such as left-right, up-down, good-bad, right-wrong. You're just Soul. So I say to myself, "This is where I was. I was below the Soul Realm, having experiences, having the Traveler take me, show me." Even though I miss not seeing J-R physically, I recognize that is putting him outside of me. When I'm Soul Traveling and moving with the Sound Current, I can tell that J-R is there, big time. There's really no difference.

Seeing J-R outside of me, putting myself here and him over there, leads to a sense of separation. When I'm truly, transcendently doing Soul Travel, it becomes an amazing experience to behold. As J-R would say, when you have those great experiences on the other side, you're not going to like it here much anymore. This Earth plane is like a garbage can—it can be really uncomfortable.

It's quite a balancing act to keep one foot in each of those realms without emotionally collapsing—being in the heart of God one moment, then here on Earth the next. The challenge is to bring the heart of God here, inside ourselves, so we can walk in this world while not being of this world.

There Is No Separation

Adriatic Cruise. Venice, 1989

"The Light is wonderful, but it doesn't come close to the Sound Current in exaltation. And when you get up higher, this becomes your manna from heaven. It's where you say you live by the word of God."

- JOHN-ROGER, D.S.S.,
ARE YOU LISTENING TO THE SOUND CURRENT

Chapter 11

Yo No Se Contar

घु

Q&A, June 2018 – Miami, Florida

When I was a kid, my stepfather used to call me *come mierda*, which means "feces eater" in Spanish. I never cared because I didn't know what it meant. I also think it was a common affectionate nickname in Cuba.

Much later, when I would audition for roles, if a producer or casting director told me I wasn't a good actor, I just continued what I was doing. I didn't care what they said; it just made me stronger. Once, while auditioning, the casting director wasn't paying attention; she was only going through the motions. This kind of thing made me strong, because it didn't matter to me.

That's what I learned by being with J-R. Whether it was my dad's insulting Spanish nickname for me, someone saying that

I'm not a good actor, or another person who thinks I am one in a million, *gracias a Dios yo no se contar* … (Thank God I didn't count …)

At a *The Love of a Master* book-signing and Q&A event that we held in Miami in June 2018, I responded to several questions from the audience. This chapter includes some of the most relevant answers and information that was shared. Unless otherwise indicated, all text below was spoken by me.

My life totally changed after J-R passed. Just before that happened, I fell in love, which saved me because I didn't want to be here. Until then, I was like a monk; it was all about the work. But finally God said, "Here, have a relationship!" I also started studying Spiritual Psychology for three years at University of Santa Monica. It was an amazing process. Earlier in his life, J-R studied psychology, too. It is so important to have some sense of psychology with awareness and observation.

For the next three years, I learned to listen. My new life would be about listening, but it wasn't about listening out there. It was about listening in here, inside. Then things started to happen.

I should have been dead a long time ago, but J-R helped me to open my mind. As an actor, my mind was restrictive, like a box. You can act with your mind or with your intuition. He also helped me with the sacred tones and Shabd Yoga, which is the connection with the Soul and the Sound. Working with the Traveler connects you to that.

(The following is a response to someone who asked about the lost art of listening.)

I was interviewed yesterday about J-R and *The Love of a Master* at the En Vivo Spanish TV studio. At first I didn't speak, I just sat in front of the camera, listening. Because once the camera starts rolling, I'm making noise, not listening any longer. An important thing about acting is that I need to listen to the other actor until they hit me with a cue, then it's my turn to talk.

When John-Roger left the planet physically, I kept looking for him everywhere. I already had a great inner connection, but it was like a muscle that I needed to exercise. After his passing, I spent two months sitting in the dark—I would play Viking movies and chant my tone.

Many of you who lived far away from the physical J-R, and hadn't spent as much time sharing with him on the outer level, are actually stronger in your inner connection, since you've had many years of practice. But I was unaware; he was right in the living room. If I had a problem, I would just say, "Hey!" Although I would confirm on the inner level, I was hanging out with the outer manifestation of J-R every day. Being with J-R, on his staff, meant a lot of physical contact, because we had to take care of him, do stuff, drive him in the car, attend seminars to be a spiritual battery for him, eat meals, and more. Even when I did my s.e.'s, I kept a focus on the outer in case he needed me.

I was recently talking to some people in Peru. This lady said, "J-R and I went to dinner. Alegre. Oh, it was amazing." I asked, "When did you meet J-R?" She replied, "Oh, I never met him." That's when I realized, it didn't matter that I was close to J-R. As a matter of fact, it could even be crippling in a way, although I did prefer and chose to be with him physically. So now I'm learning to live like some folks who didn't get to be with J-R physically.

I love talking with people who have not seen J-R for 26 years. I love traveling because of that.

J-R was just love. Being around him was like not having problems. When he left, I felt the heaviness of my karma coming back. It was like he held it off for me all that time. But now he's giving it back so I can learn to be strong enough.

Some people call this a spiritual bypass, but I don't believe in that. J-R used to say, "Chant your tone, get high, and you can see the whole thing." So I don't want to get caught up in psychology and do clearing from the bottom up. I want to chant my tone down. Most psychology courses are mental-level and involve reading a lot of books.

Whenever I auditioned, I would chant my tone until I almost fell asleep while I was waiting. I would read everything, then go in, and ask inwardly for the Traveler. But many times, I didn't end up getting the part, because I was high on Spirit. I was radical in my acting. I would see all the actors going for the same approach, and I would do it differently than everyone else. People could see it. They would say, "We don't trust you, let's get that normal actor over there."

Now I'm officially retired from acting, which was the result of a gradual transformation over many years as I slowly stepped away from it. There were two major events that catalyzed this shift in my consciousness: the first was 9/11 in 2001, and the second took place on Halloween night, October 31, 2004, when J-R fell down a staircase at Mandeville and damaged his eye. From that point on, staying by J-R's side and taking care of him became my number-one priority. Before he passed in 2014, I had a series of amazing, prophetic dreams involving President Obama, who somehow symbolized J-R. Once, in the White House rose garden, he sent me off and thanked me for my great service. Another time, he was cleaning around the toilet in J-R's bathroom and asked me to help, so I did. By November 2018, I realized that part of my life was over and that my consciousness had shifted. I heard a voice that said "there's no turning back." Acting was a catalyst to prepare me for the next great thing. Since then, I've been focused on the work, knowing that I'm on track until Spirit shifts my consciousness—sharing J-R's energy, doing spiritual counseling, and sitting in Satsang with fellow ministers, initiates, and students in MSIA.

Question: What were the keys that you learned with J-R that kept you going?

Answer: One key was visiting China twice since J-R passed. There's nothing more humbling than one-and-a-half billion people not paying attention to you. I like attention, but getting it there is impossible. I didn't know anybody and had no one to talk to … it forced me to go inward and meditate.

Another thing that has helped greatly is the Satsang I've participated in with all the ministers and initiates around the world, while traveling to places like Bulgaria, Israel, South America, China, Japan, Australia, Mexico, and Canada. I have been able to see J-R in everybody, which is such a fulfilling experience.

Chanting my tone is key, of course … nothing is better than that. In the beginning, I would tell J-R on the other side, "I want to have an experience." For the first two weeks he didn't come, but then he started showing up in my dreams. Whenever J-R would drive in my dreams, I knew it was really him. One time he was driving and told me, "Don't fall."

In another dream, I was jumping over obstacles. I jumped over John Morton, went to the bathroom and J-R was there. He asked, "Why don't you touch my feet anymore?" I knew this was the real Inner Master, because J-R knew that I loved his feet and hands. While living at Mandeville, I would often massage his feet or lay my head on them as we watched TV together. So I did that in the dream, which was incredible.

I would always wait for J-R to talk to me in my dreams about important things. Sometimes I woke up crying. He gave me a lot of clues in my dreams. These are the kinds of experiences that have kept me going over the past four years.

About a month ago, I was staying at Alberto Arango's house in Bogota, Colombia, when J-R visited my dreams and told me some amazing things. So, even if I sit here and don't know what I'm saying, it doesn't matter. Whatever I say or do, he is going to come, because it's not about me. He shows up because of all of us; when two or more are gathered, J-R is here.

I prefer to travel, so we can get together. That is sweet to me. It's like eating from the manna of heaven. You don't need food—the Sound Current feeds me. That's what J-R was doing over the past four years. It wasn't always easy. He wasn't giving it all to me, from here to there. He gave me just a bit and I have to put the rest together. I listen. When I came here, I had to bring the books with me.

Intuition is key. You need to listen inside; if you don't, the voice hides, goes away. Fear comes in through the reptilian brain. There are only two ways we can do it: through love or fear.

You have to have the awareness and give it a voice, as we do in University of Santa Monica's Spiritual Psychology program.

"Who is crying?"

"Me." But who is "me"? Perhaps the basic self or inner child.

"Why?"

"Well, J-R was like my dad, and now he's gone."

And then you continue to do a Gestalt dialogue until you get to the point to say to the child, "I am your father, don't cry." That was actually a higher part of me that stepped in, because J-R was my father.

That is where the Traveler comes in. Same with women and girls. You have to love the younger girl and talk to her with the awareness of now. This girl is sometimes controlling your life. It's usually the younger part of you that's controlling your life.

When J-R passed into Spirit, my basic self was upset, saying, "What the heck? You guys are my friends and family, and you're leaving me." Then I had to talk to it, comfort it.

Q: J-R passed with ease and grace.

A: Yeah, it was the best. I want to go like him. He never complained.

Q: First, I wanted to share that I had a dream of J-R leaving and asked him, "What can we do for you?" He responded, "I don't know, I don't care," and he left. I also wanted to ask, do you process with people during these seminars? I feel J-R here working with you.

A: I come here and do this as an MSIA minister and initiate, to represent J-R as his Ambassador, to share his energy that I am still tapped into and talk about the things I learned from him over the years. Sometimes I automatically know things because J-R would tell me. He taught me that. So I ask J-R, and he says, "Tell them this, this, this, and this." I remember everything.

Originally, I wanted to act. I never thought that I could do anything other than act. J-R taught me bigger things. I didn't really enjoy responding to emails, as they are hard to interpret, but I loved talking to people in person. One time a woman was crying because her dog died, so I complained about her to J-R, comparing her reaction to two other people who had lost their parents. He said, "Pain is pain." Yes, indeed.

Last year, my fiancée's father passed into Spirit, then another friend lost her cat; it was her second that had died. I began to judge her, but immediately said, "Delete, delete, delete." They are the same emotions, and I need to get out of my ego perception. These cats represent the person's karma. When you think like this, you feel higher, with emotional intelligence. When you start to say, "Wow, I get it." It's karma, it's bigger. To get beyond judging that it's just a cat. Depending on your level, you fall and start judging. That is why it is so important to chant the Hu or your initiatory tone. You go up, see the person with love, and can send the Light. It's not the same thing—it's a cat. I've heard J-R say that pain is a pain. "I forgive myself for judging myself for judging the lady with the two cats."

I will continue. If J-R or Spirit say go on, I go. Thank you, Mom, for having gotten sick. It's good you are not anymore. But it brought me here. Pain is pain. I think it was good to come here to Miami and do this.

Q: What is the difference between a personal tone and Hu?

A: "Hu" is the Sanskrit term for "God." I listen to the Luxor Meditation when I go to sleep, which is a PAT IV group in Egypt chanting "Hu" while J-R speaks. It's amazing. I believe he recorded the version that I use in 1988, because in it, he mentions John as the new Traveler, as well as the Peace in all people. "Hu" is for all. On the other hand, the initiatory tone is personal, charged with the energy of your Soul. You have a contract with the Traveler to clear your karma. So you become the Traveler, not with the keys, but he takes you to clear, level by level until Soul. From the Soul you can send love and Light that dissolve the rest of the karma.

There is a great seminar that J-R did called "Nuclear Radiation from Ground Zero." He says that if you are new and clear, you can radiate. Imagine doing this from the Soul—all problems go away. The problem is that when we fall, because of the karma, we are in the emotions. You can chant your tone, and you go up. You're blissed out. You start loving people from that place.

In December of 2017, I opened up. I let go of having againstness with my brothers and my friends in the Movement. And I said, "Why am I with this person and that person, but I hold this against them, and I stop my loving from them?" My intuition says, "Hug them," yet inside I would say, "But they did this and that to me." You have karma there because you withheld your loving when Spirit spoke to you. We are conductors of divine energy. I did this in December with a friend and then came down with the flu. When you are aware of this, you have to eat the karma like a hamburger. I cleared, got healthy, and started hugging.

President Trump actually saved me, because in my awareness, if you have againstness with anybody as an initiate and a minister, you're nothing. So it doesn't matter what he does. What do you do? What do you do to make this world better? We have a responsibility inside of us. We should use that energy towards good. In California, some friends are against Trump because they wanted someone else, and they are dwelling in politics. At that moment, you're done, because you are not in the level of God. You are down here.

Go up, lift yourself, become healthy, forgive yourself. Delete, delete, delete, and start sending your Light that is stronger than what you hate. Stop the againstness. Christ is in all of us, but it won't come if we are expressing againstness.

I was watching Trump on TV, feeling againstness. I said, "But I am nothing. If I am just like them, what am I doing?" So I forgave myself. I thought, "If Christ and God allowed it to be present, I'm okay. And it's not my problem, it's your problem." You can vote them out, but stop complaining. He is pressing everybody's buttons. He is incredible that way. And I don't want to give him the power to push my buttons.

At the moment, I need to cure myself. I have a problem, because my mom doesn't push my buttons. Trump doesn't push my buttons. Some people in my inner circle do, though. I have to learn. In psychology, that is a mirror called *projection*. If I don't like something my mom does, it's because I have the same problem in myself. So I don't blame her. She is reflecting my issues to me.

That's being honest when you can see it. When I see Trump, I love it, because, even if I don't know him or anything, he pushes a button and I look at all the news and the drama. I sit and meditate. I chant the Hu. This is not going to be my problem, but I will send the Light. So I am grateful for the experiences.

It's so important to take care of yourself inside and stay clear. Having againstness creates disease.

It took me three years to write *The Love of a Master*. Laren Bright helped me shape and edit the book, Teri Breier took over proofreading near the end, and Cate Kirby, Nora Valenzuela, and Lana Barreira were my translation team.

I've heard J-R say that God incarnated himself as Jesus, then killed himself and pulled it back up. That is heavy-duty. Because we're all pieces of God down here. It's so deep, this is too much for my brain. In the Moment of Peace video, *Christ: My Man for Eternity*, J-R explains the Lucifer plan and the Grace plan, and says you have to keep vigilant. Listen to your thoughts. Otherwise, we can fall.

Recently, I was in Tulum, Cancun, with Nicole. Everything was so beautiful—the sun, the beach. But I was in my mind, fighting with someone in California. Nicole said, "What are you doing? We are in Tulum. Let it go. Let's go to the beach." But I brought that argument from California to Tulum. This is what we're talking about … anybody can fall. You have to just be aware when negativity comes to test you.

At night, the Soul starts traveling, the mind stays. In comes doubt and I start having fear. I ask, "But who is crying?" It's the reptilian brain, fight or flight. At 3 a.m., I can't get to sleep and am overthinking it all. So I eat something to stuff the emotions down. J-R used to call that hidden hungers. Some people will drink or smoke or eat ice cream. I stuff it, I am vigilant, aware. But it's part of being human.

It happened especially when I was acting and the character was too hard, so it was challenging to disconnect. I would take it home and eat it until it left. You can just eat it. J-R was one of the best. He would eat the karma. He would do a seminar and right after the seminar we would go eat ice cream. That was the way he got rid of it. It felt good. Michael Hayes says, "Delete, delete" and then sleeps in the morning. J-R also went to different practitioners to clear karma and he developed the muscle testing (CKT) process in the D.S.S. and M.S.S. programs. We are not different from that. We are also Travelers, although without the keys.

Baruch Bashan.

Yo No Se Contar

Miracielo, Santa Barbara, 1990

"I am a beautiful, powerful, sensitive man, loving myself and you."

– Jesus Garcia, D.S.S.;
Insight II affirmation, 1986

"There is another level of consciousness called the basic self which resides a little deeper than the subconscious mind. The basic self can separate from the physical consciousness and project into the future. It can transcend barriers of time and space and move ahead to take a look at next week, next month, or a year from now."

– JOHN-ROGER, D.S.S., *DREAM VOYAGES*
(MANDEVILLE PRESS, KINDLE EDITION)

"Jesus the Christ, who carried the mystical consciousness that works with MSIA, said, 'I am the way, the truth, and the life: no man cometh unto the Father, but by me.'[1] He meant that it was through his consciousness, the consciousness of the Christ, that each person could be given the keys into the Soul realm, into the realm of pure Spirit. Without the help and the guidance of the Mystical Traveler Consciousness, it is difficult to move into the Soul realm."

– JOHN-ROGER, D.S.S., *DREAM VOYAGES*
(MANDEVILLE PRESS, KINDLE EDITION)

---

1   *John 14:6 (King James Version)*

Chapter 12

Discernment in the Unconscious

हू

I recently met with an older friend, who is a longtime MSIA initiate and friend of John-Roger's. I love sitting down in Satsang with elders from the church, who have the ministerial and initiation authority. There is often a conduction of divine energy that takes place. At some point the conversation becomes nonverbal. Then you can essentially tell the levels that we're in—in this particular case, we stayed primarily on the mental level, skipping over the causal/emotional. We did not get into any discussion about what we were feeling or even thinking. The strength of our connection was the sharing of J-R's love, and the love that we have for our mutual teacher.

In his best-selling book, *Power vs. Force*, Dr. David Hawkins presented the levels of consciousness on an evolutionary scale of 20 (shame) up to 1000 (Avatar consciousness). By level 500, you reach a state where the universal mind meets the etheric unconscious; at 700 and up, you become a mystic, speaking from inner knowingness, like Mother Theresa and Mahatma Gandhi; only Jesus Christ attained the highest level of 1000. At lunch with my aforementioned friend, we were basically in the realm above 500, and of course, that could be our own inner level. I'm not sure if it was the outer realms. And what if it is the etheric on the astral level? There are just so many levels within levels. But it is really nice to just get out of the mind and skate through the unconscious quickly into Soul and above.

You cannot really define the etheric level with your mind. But it's time to go into it, to really look at how the unconscious really runs us. It's like a depository or cache that accounts for everything you're holding onto in this lifetime, as well as other lives, going back for eons. It's like a debit card of karma, sitting there in the unconscious.

You've got to bear it … bare it … love it … go through it and skip the Cosmic Mirror. Or look at the mirror, comb your hair, and go past it to the Soul and the path of the Travelers. From there, you can go as high as you can, above the 27th level, to the Hu. Right now, of course, all this is a lie, because as soon as I go verbal, I am putting words on it that are not accurate. As you are reading, in a sense, you might as well throw this book away, because it's meant as something to be experienced, to experiment with, to be in it and know it.

I would like to open that up and create Light stations everywhere in the etheric that will illuminate this whole thing. Then you can be there, say "Hi," and wait for the Traveler to take you through. We can all bust in, connect with J-R, progress through all 27 levels to the Hu, and then go even beyond.

Things can get quite complicated as we journey through the fear of the unconscious/etheric level. For example, there was a night that I found myself crying because I was experiencing total separation and polarization inside of myself. As John-Roger has said, this is the Baal (or Kal) power, also called the negative power. Anything below the Soul realm is the domain of the Kal power. The loyal forces of the opposition are very good at getting you to learn your lessons.

While we were having lunch one weekend, a good friend told me that he has been working on a project for a few years. I asked, "Is it a physical project?" and he said, "No, I'm exploring the edges of the mental and etheric levels, which is the unconscious." I responded that I would love to explore my own unconscious as well—to look deeply into that abyss and face it, not fear or dodge it. For this kind of project, you need the Traveler for sure. We are blessed to have the Travelers John-Roger, John Morton, and the Christ, who can guide us through to Soul and above. And, of course, it is the Christ who heads the Movement of Spiritual Inner Awareness.

Following that conversation, I asked Christ and J-R for the Light to illuminate those dark areas of my unconscious. I realized that even in my 50s, it felt no different than when I was younger, aside from greater awareness and wisdom to notice when I am off course. Historically, when I have been in a similar dark place, I would comfort myself with distractions, such as watching television, reading, or surfing the web. Although I tried that this time, nothing seemed to shift, so eventually I did spiritual exercises and went to sleep.

The next morning, I woke up in a completely different consciousness. I was able to see that the conversation with my friend triggered some unresolved issues in the unconscious, which was nothing that I could control with my mind. For instance, I hold a perception that I come from a broken family. This is an unconscious belief that I internalized during childhood after my parents' divorce, and remained present in my psyche, even at 50-something years old. Watching my parents fight, break up, then never settling down with a family had a major impact on me. I went from having my real dad to a foster father to a stepfather and in time ended up with J-R as my surrogate father. God is the ultimate father figure, and J-R represented that for me in the physical level.

Going through the awakening, awareness, and healing of these unresolved issues is what the "hero's journey" is all about. When caught in my own unconscious patterns, I often found myself reacting automatically to other people's unconscious patterns, wanting to save people based on my "broken family" identity. This went nowhere because I was not totally present, but hooked into some unconscious behavior that set me up to go onstage and act the fool.

Doing something like that is no big deal—until the unconscious part inside judges that action. It's not your friend. J-R sometimes called this self-judgment a psychic self-attack. What we do to ourselves can get quite vicious. Going through my experience, I felt the Traveler with me the whole time. I said that I would do the work, help J-R, and wanted another 30 years with him. If I'm going to be assisting J-R in this multi-dimensional world, then this is all good. I can't say it's negative, because in the end, everything is perfect.

Insight II, a life-changing moment 1986

"*Do you know that it's okay not to always have an intellectual analysis for every move you make? You don't have to always be able to justify and explain yourself in the intellectual terms that will please another. You have the right to live your life as you intuitively know is right for you. If you make mistakes, you'll learn. Those things you need to know will become clear to you.*"

– JOHN-ROGER, D.S.S., *SACRIFICING LIMITATIONS*,
(NEW DAY HERALD, MSIA BLOG)

Chapter 13

My Etheric Experiment

ध्रू

Recently, I've been conducting my own personal experiment as a spiritual scientist to gain mastery over automatic behavior and emotional patterns. First, of course, I always call forward the presence of John-Roger, the Preceptor, and the Christ, then ask to receive more awareness in the unconscious, or etheric, level. While interacting with others, especially those people to whom I am close, I take a moment to step back and observe who is reacting, whether it's myself or someone else, and why. Usually, when an unresolved issue is triggered, it means that the unconscious is probably running the show.

In his seminar, *Passages to the Realms of Spirit,* J-R laid out the behavioral matrix and discussed the etheric level brilliantly. He said that most often, the Kal power (also known as the "loyal forces of the opposition") will set up the "final frontier" here in the lower levels that you must surmount before piercing through to the Soul. John-Roger has said, you need a Traveler to guide you through all of it. Bringing Light to the darkness of the unknown helps to dissolve it.

From what I've heard John-Roger say, all the spiritual realms are connected, with the physical body running things down here on this plane. The higher self, or Soul, touches to Spirit. The conscious self is identified with the personality and is an age-appropriate consciousness. Then at times there is a little 5-to-8-year-old kid running rebellion, which is the basic self. We all have different parts of ourselves that got stuck at a particular young age from some kind of disturbing event (such as a trauma or something a child would register as distressing).

In my case, I am 55 years old in this consciousness, as of this writing. When I lose my cool, who is it that's reacting? Certainly not my current 55-year-old self, because if he is present in the now, then there is nothing to react to except joy.

Let's say I'm having a conversation about the future when my reptilian, self-preservation-focused brain moves into concern and fear. "Oh my God, look out!" That triggers an entire cascade of sabotaging emotions that might go all the way back to when I was a scared little boy with divorced parents. The future pushes me into reaction, while my past drags me down with thoughts from that time like, "You're not going to make it; you won't survive." I only allow myself one minute for this mental chatter before I address all parts of myself with Loving.

At that point, I ask that frightened part of me, "Who are you? How old are you? Where did I hear that from?" Another important question is, "Is this issue mine or someone else's?" You might pick up thought forms from your spouse or partner, at group gatherings, or even from friends, as well as your own unconscious. Sometimes negativity gets in from outer energies, such as disembodied entities. J-R was always clearing patterns from people that came from different sources like those.

Within the unconscious, and all of the other levels, there are a lot of layers that the mind can't really figure out, because the finite can never understand the infinite. God created infinity and it just keeps going. J-R related the subconscious level to the basic self. He said that if you took the subconscious and put it on your lap like a small child and hugged it and loved it, it would cooperate with you. I find that to be true. I would add that hugging ALL parts of you, who you are and who I am, can really assist with everything.

When dealing with the unconscious, it's all about getting free. Joseph Campbell referred to this process as the "hero's journey." The best metaphor I have for the unconscious is in the original *Star Wars* film, when the main characters are stuck in the giant garbage compactor as the walls start closing in; they're being squeezed until the sewage and garbage are up to their noses.

Fortunately for us, John-Roger shared numerous techniques over the years to assist MSIA students in clearing out negativity and imbalance from their unconscious, wherever it originated. My personal favorites that I use often are the Flame Meditation, free-form writing, and daily spiritual exercises (s.e.'s, described elsewhere in this book). I also recommend listening to the *Luxor Meditation* by J-R, which can bring you into greater synchronicity with yourself. It was recorded by J-R during a PAT IV trip at the Luxor temple in the Karnak complex, transmitting over the radio to about 150 people. Almost every time I listen to *Luxor Meditation*, some conflict comes up in my awareness to resolve. In this recording, J-R talks about the new Traveler's radiant form and grafting peace into everyone from every culture and all the mystics around the world. There are several similar meditations with J-R praying from different locations, such as the Sphinx and other temples. You can find those in the *Journey to the East: Israel and Egypt* CD/DVD packet.

One of the most interesting things to observe is that people you are close to have a way of reflecting back the areas you need to work on. This includes family, friends, co-workers, and especially anyone you might identify as a petty tyrant, which J-R discussed in detail in his book, *Spiritual Warrior: The Art of Spiritual Living*. The next time you find yourself triggered, don't run away; instead, take a good look at yourself and ask, "What is this reflecting to me that is true about myself? Is there an area that I can improve?"

Not every day is the best time for deep excavation, looking at issues and dissolving negativity. Constant processing can be overwhelming. That's when I like to take the day off! Every now and then, it's good to give yourself some downtime. So treat yourself to a mundane day with no work or appointments scheduled, where you do nothing but clean up your desk drawer, catch up on receipts, take out the garbage, walk the dog, and enjoy an ice-cream cone. This can be very healing.

Some people call it a "spiritual bypass," but I don't believe in that. In the 26 years I lived with J-R, I never once heard him refer to spiritual bypass. I think it's a made-up term designed to shame people into not doing their spiritual exercises. This concept does not take the higher perspective and Grace into consideration. For me, I follow my teacher, John-Roger, not anyone else. So if you can chant your tone for an hour or two of s.e.'s, and get enough altitude, then, as J-R says, you can bring the Soul energy to your problems and dissolve them much quicker.

My Etheric Experiment

At the same time, you can also get a deeper understanding. It's still experiential in a Gestalt kind of approach. The higher you go, the wider your perspective, and the more you can see the blueprint laid out in its entirety. If I'm going to travel from here to New York, I can walk the roads with my nose to the grindstone. Perhaps I project astrally to go up higher and see the whole map. Or maybe I explore the options on Google Earth to choose the best route, and check the weather and cloud patterns. I call this getting a "spiritual advantage." J-R also said, "Use everything for your advancement."

So I don't participate in the spiritual bypass conversation. Maybe I'm misinterpreting it, but I don't believe that people can actually bypass their karma, except through Grace. Those who don't chant a tone may end up under the mental dominion of the Kal power for a while. They do all the mental analyzing, which keeps them stuck in the mental realm. They're using a finite tool to check the infinite, which doesn't work. That's all fine, since J-R said that every Soul will make it Home.

Sounds of the Realms Chart, © MSIA®

*"I am a divine soul fully prepared
to return home to God."*

– Jesus Garcia, D.S.S.;
Time Design entry after moving into
Mandeville, 1988

"If you would learn
The secret of
Soul Transcendence,
Look only for the good,
For the Divine
In people and things
And all the rest
Leave it to God."

– JOHN-ROGER, D.S.S.

Chapter 14

Experience or Information?

घु

This is an edited transcript of a presentation on August 20, 2017, at the home of Kate Ferrick and Richard Klein in Newbury Park, California.

Jsu: I appreciate all of you ministering to me. It's my first time doing this kind of event here in L.A. It looks like there are a few new guests here. So we don't want to get too far ahead, because a lot of people here are "oldies, but goodies." Not in a bad way, but they've been around the Movement of Spiritual Inner Awareness for a long time. If you are new and get lost, just raise your hand and say, "Hey, slow down!" I want this to be a spaceship—we are about to go fly. I can't go higher than what you guys want to do, because now it's an open [public] seminar. Energetically, if we have your permission, we'd like to shift some consciousness here. All right?

I'm Jsu Garcia, and I lived with John-Roger, my spiritual teacher and founder of MSIA, for 26 years. And now it's been 29 years living at the house in Mandeville Canyon, since J-R passed into Spirit in 2014. Back in the '80s, J-R founded a university called Koh-E-Nor, which later became University of Santa Monica, or USM. The school is operated by Drs. Ron and Mary Hulnick.

I participated in USM's final Master of Arts in Spiritual Psychology degree program and graduated in 2016. Many USM grads who are in MSIA congratulated me, and it felt almost like an initiation. Both USM's and Peace Theological Seminary's (PTS) educational programs emphasize experiential learning over rote memory, which J-R insisted was very important.

So many of us in MSIA were shocked after J-R's physical presence left us, trying to grasp what life would be like without him as we grieved. During the USM program, I was in the midst of my own grieving, and I still experience that even now. While participating in the trio processes, sitting in what was called the Neutral Observer's seat, I would experience insights about how J-R had worked and the techniques he used with people. As a "fly on the wall," I could not articulate a lot of the things that I saw him do in the house. But at USM, I thought, "Oh, OK. I see mentally what he was doing." I had to get above the situation, long after it happened, to be able to see that.

J-R would often ask, "Do you want the experience or the information?" and I'd respond, "I want the experience." I think information is a bit weak. When you get hit by something, you'll say, "God, I get that." But sometimes we cop out and say, "No, just give me the information," and try to take it in mentally, while it's being explained to you. For me, the school of hard knocks (and good knocks) with J-R was discerning and my way of learning the Spirit with him.

Experience or Information?

Many people tell me, "Well, that's what you needed." Sure, that's true. The USM program required the completion of a Mastery Project—mine was a book that I wrote and published in three years, called *The Love of a Master*. I borrowed the title from a beautiful man named Ishwar Puri, who is a 93-year-old initiate of the Master Sawan Singh. He may even be one of the last direct initiates. After J-R passed into Spirit, I fled Los Angeles to spend time with this Master and new friend, Ishwar, only to realize that I could not escape the grieving process.

In many recordings, I have heard J-R say something to the effect of, "I don't let my initiates grieve or get into that level." Now I understand the reason is because you can get trapped in the astral realm and over-emote in the causal level, where the Traveler cannot inflict. I didn't want to judge myself, but I recognized how deeply I was going into the feelings of grief that were trapping me there. I went to be with Ishwar and his wife, Toshi, to celebrate their Master Sawan Singh at the annual Bhandara gathering, celebrating his passage into Spirit on April 2, 1948. We spent many days together with other MSIA friends. He would tell his curious congregation that "we are the same as MSIA, only they eat meat and we don't."

I experienced that J-R was using him to send me messages. It's similar to when the Dalai Lama dies, and everyone is looking for his young reincarnation, with tests like, "Will he pick that same toy?" Somehow, Ishwar said things that only J-R would say to me. He tapped me on my face exactly the way J-R did. A while ago, Leigh Taylor-Young interviewed him here in Los Angeles, and I was present at that dinner. We had a private moment together, when he gently slapped my face like J-R did, and said, "I'm your friend." Then I just cried. I started to have experiences that J-R was in everyone else, but not in me. First I had to see it in other people and the things they said.

The Dreams of a Master

It's been interesting to watch John Morton take on more of the Traveler consciousness since J-R passed. How many people have noticed that? I saw it in many people, like Michael Hayes and Paul Kaye, and then I recognized it in each one of us who were individualizing. I was reminded of that Moment of Peace video where Michael Hayes asked J-R about J-R's energy that is individualizing in all of us. There's one Traveler with the keys, John Morton, whom I acknowledge as we all do. Yet as J-R's initiates, we all have a part of J-R inside, somehow, because we're all connected. We are all becoming like J-R. Then I started to look at you guys differently than I used to. I realized, "Oh my God, he's been there forever," and I had so much appreciation for the initiates and ministers in MSIA. Once I asked J-R who was going to run MSIA in the future, and he responded, "The ministerial body."

Most of you know that I was a film actor for many years, but I'm not getting any intuition regarding continuing acting. Something switched when J-R transitioned. In fact, after I finished the *Mystical Traveler* movie, I was exhausted. It was the hardest thing I ever did. I was with J-R in the kitchen at Mandeville, the editors were in the back, and I said, "J-R, we're done." Then he said, "You'll probably never want to do another movie again." This was about a year or two before he passed. He was right, my awareness wasn't the same anymore. My consciousness is different. Of course, if Steven Spielberg walked in right now and offered a role, I'd do it, because J-R always liked him.

Now my life and ministry is all about sharing J-R's work. So far, I have done a few workshops and off-the-cuff Q&As in South America and Bulgaria, free from criticism. However, as J-R said, "When the baboon gets high enough, his butt can be seen." So you will be seeing a lot of my behind and I'm not going anywhere! I really enjoy traveling around and will continue until

Experience or Information?

it's not clear to travel any more. I get the opportunity to initiate new people into MSIA, as well as others in remote areas that the Staff cannot normally reach. I do that on behalf of J-R, John, and the Sound Current supporting the business of MSIA, which is Soul Transcendence. That's my ministry—I need to share J-R wherever I go. It keeps me from falling asleep and supports our initiates around the world to keep from falling asleep themselves and getting jaded without J-R still present on the planet. Speaking for myself, it seems like this hunger is everywhere in the world.

Together, we can be alchemists. As J-R often quoted, Christ said, "You too can do these things and even greater, because I go to the Father." That's the way I saw J-R. We can be as good as him because he went to the Father. I just believe that in our own way, we too can move to that level. When two or more are gathered, there's the Spirit, there's the Christ. That's what I like, especially when initiates and ministers get together. They already know what to do, so the magic happens. Even with new people. It's not about new or old, it's "two or more." When Kate invited me, I said, "Yes, I'll do it."

Last night I was up until 5 a.m. at Mandeville, the house where J-R lived forever. There are beings there that come in and out. Most people wouldn't know how to handle that and would probably run away. But I just sleep on the couch, and they come in and fly around the living room. It was really crowded last night. I was trying to sleep, and it can be spooky. Turn on the light and everything disappears; turn it off, everything moves in. The house pulsates, moves, creaks. Doors shut on their own. I thought maybe it's because I'm doing this talk here today. It might have been the sentient beings saying, "Let's help him out because he doesn't know what he's going to say tomorrow." So I invite that in, and I always invite J-R's energy and the Christ above all.

My process lately has been packing to move out of Mandeville after living there for 29 years. I can't stop talking about it because it's quite an experience. In my life so far, I've awakened somehow to things that other guy, Jesus, did; I've done these things under the umbrella of John-Roger. Over the years, people would have feedback and would write J-R letters about me. I used to sit there with J-R while he would read those letters. At one point, he gave us, as staff, the permission and energy to read his correspondence, because he only had one good eye. Back when he was reading emails, he would ask, "Zeus, did you do this?" and I would admit, "Yeah, I did." And he'd say, "OK."

With J-R, it was important to confess. We learned not to argue or defend, as J-R would call that, "arguing for your limitations." Denial or back-pedaling essentially meant excommunication; your head came off and then you moved out. I was talking with a guest up at the house about the standards of Mandeville. If you ever dropped below a certain level of impeccability, that was it, you had to move out. There was also a high standard of communication between all the residents. We would have discussions and share about whatever was bothering us—this sometimes led to arguments and telling each other off. But we would always clear the air and apologize. He that apologizes first wins in J-R's world. John was great at that.

During a trip to Norway in 1988, John said something, I said something in response, and J-R said, "Sit down," to me, because John's the Traveler. Then John walked away, came back, sat down, and said, "I'm sorry." So J-R looked at him and said, "That's the man, that's 16 Tons" (referring to John Morton's walkie-talkie handle). From John at Mandeville, I learned the importance of the principle, "Say what you mean and mean what you say." It's different from the rules at PRANA. But you had to act at that level. Anyone who withheld or lied would be gone, instantly.

Experience or Information?

After that incident, I tried to one-up John—if I apologized first, I'd win. Then all the staff became quick to apologize if we'd fight. "Sorry man, sorry about that." J-R would see it and wink because the negativity was immediately gone with the apology. Sometimes he would make us all wash each other's feet. We washed Erik Raleigh's feet once, which was quite humbling. Nat Sharratt, Mark Harradine, Erik, and I always acted like boys trying to outdo each other. We had arguments over what kind of detergent was better for J-R—only the best for the Master. I'd suggest Tide, then Erik would say, "That's got junk in it." J-R taught us to agree to disagree and keep the loving going. If I were off, J-R would give me instant feedback. Sometimes he said to us, "No apologies only change of behavior."

As I went through all the boxes to pack up my things, I found lots of papers and other stuff. For instance, there was a great prayer from our Time Design organizers that I sent to John, asking "Who wrote this?" He replied, "I did."

PRAYER

Father Mother God
I pray for the Light of the Highest Good
To fill me, surround me and protect me.
I ask for the presence of the Mystical Traveler
and Preceptor Consciousness to enlighten my
being fully on all levels as a conscious awareness.
I ask that any negativity within my consciousness
be removed at the highest rate and placed into

the higher light to be transmuted and cleared.
May my conscious awareness be restored
and established in the Soul Realm.
I ask that whatever blocks stand between
John-Roger and my Self be removed.
I ask for the discernment to bring forward
the greatest blessing of God.
I ask for the strength to carry forth
the choices that answer my prayers.
I forgive myself for any past transgressions
against the Perfection of God.
I ask for the Spark of Joy to be rekindled
and sustained into my expression.
May my presence bring ever greater joy
and peace to John-Roger and all else.

AMEN   AMEN   AMEN

Those Time Designs were state-of-the-art systems in the '80s, way before smart phones and Google. If you were sophisticated, you had the really cool zipper closure around the outside. There was something called a MAP Training with David Allen to get clear on your next steps, which eventually became David's "Getting Things Done" system. Just deciding how to start your day with Time Design was a minefield of a matrix. As technology changed, we got more electronic gadgets in the house, like the

Experience or Information?

Palm Treo and other Palm Pilots. Today, you can still apply the same system to evolving technologies.

But back then, it was all on paper. Every morning, we would get J-R's schedule from one of his assistants, print it up, and tape it on the mirrored sliding door in his room. We'd leave trails of paper down the hallway to remind us to pick it up and start our day. That was our secret. As people get older and forget things, putting a note on the floor, like "10 a.m. doctor's appointment" can help them remember, because they will notice it lying there and pick it up. I loved leaving notes under J-R's door; it was an amazing way to keep him updated on my whereabouts long before texting and smartphones. He would call me later, and we would plan to rendezvous.

Years ago, J-R suggested, in person and in dreams, that I do muscle testing, or kinesiology. Early on, around 1988, when I was 23 years old, J-R would take me with him on his visits to Dr. Ed Wagner, which is when I was first introduced to this technique. Dr. David Denton would do cranial work on us. I saw Bertrand Babinet do this deep work with J-R, as part of his Babinetics practice, near Victoria Lake on a trip to Africa. Then it seemed like everyone in MSIA started doing muscle testing, but I was very reluctant and avoided doing it for many years. For some reason, it was really annoying to me at that time, so I rebelled against it. But finally I started using muscle testing in the M.S.S. and D.S.S. programs and loved it. I still use it in my life now, although I am able to check inside energetically without using arms, hands, or fingers.

Michael Hayes spent many hours working with J-R, sometimes for 17 hours at a time. We were witnesses to it, especially Nat Sharratt. As a young man watching, I thought, "This is crazy." But that was how they worked. Finally, I took the Doctor of Spiritual Science program (D.S.S.), completed my Practical Treatise, and graduated. Now I think muscle testing is the most amazing technique ever—I'm really good at it and love doing it.

Back in 2012, J-R asked me to go up on stage at the Living in Grace retreat and I wouldn't; in fact, I got really annoyed with him. We were all gathered around his bed when I asked, "Hey, can you go on stage? People want to see you." He said, "No, you do it." I said, "That's ridiculous and I'm not doing it." Partly I felt unworthy and partly I wanted to excuse myself because I was focused on acting and wanted to do that. That was probably the last opportunity that J-R had to go up on stage. Eventually, I did go up that night to sing and tell this story to the group. Since then, I've continued to get up and share on stages, at home seminars, book events, or wherever, because at that moment, I got that J-R was really encouraging me to do this more and more.

He taught me so many things that are still percolating inside. Over the years, when people called Mandeville, J-R would say, "Pick up the phone," and I'd have to translate to him what they said. After a while, it became automatic; I had a template of similar situations, because I learned from the Master. Now, when people come talk to me, it's different, because I am relating as myself.

I was never on staff with the Movement of Spiritual Inner Awareness (MSIA). I was on John-Roger's personal staff and worked for 29 years with a vow of poverty; 26 while J-R was on the planet. They took care of me very well in that time. I'm not the one trying to do anything or take on any karma; I'm just an initiate of John-Roger. Above me is J-R and the Christ, and if anything gets tough, I give it to John-Roger. "You take it." Together we can talk about releasing things and it goes to the Spirit.

Experience or Information?

Moments with J-R in Japan, 1998

That said, I'm not going anywhere. I'm here to serve. I love going around initiating people for John and J-R. So if there's anything I can do, let me know. Do you have any questions?

Question: Can you talk about your book?

Answer: My book is called *The Love of the Master*, named after the seminars that Ishwar Puri did with that title. I have visited with Ishwar and his wife, Toshi, several times. They are Sikhs who were born in India and follow the Sant Mat. Ishwar was an initiate of Sawan Singh, who was a Mystical Traveler, and Toshi was an initiate of his successor, Jagat Singh. Ishwar told me a story of Yogi Bhajan asking him to do "The Love of a Master" seminar, which he did. I said, "I'm going to steal that," because J-R loved Yogi Bhajan.

It's fascinating to talk with someone in a different religion who has the same spiritual practices that originate from Sant Mat path of the Masters. I was riding in a taxi with a Sikh driver and asked, "Hey, you do the same thing we do, right?"

He replied, "You can't say it out loud!"

"No, I'm not saying it out loud, but it's the same, right?"

He said, "Yes, the same thing."

At its essence, *The Love of a Master* is really the heart of what J-R left to all of us, but I'm speaking about my own experiences. You could read the book and might disagree with it, since it is from my own viewpoint. I had a lot of help with transcribing, editing, and proofreading along the way.

I share a lot of little anecdotes about hanging out with J-R privately. One of the stories that didn't make it into the book was

Experience or Information?

about Liza Minnelli. J-R loved entertainers, actors, and movies—somehow, he would get invited to the strangest Hollywood parties. Sally Kirkland, a great friend and initiate of J-R's and still a great friend of mine, was one of the actors who was often inviting us to parties. For a few months in the early '90s, we went every weekend to Liza Minnelli's house, who served cocktails and sang songs all night long, with her husband playing the grand piano. She was imitating Sammy Davis Jr.'s home concert events. A lot of Liza's songs were written by friends, many of whom had not survived the AIDS crisis. Songwriters at the party would say, "Yeah, we wrote that song" or "Oh, Mike wrote that. He died seven years ago." Scott Baio, who played Chachi on Happy Days, also attended these gatherings. We were just there, hanging out with Liza Minnelli. That didn't make the book because there's nothing to get out of it except a cool story.

I always remember the stuff I did with J-R, like driving him to different places, especially the late-night drives, which I talk about in the book. Other details come back to me when I watch seminars now. "What's he wearing? Oh yeah, that watch! Nat put that tie on." Or "Right, that's when we didn't want to cut his hair. He's got that long curly hair." Or "Oh, that was a horrible night. We went to Izzy's Deli and his eye was swollen." Sometimes, watching seminars is almost like having PTSD.

On Christmas in 2004, we were up all night with Michael Hayes at his home in Topanga Canyon, after the big 9.1 earthquake and tsunami hit Indonesia. Michael and J-R spent 10 hours, locating, naming, and clearing the source of the negativity to disperse the energy on the island of Krakatoa using the Light of the Christ and Traveler, from 5 p.m. until 5 a.m. the next day. Then we went to eat breakfast at Jerry's Deli in the morning. That is the kind of wild adventure I included in my book, although I didn't share that exact story in *The Love of a Master*.

Traveling now is sort of like chasing J-R's fumes, if you will. There is actually a perfume or scent that is the Spirit, which is what I chase; it's really there. This scent is very strong at the 2101 building, PRANA, and Mandeville. When I travel and smell the perfume, the ambrosia, I think, "Yeah! That's why I'm coming here." I was in the USSR with J-R in 1988, where many of us got drunk on the Spirit. We had a stopover in Amsterdam. J-R loved to go through the red-light district and plant the Light.

As I wrote in the book, I never took J-R cruising through Beverly Hills or to wealthy neighborhoods. He would say, "Make a right here," and we'd tell him, "J-R, we're in the ghetto." "Make a left here. Go straight and pull over there. Get me two doughnuts and an éclair." How the heck did he know how to find that place? This was before GPS and he didn't have a map. J-R was great at finding parking spots, too. The other day, I drove John Morton to the airport and he was starting to do the same thing as J-R, giving me directions: "right here and left there." It's funny, because we were both J-R's drivers and now I am driving John, too. That came out of the J-R training we both had.

Q: John mentioned that on the last Israel trip, J-R came to him and said, "I'm dying." Did J-R talk to you guys about that?

A: I would have to defer to John. A Traveler always knows when he is going to die, so he probably told John. We kind of got it, though; we were in it day to day. Of course he would need to tell John, who was out there doing the work. Meanwhile, as his personal staff, we were in the bubble. I told Nicole, "I would move mountains for J-R." You just kind of know it's coming to the end. You know the wheels are coming off, so Nat and I could not take our eyes off the ball.

Experience or Information?

You could probably see it at Conference that year, in that video where he looked so weak. Nat's and my job was to take it to the end. I would ask J-R, "Do you want to do this until the wheels fall off?" "Yeah," he'd reply. He was all there, but just slow. And then he would motion to me to come close, lean toward my ear and then say, "Are you taking care of yourself?" I admit that my ego was definitely invested. I used to tell J-R, "My ego is all over this," and he would say, "You need your ego to get it done." You can't kill the ego or who's going to do it?

Given that, I was invested in finishing the bookings for the Israel trips and bringing J-R there. He almost passed away three times that year, but Nat and I would simply not allow it. In some crazy way, he would not go until he knew that I'd be OK. In Israel, J-R took care of me by being a matchmaker (like Yente in *Fiddler on the Roof*, which he loved) and setting me up with Nicole. I fell in love; for the first time in 26 years, I wasn't entirely focused on him. And that's when he went. He couldn't leave otherwise. Thinking about this gives me goosebumps.

Sometimes I wondered, "Well, did I create it? Did he create it?" Looking back from a higher perspective, I can see that he definitely set me up. While I was stuck in the astral/causal levels of grief, I didn't know anything. I felt awful, which triggered a victimhood pattern that was part of my childhood. Then I panicked and blamed everybody—"Oh no, how can you do that to me?" Once I got out, I could see the whole situation from the top down and recognized that J-R left me with invaluable stuff, inner gifts that were worth much more than money.

When I traveled the world not long after J-R's transition, most people I met in the local MSIA communities were going through the same thing. I did a lot of spiritual counseling. Some people were acting out the loss of J-R with hurt feelings, while others just mourned quietly. Everybody was essentially grieving that "Dad" had transitioned into Spirit, and all the brothers and sisters were having disagreements, while "big brother" John did his best to reassure the whole family. After two years, those rampant emotions finally calmed down, at least from my end. J-R always said any situation required two years for full clarity and understanding. So I gave myself a break and everyone else, too.

Things are good now. Of course, it's not the same, because J-R was the Dude. But I know and have experienced that we can access J-R whenever we want, and we help each other with that. John's really doing great, maintaining it all. He's a rock; that's why J-R chose him. J-R chose the three acting MSIA co-presidents, he chose me, and every one of us. And now, I choose you back.

J-R used to say something that drove me crazy. I would feel him detaching himself from me, then he would say, "The freedom I give to you is the freedom I take." "Ugh! What does that mean? Did something happen? Are you getting rid of me?" He just kept giving me more rope and I had to be careful that I didn't hang myself with it. But now, that's the way I look at everything I do. The freedom I give to everyone is the freedom I take. So I take my freedom and I'm really glad to be here. As I launch my book, I'm coming out as an author. I'm not ducking or hiding. I really want to talk about J-R as my master teacher, because he is *our* master teacher. The things that are being revealed to me now about J-R are unbelievable. Master teachers say that you know a master teacher when he talks from his totality. J-R was the totality. He was the total of it. And through his manifestation of the Preceptor Consciousness and Christ, that went to an even higher level.

While J-R was transitioning, the living room was a massive ball of pulsating Light energy, with him at the vortex. When I walked into that room, all my "stuff" disappeared. I saw lines from all of us, as his initiates, bridging to him above the 27 levels. A longtime MSIA minister told Nicole and me something about this when we visited him in Santa Barbara recently. He said that if Christ was the one who bridged us all to the Soul level, J-R was the bridge to the 27th level and above. Out of his mouth, J-R came out, and it was the most mysterious, mystical Windermere moment. I was crying. I used to judge this guy as being pretty "far out," but he is a beautiful being whom I tapped into when J-R told me inwardly to listen. So I'm listening.

Q: How did you get into MSIA?

A: It was definitely guided by John-Roger, back in 1986. A girl in my Insight II seminar gave me some early John-Roger books. Then not long after my graduation, my facilitators Lawrence Caminite and Terry Tillman said I needed to get on Discourses. I wondered, "What is going on here? Whatever it is, I have to do it." Soon after, at Lawrence's home seminars, I met Ruben Paris, who sold me cassette tapes with group s.e.'s chanting, which were mysteriously erased after listening to them; I could swear they had chanting one day and were empty the next. He said, "I love you; I know you from another life." I, too, loved him and recognized him from some faraway place. I was pulled to do the home seminar circuit, so I went to Laren and Penelope's MSIA seminars, got hooked, and subscribed to Discourses.

Years earlier, in 1980, at the age of 16, I had attended a teen seminar at Leigh Taylor-Young's house with David Raynr and Joey Hubbard (who, along with their mother, Patti Rayner, supported me throughout my gradual process of coming into the Movement). I was stunned to see a photo of John-Roger wearing a three-piece white suit on the mantel at Leigh's home, long before I met him in person. As I shared in *The Love of a Master* book, I first saw J-R's radiant form at age eight and then around 12—wearing that exact same white suit. Much later, J-R confirmed that he had shown me his radiant form during my childhood, as many masters do. However, after that first seminar, I was so moved and shaken that I didn't return until I was in my 20s. I loved the energy and was afraid of it at the same time.

It was only after his death that I started to understand the radiant form of J-R. If you really listen to the words of the Luxor Meditation, he says, "The radiant form is above you." Then I realized, "I was there with J-R." He did several meditations at the Temple of Luxor in Egypt on the PAT IV trips, but I was present at the one in 1988, which was made into the recording.

After going on Discourses, I began to study more and more, listening to his early seminars, which I highly recommend if you haven't heard them in a while. He talks about all kinds of esoteric things, like Radha Swami, Shabd yoga, and the spiritual levels, so it was pretty intense for a neophyte. Facilitating the J-R video marathons have helped me tremendously because I whip out those old-time seminars that he did at PRANA for several years. Sure, I got to play at being a cowboy with J-R at Windermere post-1988, but there's that three-piece-suit J-R in the '70s seminars explaining all the levels; when you personally experience them, it can be mind-blowing. There are still quite a few people around who had the blessing of attending those early seminars. After 40 years, you see those same people in the video, in the room where I'm screening the J-R seminars. It's a bizarre mind-blowing awareness.

In 1988, I attended an MSIA seminar in Florida at the home of Lin and Larry Whitaker and shared that I wanted to work for John-Roger. Speaking about that memory with me 29 years later, Lin said that I had been on fire. Indeed, I felt that I was on fire—I knew what I wanted so clearly, and from my experience in the acting business, I knew that intention was more important than method. The method would show up once the intention was set. Later, I would learn from John-Roger that Spirit meets you at the point of action.

Lin asked, "Oh, do you know what's going on in Los Angeles?"

"No," I replied.

"Well, John-Roger has passed the keys of the Traveler Consciousness to John Morton."

As soon as she told me this, I went cold and felt like someone had punched me in the stomach. "What?"

It was like I regressed to being a distraught and panic-stricken little boy. That evening, I called J-R from my father's house, crying. I was really depressed to be in Florida, not doing what I needed to do, when I would much rather have been in Los Angeles with J-R. A few days earlier, I had auditioned for a film role in New York that I would ultimately get. As I explained in *The Love of a Master*, the proceeds from this role would help me finish paying for the summer PAT IV trip to the Middle East. Near the end of that trip, I would finally be invited to join J-R's staff.

When I had my third aura balance that same year, before going on the PAT IV trip, I drove 100 miles an hour to Las Vegas to make it on time. J-R physically came into the room and touched the tips of my feet. Then when J-R transcended into the Realms of Spirit, I was touching the tips of his feet while John held his head. It was a vision I experienced when J-R was ready to leave the planet. I was the lead on his Healthcare Directive and didn't want to let anybody in.

In caring for J-R and during my earlier years with him, I learned not to move until that hesitation shifts, even to the death. The bandwidth between what is clear and what is not clear is huge. It either closes or goes clear. I never need to muscle test any more … it's all inside of me. "You want to go eat?" "No." That's how quick the awareness is. I don't need to check between this and that—no judgments on those who do. A few days before, John invited me to come up and share in front of a group. As soon as John called my name, I immediately saw a vision and intuitively knew that I needed John to say something to me. When he did, I saw John at J-R's head, the MSIA presidency triune ("Prez")—Paul Kaye, Vincent DuPont, and Mark Lurie—on his right side, Nat on his left, and me at his feet. So when the moment of transition came, that's what we did; it was an amazing experience.

We were chanting the Hu tone and playing the old MSIA songs by Michael Sun. It was incredible to watch John as the Traveler take another Traveler through to the other side. I remember during one PAT IV trip, J-R kind of slapped me and said, "I don't want you leaving through your feet!" At first I didn't know what he meant, then I realized that when people go unconscious, they can drop and go out through either their feet or their crown. So when you go to sleep, be sure to close the feet. So I said, "I'm going to take the feet. Nothing will come in on my end." The Prez held strong, Nat held strong, and John brought the strength of the Traveler.

J-R had said he wanted to be burned in three days after leaving his body. But legally, you can't cremate someone in that time, because there is paperwork to submit for approval. I did it in seven days. Nat and I saw his body as it entered the crematory. Some of Yogananda's devotees used to say how vibrant their Master looked after his death. J-R actually looked a hundred percent better and

Experience or Information?

healthier on the way to cremation than when he passed away. His cheeks were red, his eyes were clear, and it was like there was still somebody in there. That memory gives me goosebumps. Nat and I kissed J-R and then we burned him. We were just soldiers, the two of us, carrying out our duties. But afterwards, I had PTSD for a while. For the first year, any time I touched the handles of his wheelchair, I would start crying. I would see photos of J-R or his clothing, and nothing. But when I had to move the wheelchair, I wept. There cracks the soldier. With USM, I cracked even further. I don't think anybody survived the loss of J-R intact. Personally, I've seen that most people in our communities worldwide are still wounded. It's a wound that needs loving and healing. This probably comes from an ego place, because I recognize that my ego will be left here while my Soul and consciousness go. So it's my ego and my inner little boy that miss J-R.

Q: Did J-R say what he wanted done with his ashes?

A: No, it was kind of a default decision. We were thinking Bora Bora in Tahiti, because it was J-R's favorite place, but I said, "Well, we can't afford to go there." John said, "I'll go to Bora Bora and take care of it." However, when I went inside, it was clear to scatter his ashes at our annual Living in Grace retreat, held at the Asilomar Conference Grounds in the Bay Area, which was J-R's second favorite place. We realized that, while not everyone can get to Tahiti, they can come to Grace, so there would be more people present to enjoy the energy and participate in the process. We all went out on a boat together and gave the ashes to J-R's brother and sister-in-law, Delile and Elda Hinkins, to toss overboard into Monterey Bay. Letting go of him, it felt like the world went upside down for me. But now that I look back, it was all perfect. J-R left me a lot of stuff here, inside. I got my ego and that's all right. And I got my Soul and that's all right.

However, I want to give back even more. Recently, an MSIA old-timer requested a spiritual counseling. Spirit threw me a line, asking, "Do you want to do this?" I said, "Yes, I'll do it." And J-R spoke again through this old timer. That shook me and I recognized how powerful it was. So now, I am staying aware to find out who J-R speaks through—this can be anybody in the Movement who is connected to the Sound Current, and even those who are not. I believe that someone who hears J-R's name or sees his face in a photo becomes initiated.

Q: You recently went to Bulgaria. How do people find MSIA in Bulgaria?

A: Insight Seminars is rocking and rolling over there. Here in L.A. people ask, "When is the next Insight?" Insight in Bulgaria says, "NOW!" I'm telling you, the world is a hundred times hungrier for this work now—much like J-R's original students were back in the '70s. From what I hear, the energy then was turbo-charged, with people fired up about the Light Castle house in Whittier, then the acquisition of PRANA, and building on the Lake Arrowhead property. Bulgaria has this energy now, Russia has it, and Aruba in South America had it about 10 years ago; in 2007, 500 people from Insight Aruba came to see J-R. It just keeps going and it's incredible.

Q: So usually it starts with Insight, probably in Europe, and then they go into MSIA, the spiritual teachings, right?

A: Yeah! J-R was right. It was Russell and J-R who set that up 40 years ago. I'm in MSIA because I did Insight first. Those Insight seminars and USM courses open you up to get connected to the Sound Current. Michael Hayes' workshops are great, too. He helps introduce guests (many of whom are USM students and grads) to the spiritual awareness, decompress them, and then usher

Experience or Information?

them into MSIA. Many other MSIA ministers are now providing great opportunities to experience J-R inwardly through their outer ministries, including Alisha Hayes, Zoe and Eric Lumiere, Richard Powell, Greg Stebbins, David Allen, Cheryl Mathieu, Ed Wagner, Bertrand Babinet, Bryan McMullen, Melba Alhonte, Robert Waterman, Karey Thorne, Nat Sharratt, and many more, the list is long.

The University of Santa Monica continues to expand; its program is powerful and informative in an experiential way. I'm going to take Consciousness, Health, and Healing (CHH) this year [Ed. note: Jesus since graduated CHH in 2018]. Many USM students and grads are on the fringe of MSIA and J-R. It's funny to be at a USM class or event where someone will share, "Oh man, I popped out and saw J-R. There was purple everywhere. What do I do?" And then Mary says, "Just see me in the back on the break. We'll talk." Next thing you know, they're subscribing to Discourses.

At USM, they are working with Robert Holden, a best-selling author who spoke at my graduation and later endorsed *The Love of a Master* with his wife, Hollie. He often mentions John the Beloved and Francis of Assisi, which reminds me of one of J-R's recorded seminars about John and Francis. Robert loves J-R and supporting Drs. Ron and Mary Hulnick. I think this is a great thing, because he is younger, with a younger following, so he is helping to keep J-R's energy moving. We are all getting out there—Nat Sharratt is doing things and I'm doing things and traveling everywhere around the world. I will even be going to Siberia soon.

Going to the terminal at LAX is exciting. I now have Global Entry. "Keep my shoes on? Thank you, TSA. Thanks, J-R!" As soon as I reach the gate, I feel like a little kid traveling with my dad, J-R. That's why I travel—my globetrotting is therapeutic for me. On a plane looking out the window, I'm with J-R or with

John. We all used to be on the road constantly, six months out of the year. There's nothing better. I'll be in Moscow showing the *Mystical Traveler* movie September 28, in Siberia the 30, London on October 6 (my birthday). Then I return to Germany and maybe I'll just keep going. J-R and John have been my mentors for traveling for many months out of the year, serving and sharing the teachings around the world.

Q: How's MSIA in Germany?

A: John was just recently there. There are a few Discourse subscribers. It's close to Switzerland, which has a small community and an MSIA representative. People in Germany are super spiritual.

Q: So you don't travel with John, you just do everything on your own?

A: It's a matter of going inside and checking with J-R inside to ask what's true for me, and it wasn't clear to go to Spain [in September 2017]. Israel was clear. I wanted to work with John in the Italy portion of the trip, but Spirit directed me to return to Israel.

Q: This morning when I woke up I was feeling pretty good. I got up and I felt awful. I know it wasn't physical; I needed to get the house set up for your visit today. So I played some meditations, but that wasn't doing it. Then I said, "J-R, help me out here," and saw the *Journey through the Spirit Realms* meditation. When I came back, I was feeling really good. I just wanted to share that experience and say how much I appreciate you. I love you. I really enjoy your joy and the love you have for J-R, that you're doing this work ...

Experience or Information?

A: Yes, it's important for everybody to clear themselves from what's going on in the world. J-R and John use us, if you didn't already know that. If you're feeling off, turn on CNN, and you'll realize why. It isn't just you being absorbed by your own life. As initiates, we are put here to be conduits. J-R did a public seminar called "Re-Creation: Conducting Divine Energy" that I recommend.

It's like we are being used here. Everyone's an initiate, everyone's connected. Which means, in a group, especially when John is leading one of the trips as the Traveler, it's on. Sometimes it can be even more intense for the people who live the furthest away. Spirit says, "Let's use them—they seem to be comfortable up there. Come on!" So this initiate is on and that initiate is on and maybe I get a bit irritated or something's up. In the clearing process, J-R and the D.S.S. class suggested asking, "Is this mine or someone else's?" That's number one. Often it's not you. It could be your spouse, because you sleep together.

I've learned that in a relationship, you are dealing with two consciousnesses and two sets of karma. There was a couple I recently counseled. The guy was worried about something; he gave it to his partner and she woke up the next day with a cold. If she had problems, he got the cold. That's when you clear it and check, "Is this hers or mine?" It's not meant to be a negative judgment. You don't say to your partner out loud in public, "You attacked me last night." Just clear yourself as the minister in the family. "OK, I took that on. Great. It's her stuff. Let me send her Light." Or maybe you'll discover it's yours after all.

You can also pick up things from the world as you're watching the news or reading headlines online. Some people like to stay up late. That's because there's a part that chooses to be up late to work the karma. Those are the "Night Watchers." No kidding. It's like being the Watcher of the Universe, because it is so much quieter at night. When you eventually fall asleep, you may wake up at 6 in the morning to hear about a major earthquake or terrorist attack. While we're on the topic, I think we should all send love and Light to Trump. I'm not in againstness nor do I hate anyone. I think he's good for our country because he brings out the Loving. Because of him, we're going to end up choosing our better natures and the higher parts of ourselves. We need to love, not hate.

I see nothing but great demonstrations of love and I hope we can push that love. I don't want to be political, I just think that againstness doesn't work. I recently heard someone say, "I don't want him to go away, because I want to see the head of the snake." The negativity is the head of the snake. Let's not put the negativity down. Put Light on it. Let's talk about it. Let's clean the feet. Pope Francis has cleansed the feet of people from all races and backgrounds. We need more of that, more love. I want to just love everybody—I'm not a hater. Even when Trump won, I was not a hater. It was like the winds of change came in. The thing that changed it inside of me is that I wondered, "What if Spirit chose Trump?" If Spirit allowed Trump to win, then I'm okay with it.

If I've got an unresolved issue, as USM describes it, I'm going to be complaining out there in the world. Sure, I have problems, but I'm not going to complain, I'm done with that. I just want to do constructive work. I want to pivot. If an initiate needs their next initiation, I'm going to go do that for them. We need Discourses in Venezuela—let's go. Let's pivot, pivot, pivot away from the againstness, that's my philosophy. Facebook turned really crazy when Trump won. I was thinking, "We need to love and not judge," so we can move the energy. Martin Luther King said something like this, "You can't fight hate with hate." Especially as initiates, we need to bring love forward. We are so powerful in our positive natures. I used to tell J-R, "I feel like I'm attacking you." He would say, "You're not that strong, you're not that powerful." That really crushed my ego in a good way and shut me up. We're not that powerful. Just do the work.

Q: Sitting here, I'm remembering how every time I've seen you, particularly since J-R left, I can feel him loving you when I see you. It touches me so much that it's almost hard to tell you now without crying but I'm so thankful that you and Nat were chosen to be there with J-R.

A: Me too. I'm still kicking myself, thinking, "God, I was with the Dude who had all the answers. I was with the It of Is-ness. What did I do? Why couldn't I ask him all those questions?" But I realize that I did ask them, but he would not give it to me. He just would not give me the answers. He was so smart. I would be asking, "What about this? I need to know about that?" And he'd say, "You just killed four universes." "What?" "You just killed another one. Shut up and get me a tuna sandwich." That story is recounted in *The Love of a Master* book.

Once, as J-R was flipping through TV channels, I approached him and said, "Hey, can I ask you something?" "Yeah." "So about my initiation, am I going to feel ... " He cut me off. "Can you give me a tuna fish sandwich? Make sure you toast it and add some pepperoncinis. Then quarter it." I returned with the sandwich and continued, "Here, J-R ... so anyways ... " "Hey, can you put some chips on this?" "So J-R, I was asking ... "Can you get me an Arnold Palmer?" "OK, J-R, an Arnold Palmer." Then I sat down and started again. "I wanted to know if I get to the etheric level ... "Hold on a second ... can you call Betsy? I need something." By then, I just thought, "Forget it, we're done."

Now Timothea Stewart, on the other hand, could get anything out of J-R, any time, 24/7. We'd be out to dinner when Timothea started off with a question like, "J-R, who created the universe?"

Then J-R would discourse for two hours straight at the restaurant. He was famous for clearing out restaurants. At 8:00, J-R would look around when it was busy and say, "I'm going to clear this restaurant by 10:00." Sure enough, at 10:00, it was completely empty except for us and the waiters, who would look at us like they wanted us to leave. But at that point, J-R was still discoursing as if nothing else mattered. I'd sit there thinking, "He doesn't do that for me at home."

In my book, I share about some of the weird entities and beings that messed with us at the Mandeville house. They would often hide small objects, especially when we needed them. Things came in and moved stuff for J-R and me and everybody. Once, I couldn't find my credit card and I looked everywhere. I'll scream at those little trolls; they're in the house but invisible. I'll say, "This is not OK; you'd better give me my credit card. I will tear you guys apart." Meanwhile, I know they're laughing at me. The next morning, my dream says, "Go check the trash."

I always tell clients in my spiritual counseling sessions, never negate that little voice inside you that says to check it out. Many people respond, "No, I'll do it later." Careful … that voice will stop talking to you eventually. J-R always told me, and I'll tell you, to go check it. So that morning, I went to look in the trash and the credit card was in there. I ran to J-R and said, "I got my credit card. Somebody here is doing this." I told that story in my book.

They would do that with his keys, too, so we all went around chasing invisible things all the time. After a while, I became the king of finding lost items, and Nat got good at it too. Just today, I got here later than I wanted, because one of those trolls moved my wallet. So I walked to the car and said, "Seriously! I've got to go, I have something to do." Then my wallet appeared again. Jason Laskay was right there as a witness. I said, "Jason, I can't

Experience or Information?

find my wallet." I left, came back, left, came back, and suddenly the wallet reappeared.

Before the Internet, J-R loved watching TV infomercials and ordering items from catalogs. When I moved into Mandeville, he had boxes of stuff all the way down the hallway to his room, crowding my space in the back. At that time, I was extremely picky about cleanliness and clutter, so I wanted it gone. "Mail Number Three" was our shorthand that referred to the unread catalogs, at least 30 boxes full. It took years to go through them all, because we could never toss anything without asking J-R, "Can I throw it away?" "No, I'll look at it later." "You're not going to look at it later." Every now and then, though, I'd get J-R to go through Mail Number Three. We'd start with one box—he looked through every page of every catalog. It never ended—J-R would glance over one or two pages, get hungry, and put it down again. We would also get interrupted by six months of staff travels every year.

And that was just the catalogs. The amount of stuff that accumulated over the years was frustrating. We still had electronics from former staff in the early '80s, and dating back even further. One particular day, sometime in 2011, I finally got a green light. I pleaded, "J-R, c'mon man, let me throw stuff out!" J-R said, "Fine." So I called my guys with a pickup truck to cart away all those electronics from the '60s. J-R loved technology and collected so many gadgets over the years. We still had an old-style intercom in the house that was no longer connected. I suggested, "Let's throw that out." J-R said, "You touch, you leave!" When I asked what was so special about it, J-R said, "I communicate that way." That totally tripped me out—it's like he had a telephone between two worlds. To this day, I can't touch that intercom. When we re-did his room, we left it alone. When I moved out, I told the Prez, "Don't touch the intercom."

J-R would be in his chair flipping through channels with the remote control while I sat on the couch. One time in my acting days, I asked him to stop on *The Godfather*, but he flicked right past it and kept changing the channel. He said, "You've got a TV in your room, watch it there." Now I've become a channel flicker just like him. I didn't realize until much later that the flicking was J-R's way to trick the mind. If his mind got too involved in something, it would override his Soul's focus. My theory is that by flicking, he distracted the mind so he could look where he needed to look. It might look like J-R was watching TV, but he was actually gone. Later, I started to realize that I could do the same thing. I was always the most creative when J-R was talking because the mind flipped and entered into creativity. The same thing happens now when John talks. So I whip out the computer intending to create—not to play games or distract myself. That's when notes come in, ideas come in. When the Travelers speak, the door opens to creativity. I believe that was a technique that I took advantage of, so now I'm flicking. I actually use CNN's disastrous news broadcast as white noise, playing in the kitchen. My mind goes, "Oh my God, disaster!" but then I'm off somewhere else, into the total Spirit and creative source. It's similar to spacing out on the freeway and missing the off-ramp but safer.

Q: I want to thank you for your service, Jsu. I'd like to ask about the time when they finished the September 2014 Light Tour in Israel and then it was you, J-R, and David Sand, and maybe the nurse. You were wheeling him around and he's half gone. I am a nurse, and no doctor in their right mind would say that this is OK.

A: Laurie Lerner's contributions made it possible to support J-R at a very high level on that trip. We were able to turn his hotel room into a hospital. We had four doctors with us in Israel, communicating with the doctors in L.A. It was really critical to keep the supply lines open, and I didn't do anything without J-R's approval. Despite how it may have looked, J-R was there. I'd say, "Hey, Hamas is bombing Israel with rockets. Are we good?" And J-R responded, "We're good." J-R started off in E.R. when we arrived after the 15-hour nonstop flight, which Laurie paid for. Nat, J-R, and I even flew first class. We never enjoyed it because we switched off between watching J-R and sleeping. But it was suitable for J-R, because of the larger seats, aisles, and lavatories. Once we landed, I arranged for all of the equipment, supplies, and prescriptions to be sent up to J-R's hotel room. Oxygen tanks, breathing masks, and other gear. Mostly, I built a hospital in his hotel room. For acute care, we had two nurses with us 24 hours a day. If we had to take him to an actual hospital at some point, we would have.

Q: The nurses went on all the trips with J-R?

A: Yes, at least two at a time. They worked hard and some of them burnt out when they couldn't get at least 10 hours of sleep. Nurses have a shelf-life. Nat and I too; by the time J-R passed, we were fried. It was tough. J-R only slept around two hours at a time, so Nat and I switched off. I was up all night and then I'd sleep during the day.

Our nurses were the best. Before we hired them, J-R told me, "Angels are going to come be with me now." He was right and we couldn't have done it without them. Nat and I got schooled. When the nurses ring the bell, you'd better pay attention. That's your tithing dollars, by the way. All the donations you made since 2007 paid for a lot of J-R's medical care and nursing. So thank you.

There comes a point when you're taking care of somebody when you must have the common sense to say, "It's beyond my means now." And it wasn't yet. Although J-R looked it, I knew what his boundary was, and we had experts with us. There were doctors going in and out of his room and conferring over the phone. The nurses were my protection. I'd ask, "How are we doing?" "He's good." "If he isn't, tell me. Ring the bell. That means we'll go home." We got back to Mandeville and he was still fine. Then a few weeks later, he found the time to go and he left. I never felt blame for anything. I think that last Israel trip was the greatest thing ever. I think we broke a record with 141 people. We got a room at the David Citadel Hotel that faced Jaffa Gate, the Tower of David, and Mount of Olives. Every morning, J-R rose at sunrise. He'd look out the window and say, "I love this." That's all I needed. It was incredible.

I have a sense that the initiates and ministers who were there did something with J-R and John that will show itself later, some kind of covenant. Then J-R was done. I looked at it as if there was something bigger at play. "What can I contribute here? Am I out of line?" And I would always ask J-R. The thing that we could never do with J-R or his basic self was to exclude him by holding secret meetings about what we were doing. It's called withholding. It would instantly backfire on us. So I was always having meetings with J-R, even when he was out traveling, his consciousness was still present. "What are we going to do?" He canceled the trip in January because it wasn't clear, and I was upset. "Damn, we'll never go to Israel again. It's over." But then in July, I asked, "Is it spiritually clear to go Israel? And J-R says, "Yes." So we were on. Nat was right there, my right-hand man. We went to the wall.

It was tough, but now I know how to help people for the highest good and discern when it's better spiritually to stay clear and just hold the Light for them. Someone else was sick recently, and I knew what to do and what to say. My 33-year-old niece recently died in Miami from an overdose of fentanyl and heroin. I went on automatic pilot, flew there, and paid for her cremation. Everyone was crying, but I just did my job and I didn't feel anything. She was a good girl and had met J-R. That's why I think I was OK with it all. She met J-R, the initiation happened, and I'm hoping that she Soul Travels with him.

One last question.

Q: I remember J-R working with another spiritual group. Once we saw J-R at Urth Caffé; we were talking to some guy who was trying to sell us something, and said, "That's our friend, John-Roger. Do you know him?" He says, "Everybody knows him." When we went into the restaurant, I told J-R and he said, "Well, sometimes people know me who are not in MSIA. They are with other spiritual groups that I work with." "So who are they?" "They're the Silent Ones. They have names, but they're called the Silent Ones." Do you remember that?

A: No, but that tracks with the seminars I've heard where he works with Great White Brotherhood.

Q: But it sounded like they were in physical bodies ...

A: I believe it. I think J-R was the conduit. He was the Light that connected to everything. So if you plug into him, you're working with him, although you might not be aware of it. I find it interesting that Ishwar Puri's schedule looks like the exact same itinerary as John and J-R's that we've always had when we travel the world. I wondered, "How did this guy come out of nowhere when we've never heard of him before?" J-R passed into Spirit and then Jan Shepherd found Ishwar—who was the initiate of Sawan Singh, one of the Travelers before J-R—on YouTube. When I was out visiting with Ishwar, I asked, "Where do you want to eat?" He said, "I love pizza" and I could swear it was J-R answering.

It's interesting how the Traveler's energy is available to all groups. Even Scientology, in some odd way, because many of my Hollywood friends have been a part of that. It seems like, in every religion, there is always someone to whom J-R is connected. When I was doing the research for the *Mystical Traveler* movie, I was listening to old audio tapes. He knew everybody: David Spangler, the Findhorn group, Werner Erhardt, Tony Robbins, when he was starting out—they were all connected. I think J-R might be the only one I know who met everybody. They came and went—J-R sprinkled magic dust over them, and then they would go off, doing their own thing. For a while, we were following Benny Hinn, an Israeli-Christian televangelist that J-R really loved. He spoke really well and did faith healings where he would touch someone, and they'd fall down. J-R told me that long ago, he was an usher for Kathryn Kuhlman's healing services, and Pauli Sanderson confirmed that J-R would go and work with her. She was a very dramatic faith healer like Elizabeth Clare Prophet, whom J-R also knew.

Neva Del Hunter was fascinating, too. And seeing Robert Waterman win the Minister of the Year award at Conference was great. When you learn the history of MSIA, you realize how plugged in J-R was. He was just tuned in to everything, on all the levels. He knew where people were coming from, what all the connections were, and so on. My early years on staff with J-R were basically watching Pastor Gene Scott on satellite every night, especially during the Windermere era. There was really nothing he didn't know.

"Sometimes one of your biggest challenges will be to keep your mouth shut and let people make their own decisions and travel their own path. It's important. Sometimes you'll 'know' that you can see what is best for them, and it will be so tempting to lay it out for them and tell them what it is. Don't do it. Let them come to their own realizations and their own awakenings, in their own time."

-JOHN-ROGER, D.S.S.

"Cherish your visions and your dreams as they are the children of your soul; the blueprints of your ultimate achievements."

– Napoleon Hill

Chapter 15

Consciousness, Health, and Healing Prayer

ॐ

After earning a Master's Degree in Spiritual Psychology from University of Santa Monica in August 2016, I enrolled in their third-year Consciousness, Health, and Healing program for the 2017-18 academic year. One of the most powerful assignments was to create our own healing visualization prayer that can be repeated daily for radiant health and well-being. If this is something that moves you, I encourage you to write your own healing prayer.

My prayer showed up spontaneously as a download from Spirit as I was on an airplane flying to my next destination. After boarding, I asked for the Light to be inside me and for John-Roger's energy to surround and prepare me for this flight.

They've just closed the door. The air in the cabin is very nice and the seat is quite comfortable. I put my seatbelt on. They have lowered the lights and I can see the window, noticing how dark it is outside with the lights. I'm hearing the sound and hum of the engines, which is similar to the Hu tone. It sounds like HUUUUUUU ... The engines are revving up with high RPMs that seem to contain all of the sacred tones, my five initiatory tones, and the Hu. The cabin is dark with a lot of purple light at the ceiling to gently illuminate the aisles. Now the aircraft is signaling purple, which means ready for takeoff. As the plane—or my Soul or my body—begins to take off with the sound that's coming in, I start hearing, among other noises, the honeycomb buzzing of bees in the millions.

With that, I have the sensation of purple Light entering the areas of my mind, all the areas that have been hurt and those that have memory and reaction; all the parts of my mind that have patterning and pattern interrupts get filled with this purple Light and also a yellow Light that just came in. It clears out, then becomes filled in with the purple lapis color. The honeycomb is made up of all these little tiny slots, but it continues on infinitely, as big as universes. It doesn't stop. It's almost like you can go inside the cone and be inside an atom that has endless space inside.

The sound is very strong as I'm lifting and going higher. I can feel through every cell of my body the Sound Current flushing me like warm, warm water all over my body. It is coming through the honeycomb of my mind, then it keeps going down into the cells of my arm and my chest and my heart and my legs and my torso and my hips.

It's almost like having a laser surgery with some kind of spiritual material that creates rivets, cracks, and seams in deteriorating areas of my body. It's as if I am being 3-D printed in my hip and reproductive area, my upper and lower back—everywhere that hurts. All of a sudden, the Sound Current has entered another level and is hitting all the nerves in my neck and back of the head. The color is purple, which is perfect because it goes into the nerve that is shaded blue. I keep hearing the word "saffron," connecting back to the yellow Light that appeared earlier. I envision the saffron dissolving in the warm water as if it is a dye.

It starts in my stomach and goes all the way, like tie-dying a white shirt by putting rubber bands around it, then dipping each area in different colors. That's it, I can see the purple inside me now, opening up and flooding my body all over. I am at one with myself and my mind, my Basic Self, my True Self, and the greater part that is inside me.

Baruch Bashan.

Soul Traveling 2019

"Delicious loving, Spiritual awareness, Silent listening, and Alignment to J-R."

– Jesus Garcia, D.S.S.;
Master of Spiritual Science program
Affirmation, 2003

"Do not spoil what you have by desiring what you have not; remember that what you now have was once among the things you only hoped for."

– Epicurus

Chapter 16

Manifesting Abundance

New Year's Eve webcast at my home
Santa Monica, California, December 31, 2018

I learned a lot from John-Roger about manifesting abundance through seeding, tithing, and money magnets, and I wanted to share some of that here from my perspective. Much of this information was included in his classic book, *Wealth and Higher Consciousness* (available in the MSIA.org online store or on Amazon).

Money Magnet

I strongly suggest that you start by creating a money magnet. In *The Richest Man in Babylon*, a book published in 1926, author George S. Clason relates the parable of a wealthy man who gave himself 10 percent of everything he earned. In his book, *Wealth and*

Higher Consciousness, J-R called this a "money magnet," saying it was important to give yourself 10 percent of whatever you receive. Your basic self needs to know that it gets something from all of your hard work, and you're just not giving all your money away to others. Once your basic self realizes that it is making money, it will cooperate more and more with your efforts.

Basically, how it works is, from each dollar that comes in, give yourself 10 cents first. If your paycheck is $500, take out $50 in cash and save it in a hidden place at home. Did you ever wonder how banks consistently pull in money? By holding on to money, they have created a magnet that attracts more money. So you don't want to deposit your 10% in a bank or leave it at someone else's house—keep it very close to magnetize the money directly to you.

Remember that this cash is for saving, not spending. Even if you are broke near the end of the month, don't touch it! Saving up for a new house or a vacation is not a money magnet, either. Keep it safe or carry it with you. The form doesn't matter—it could be paper bills, coins, or other items of comparable value. Some basic selves love the feeling of collecting silver dollars, gold or silver coins, even jewelry or rings. Buying stocks also can act as a money magnet; print out the stock certificate or paperwork and keep it with the other items in your home. The key is to nurture your money magnet over time with energetics that support large amounts of money flowing to you.

As it grows, your money magnet has the power to magically attract abundance in all of its forms—in addition to financial wealth, there is tremendous value in good health, nutritious food, a loving relationship, children, happiness, security, and peace of mind. I have kept a money magnet for a long time and believe that it helped me get many of my well-known roles as an actor, along with seeding and other support that J-R provided.

Tithing and Seeding

J-R said that tithing is giving back to God in gratitude for what we have already received, and seeding represents our appreciation in advance for what we want to create. He suggested that we tithe and seed to our spiritual source, whatever that may be. For instance, someone who is Jewish would give to their synagogue; Christians to their church; Muslims to their mosque. Those of us who study in MSIA tithe and seed to MSIA. Personally, I seed to receive the Traveler's energy through J-R and John Morton, and MSIA is the organization that represents this.

Although tithing is most commonly recognized as a Biblical concept, it is actually based on a universal spiritual law of abundance and not tied into Judeo-Christianity. Tithing involves giving 10% of your "harvest" or financial increase to acknowledge God as your partner in co-creation. While some people base this percentage on their net income, personally, I tithe on my gross income in full appreciation for what I have received. I also choose not to write it off on my tax return as a charitable donation, because to me that goes against the spirit of tithing, which is a reminder of God's grace. There is no reason to overcomplicate this process; just keep it simple.

Seeding, on the other hand, symbolizes your trust that you will receive whatever you are envisioning. In short, the idea is to hold a clear intention of what you want to create, energize that vision, determine its value, and "seed" 10 percent of that amount as a kind of "down payment"; then you let it go so Spirit can handle it for the highest good. Often, you end up with a reward from Spirit that is even better than your original vision. Sometimes the value of what you are seeding for shows up as abundance and healing, rather than a material item or money. There are many miracles in life that God supplies to us in various ways. And it's important not to treat God as "the great bellhop in the sky," which is something that J-R often told us.

I used seeding a lot in my acting career to get roles that I desired, but it took me a while to learn how to seed successfully. I learned that it was critical to be as specific as possible while planting the seed. Let me illustrate how that works. The first time, I really wanted to be in a movie. J-R told me to find the projected value of what the movie would be worth, then seed a percentage of that; so I seeded around $500. The way that I worded it was, "I'd like to be in this movie." Sure enough, I got cast, we filmed, then upon its release, my part had been cut out. I went back to J-R, who said, "Well, you've got to really put all the details out. God knows what you want, but if you're limited in your scope, then you're going to get exactly what you asked for and then some."

I seeded again, saying, "I'd love to get a role in movie that I'm not cut from." Once again, I got cast in a film, and this time, I wasn't cut. However, the movie did not turn out to be successful. This is how Hollywood works: you can be really bad in a popular movie and continue to work, or you can be really good in a flop and never get seen at all. Actors want to be seen, do well, then get their next role and the next one and so on.

Finally, after learning through trial by error, my third seed was a request to get cast in a blockbuster movie (earning over $100 million dollars or more, according to *Variety* magazine) where my role wasn't cut in the released version. Next thing I knew, I was shooting *Along Came Polly*, co-starring Jennifer Aniston and Ben Stiller. My part didn't get cut, I did really well, and it was a huge hit, earning $172 million dollars plus cast bonuses. J-R told me, "Put your hands in the air and just receive." I did that and WOW! It was a really amazing experience and I was flying high.

Manifesting Abundance

You can use the same process to manifest just about anything. Many people visualize and energize their seeds with a vision board, an ideal scene, or a mind map. You might say, "Oh, I'd really love a house." Well, you'd better be very clear with exactly what you want—detail your vision as best as you can, then hand it over to God. If you just say "I want a house," it might end up being in Utah with termites or rusty pipes; so you get more than you bargained for and have to pay for repairs. Many of us in MSIA have heard J-R's favorite warning, "Be careful what you ask for, because you might just get it … and everything that goes along with it."

In my counseling sessions, sometimes women say, "I'd love a relationship." But what does that mean? You can have a relationship with this thing or that person, and it doesn't necessarily mean a romantic partnership. So get as close as possible to the vision you have for that relationship. How does it feel inside, how does it look, what are you doing together? The more vividly you can imagine it, the more powerful (and accurate) your manifestation will be. After you plant the seed (a percentage based on the value you determine), it also helps to hang out in places where you might meet the man or woman of your dreams. J-R used to say, "If you want to meet a doctor or dentist, head up to Mammoth Mountain or Big Bear for a ski trip, where the doctors and dentists go."

These are examples of things that you can pursue in the world; they're not bad, but always remember to ask for the "highest good." J-R ingrained that in me, because you don't want to manifest something from your will that might be too much to handle karmically. Some people can't handle owning a house, or find other things difficult. As you become more responsible, more things are given to you.

Along with many other ministers and initiates, I used to seed a lot for J-R's health, which was magical, in my opinion. I continue to seed for J-R's Soul and more. While he was still on the planet, I saw him get one extension after another; he kept living and getting healthier, and we would find new practitioners to support his well-being. To me, as a spiritual scientist, this was proof: one day he wouldn't be feeling well, I would seed, and the next day he was fine. Or we'd get a call from a doctor in another country with a new treatment that gave him a few more years. There were just so many miracles that happened on a daily basis.

As mentioned earlier, tithing was first mentioned in the Old Testament when Abraham gave 10 percent of his harvest to the priest, Melchizidek. I tithe quite often to MSIA—I love it and it feels great to me. But that's my private business between me and my source: J-R and the Christ. The MSIA teachings about tithing, through J-R and John Morton, refer to it as a partnership with God, which has always been my experience.

Some people find it difficult to tithe 10 percent of their increase, or income. It's fine to start slowly at 1 percent or even 0.5 percent, then work up gradually to 2 percent, 5 percent, and so on. Some people go in the other direction and tithe a double portion, 20 percent. Just do the best you can; it isn't really a numbers game. It's more like a marriage game, because you're with the source and having this experience. Your mindset is the most important thing. In MSIA, we've talked about being a "joyful giver." If you can tithe with joy and gratitude in your heart for what you have received from God, even if you are tithing a penny, you will be ahead of the game.

In the old days, everyone would write checks and do an inner process of thanking God. You can still do this and mail it to MSIA (or wherever your source is). But nowadays, it's so much easier to tithe and seed through our mobile MSIA app; I still do the same inner process as I'm clicking and swiping.

Recently, I gave a large tithe to a person in my spiritual community who needed the money. Sometimes, if I am aware of someone in the Movement who is older or going through a tough time and doesn't have enough to pay for food or Discourses, I will tithe directly to them instead of the church. If an action feels clear inside of me, I do it, taking full responsibility. I know what I'm doing, because I am in contact with J-R, and ultimately, it's between me and God. I'm not suggesting that you do anything like this, but if you do, I'd encourage you to check inside to see what is in alignment for you, with Spirit.

So I do seeding … I do tithing … they are both ingrained in me, so I do them as part of my regular routine. I can't stress enough that the money magnet is actually my favorite tool of the three. I feel like a little kid—"Ooooh, I just gave myself a dollar!" You can begin your money magnet with the first coin that you get, or the first bill. But it doesn't even need to be currency; it can also be a gem, a ring or other jewelry, or anything of monetary value. Again, this is a sacred process that you don't want to share with people; keep it between you and the source.

When you start communicating and being partners with God and become a co-creator, it starts to get pretty incredible. Eventually, you might find you can manifest something instantly by just thinking about it—always asking for the highest good. I've heard J-R say, "The soul observes and the mind talks." That's why I am very careful about what I ask for, because I will get it and never want to end up with something I don't want.

So the bottom line is, when you receive, contribute 10 percent to your money magnet first. Then if you want to be in partnership with your source, tithe. If there is something you'd like to manifest, seed. Then use the rest to pay bills, save, invest, buy groceries, and live your life.

Insight IV, Sofia, Bulgaria, 2019

*"If your mind plays questions, you can, if you wish, use the spiritual law of assumption:
to assume right now that you are in Soul consciousness.
In this place of the Soul, you
experience unconditional loving for yourself and
everything around you. Any disturbances
are dissolved instantaneously in this awareness and it
all becomes energy that's added to
you for your strength and your purpose."*

– JOHN-ROGER, D.S.S

Chapter 17
Influence and Assumption

हू

This is an edited transcript of a presentation on October 29, 2018, which was my second talk at the home of Kate Ferrick and Richard Klein in Newbury Park, California.

Question: Jsu, I've heard you say that your life was weird before you met J-R. What do you mean by that?

Answer: Show of hands, how many of your lives were weird before you met J-R?

It felt like the world was harsher because I had a bad attitude and outlook on life. Even though I went into the acting world and knew what I wanted, I wasn't really focused. J-R told me that nothing actually became different after meeting him except my attitude and judgments. When I studied psychology much later, I realized that I was running away from something at that time. Then I meet J-R, who was the most authentic person ever. I have a very addictive personality, so I went from doing drugs to selecting the best vitamins, weighing my food, and researching what kind of blender we should get for the protein drinks. I reframed my addictions years ago.

My life before was totally "not J-R," and now, after 26 years together, I can't live without his constant influence. I am constantly spinning the jukebox with my fiancée, Nicole; I drop the needle and it plays J-R. I get nostalgic, especially when I'm driving somewhere or listening to music that reminds me of all the things he said and did. "Oh, we always used to eat at this Denny's on our way to and from Windermere Ranch in Santa Barbara. We would exit at Wendy Drive and order hash browns, two eggs over easy, pancakes, and coffee. Thirty minutes later, we'd be back on the road." Sometimes we'd go to In-and-Out Burger instead.

J-R often said that "Ordinariness is a prior condition to God." He demonstrated that all the time, because he was so simple. He had a cup of coffee with one teaspoon of sugar and stirred it exactly the same way, every morning, followed by two eggs over easy on hash brown potatoes or corned beef hash. From the beginning, when I took over as J-R's driver, that was our routine for many years: breakfast, lunch, dinner, meetings, health visits, and MSIA events.

In *The Love of a Master*, I share the story of when I first saw J-R in person, while attending a relationship workshop with Drs. Ron and Mary Hulnick at the Sheraton Universal Hotel in January 1988. At that time, I had already read J-R's great *Relationships* book, and I was trying to hold my marriage together. An old, brown, four-door Lincoln with "Mystical Traveler" abbreviated license plates pulled up next to me; J-R sat in the back seat doing paperwork. He rolled the tinted window down and I said, "Hi, I'm

Jesus, an actor, and I was just in *Gotcha*." J-R said, "I know, I saw you in it." Of course, when actors are starting out, they crave any kind of recognition; but I couldn't believe it. "What? He actually saw my movie?"

I am very competitive and when I saw John driving, I thought, "I want to do that." So when I got called on to share with J-R in front of the group, I stood up and asked, "How can I do what John does?" J-R told me to go talk to John. At that time, I had long hair and was very cocky. If you think I'm arrogant now, I was super arrogant then. And I knew what I wanted. Along with that arrogance came determination, and nothing could stop me. I was like a pit bull locking his jaws on a bone, if I wanted something. I was determined to be J-R's friend and the rest is history.

How do you navigate once you lose someone physically like that? We'd had such a powerful connection. Then, he started to show up in dreams. When you're dreaming, it's a really smart idea to confirm whether you are encountering the real J-R and John or the counterfeit versions who try to fool and mislead you. So I would have a dream, see J-R, and get all excited. "Oh my God, it's J-R!" All the guys would rush over to him, sobbing. We got initiated, then he sent me away. I said, "That can't be! No!" Then he looked over and said, "That wasn't me." I responded, "OK, but it seemed so real and sure looked like you." In my experience, the inner and outer Master don't contradict each other, which is how you can start to be discerning.

For many years, I had the privilege of confirming with J-R directly whenever I had an inner experience. After he passed, I was left with my own process of tracking, from the Peace Theological Seminary's Master and Doctor of Spiritual Science programs. Tracking was also a tool included in the original discourses, which had calendars in the back for checking off spiritual exercises, highs, and lows for the month. There is nothing better than tracking—I've tracked for years like a maniac. After I have a dream, I'll try to connect all the dots. "Wait a minute. If I did this, then talked to her, and I did that other thing, and now I have the flu … let's go back. I was responsible for it. What did I do?" From J-R, I learned how to confirm outwardly and inwardly. University of Santa Monica (USM) provided me with some excellent tracking processes, too. The part that was most valuable in USM was sitting in the Neutral Observer seat during trios, just observing and listening. This was always very hard for me to do.

When I first moved into J-R's house, he gave me a book called *The Listener*. I said, "What is this? I don't read books!" At that point, in my 20s, I had only read three books in my life: *The Godfather*, *The Once and Future King*, and *The Fountainhead*. Those three books ruined and made my life. *The Fountainhead* by Ayn Rand changed me. *The Godfather* by Mario Puzo explained the streets. *The Once and Future King* by T.H. White was all about Merlin, King Arthur, and underneath it all, the Traveler. Those three books set the tone for me to meet J-R. Of course, once I was on the MSIA Soul Awareness Discourses, I found them amazing, along with every other book after that. However, *The Listener* by Taylor Caldwell was just incredible—I read it again after J-R passed. In fact, I've become a student since his transition, doing the USM programs and studying more on my own.

Before his transition, I was a caretaker, a helper, a luggage packer, a driver, a fixer. Whenever something broke, I had the knack of fixing it. The biggest crime at the Mandeville house was not reporting a broken item, for fear of retribution or getting blamed. If J-R learned that one of us knew about something that we didn't report, he would ask, "How long did you know about this?" If the person answered, "About three months," J-R would say, "You're fired. Call PRANA, you're moving in tomorrow."

One of my fellow J-R staff members was notorious for running into and breaking things. We used to laugh and tease him; his stories entertained all. Then I became famous in our house for locating missing stuff, finding broken items, and repairing them. We were taught, if it's broken, fix it. J-R didn't care who broke something, as long as it was immediately repaired or reported. When the pipe burst or the refrigerator drawer cracked, or the coffee mug handle broke off, I always seemed to be the one to discover it, then I would do my best to fix it. Eventually, J-R made me responsible for everything. There was always something to handle around Nat and me—drive the car and get a flat tire. So, with J-R, it wasn't about dodging who did it, it was, "Did you fix it?" We would say, "Yeah, all done." Then he never brought it up again.

One of my favourite stories in *The Love of a Master* was kind of brutal at the time. During PAT IV trips and staff travels, J-R would carry an Italian leather satchel with thousands of dollars in cash for emergencies, tipping, taxis, and other travel expenses for our group. Near the end of my very first PAT IV trip, J-R put me on staff and arranged for me to travel onward to other countries with a smaller group. I had no idea what that was going to be like. At the airport in Amsterdam, he asked me to watch his bag, and I thought, "Oh, this is simple." He went to the KLM ticket counter to check in for our flights to Russia, and I took my eye off the bag for a minute. He came back and asked, "Can you get my bag?" But it was gone. My stomach fell straight down to the floor. I felt awful. There were literally thousands of dollars in that bag. J-R just said, "Looks like that guy needed it more than me" and never brought it up ever again. He never put me down about it or anything. That was a heavy lesson, but I got it. Ever since then, when I'm at the airport, I always keep my eye on the bag. I've done trips with 150 people when I've been in charge of baggage. We watch everybody around us and count all the luggage twice. So I'm ready now.

Q: Can you share about the Israel trip? You said you had some amazing experiences, and my antenna went up on that one.

A: I loved the trips that John was doing. When J-R passed away, I grieved and asked, "Why does this have to stop?" Then in the USM Consciousness, Health, and Healing program, we were assigned to create ideal scenes around our clear intentions. One of my intentions was, "I want to continue doing what I was already doing before." What was that? Group trips. I had been leading various tours with J-R since 2007, so I decided to continue traveling and sharing the experience of J-R, in order to learn to walk with the presence of J-R, my inner master. I realized that any hesitation I felt was related to a lack of confidence from self-esteem issues. If you ever feel like you don't have what it takes to do something, it's just your self-esteem, which you can acknowledge and bypass. Then you find that the willingness to do gives you the ability to do, as J-R always said. So I decided, "OK, I want to go back to Israel in September 2017."

All of a sudden, David Sand designed a digital banner to promote the trip online, then everything started to kick in. We got T-shirts; we got creative. Nicole and I had already bought our tickets, and I gambled everything. We needed to hit a minimum of 15 for the trip to pay for itself. As the organizer, I wasn't intending to make any money from it, but I needed to at least go. I decided, "You know what? I don't care if just we two end up going to Israel." Then Wendy signed up, and then two more. The momentum was building, but I didn't want to get cocky like the Olympic snowboard athlete who said, "I won!" just before falling at the end of her run and losing.

Then I went to Chile and seven Latin women came on board for the Israel tour. I said, "Oh my God, I've got to do translations!" So with my own money, I subtitled a couple of J-R's videos. Then more people wanted to come. One woman donated money, even though she didn't come on the trip, which was amazing. Debbie decided to come; we had 15 and there we were. It was a wonderful trip. The best highlight was celebrating J-R's birthday on September 24 at the Notre Dame Hotel, overlooking the Old City of Jerusalem at sunset, six o' clock. Everybody looked beautiful and dressed up really nice. We could all feel the love of J-R so strongly.

The trip wouldn't have been the same without Benji Shavit, our tour guide in Israel. He's known J-R for over 30 years now. Zahava, his late wife, passed away from cancer. We gathered in what had been her studio at the base of Mount Tabor (also known as the Mount of Transfiguration), where Jesus is transfigured, and he speaks with Moses and Elijah. There's a magnificent Franciscan church nearby. I played a J-R seminar called, "How to Transform Yourself," which was recorded there. In it, J-R says, "I did that one for you." In the bus, we shared stories. It became a tour of walking in J-R's footsteps, which also coincided with Jesus's footsteps most of the time. It was like, after Christ passed away 2,000 years ago, if four of the disciples had traveled together in an ox-driven cart, saying, "Over here to your left is where Jesus walked." It was very cool.

At Mount of Olives, we did our traditional toast. It was a pleasure to say to everyone who hadn't been to Israel before, "This is kind of how it was back then." Even though it was only 15 and not 150 people, I always sensed that J-R was sitting in the front, with Michael Hayes working on him energetically. It really felt wonderful. We went to Bethlehem and to Jericho, in Palestine. It was incredible to experience both the Palestinian and Jewish sides, as well as the Armenian and Christian quarters.

I told John over lunch the other day, "I'm going to do J-R." All I want to do is be in that Satsang. I've planned virtual tours to Nigeria and Israel for the summer and fall of 2019, where people can travel along with me vicariously through a private Facebook group. Whenever we get together, like this today, whether it's playing an old video or doing a Q&A, I like to be the catalyst. If someone else wants to go ahead and do that, I will shut up and sit down. But I want to be the one to say, "Hey, let's show some videos."

We were recently in Santa Barbara for a video marathon, playing 16 hours straight of J-R. I like to celebrate the day he passed and his birthday. It's similar to celebrating the birth of Christ in December and his Crucifixion at Easter. Many of us knew and know J-R, others don't, but there's an inner feeling you may have. Perhaps you said you wanted to start anew and to know your path. That's the way the Traveler works inside of you, even if you're not consciously aware of it.

Q: Can you talk about the Law of Assumption?

A: Yes. Recently I was hanging out with a friend in Santa Barbara. Since the interviews I did for the *Mystical Traveler* documentary, I've been connecting with the old-timers, or Experience Masters, as I call them, such as Ted Drake, Rama Fox, Beverly Terrill, Jack Reed, David Allen, Robert Waterman, Phil Danza, Russell Bishop, and others who were there at the beginning with J-R. At this point, I declare that they're all Masters in their own right; we are all Masters, too. When I picked the brain of one of those people, inside of me I said, "Alright, J-R, I want to know about the unconscious." I'm fascinated by things I don't know, and lately, I have become very proactive to learn as much as I can about the unconscious level. I find it very interesting that it's essentially the gateway of the Soul realm.

One facet of the Law of Assumption refers to how your experiences are influenced by the thoughts you hold in your mind. I remember that J-R often said to hold in your mind pictures of what you want more of, and to act as if you have already received it. Because what you think about habitually, you become.

In the Moment of Peace video, "Christ: My Man For Eternity," J-R explains that the mind is Lucifer's domain; not evil, but something that we choose to focus on. There's the Law and then there is Grace, and it's our choice. The mind can be tricky, and I've experienced it in everyday communications through Facebook, texts, emails, etc. For instance, my ego is speaking right now, which is completely full of B.S. It's like I'm trying to bust through, so that energy comes out. I trick it by saying, "Yeah, I'm writing a book, I really want to get out and do all this." I trick my mind by watching CNN and other things to distract it while I do the spiritual work, like J-R did.

The mind is always listening and is easily influenced by things like the news. We are all suckers for the reaction that the media wants us to have. Not tragedies and terrorism *per se*, but the continuing cycle of againstness and judging that is the negative power wheel. It doesn't get us anywhere. Something I do when it comes at me, rather than take it on, is to quickly pivot my focus, and just keep going in that direction. If you fight with a skunk, you end up smelling. So you run. What do I do? I pivot.

The Dreams of a Master

Post-PAT IV trip on a break in Finland, 1988

"Oh, there's something negative in this email, I can feel the vibe." I open it up anyways, and regret it, then I'm off and judging myself again. Young people in particular get caught up in this with texting. I helped a 21-year-old and fell into it, too. "Hey, what are you doing?" "Nothing." "You want to do something tonight?" "Yeah." "Let's go eat at 6 o'clock?" Pause … "Hello?" Twenty minutes later … "Hey, are you there?" Three hours later … "Sorry, dude, I was showering." It's like an infinite, open loop. I don't like it when someone leaves me hanging; I want to close the loop and get it into my calendar. Otherwise, I'd rather not talk to them anymore; they will have to call me. That's how I clean up my act.

I am careful about the theater in which the negative power plays. Sure, we have to go out, make a living, and do stuff in the world, and so much of that is a left-brain, analytical process—like trying to read or create a spreadsheet, which pulls on my left brain into self-preservation mode. In her book *Leap of Perception*, Penney Peirce discusses the direct knowing that comes from the creative right brain. Activities like painting, singing, or being near the ocean can stimulate our right brains. Walking in parks or on the beach helps to reboot me.

Meanwhile, the reptilian brain is all about self-preservation and survival. "Oh my God, what are we going to do? What's the 5-year plan, the 10-year plan? It's going to be awful—it doesn't look good!" We forget that we are completely connected to God. But the Law of Assumption takes over and convinces us that we are not worthy, we are not divine, we are against Trump, and the whole United States is going to hell. That's fine for normal people, but it's out of balance for someone who is conducting divine energy as an initiate in the Movement of Spiritual Inner Awareness and an ordained minister in the Melchizedek priesthood. We can drop down to the astral level very quickly.

Q: There are two sides of the Law of Assumption; what you describe is the Law part. There's another part that you were describing with Nicole. And there's the assumption that everything I need is here and now—I'm totally taken care of. Can you speak about that Assumption?

A: Well, I would say that is direct knowing, not assumption. I admit that I changed the wording. J-R says to mock up the Soul, so I do it! During the Insight I seminar, we go into our inner Sanctuary and put on ability suits that give us the knowing and skills to do anything we want. We see it happening on the television screen.

Before the celebration of J-R's life that MSIA held five weeks after he passed, I asked him to send me energy. Inwardly, I saw a superhero in a rubber suit hit me in the head and I got it immediately. The message was to put the superhero suit on, which is the Spirit suit or spiritual body, and go. Don't assume it, know it. That's direct knowing. I was in Ashford Castle's Mystical Forest in Ireland when trees and plants started talking to me, which put me in a whole different level. That has happened in the small town of Ojai, California, too. I don't like to have too many conversations with plants; but if you go into nature, and you're in the knowingness, you can get plugged in. The best way to say that is you're in the zone. You can also get there by going down on all fours and barking like a dog or meowing like a cat. In other words, acting outrageous can help you break through whatever is making you rigid and shut down.

Whenever I am in contraction, I go to a karaoke bar. I act the fool and sing stupid songs, because it breaks me from the negativity that tells me I'm not going to make it; that I won't be able to pay my rent. J-R calls it a psychic self-attack when I get self-critical and judgmental. When I'm aware that I am hurting myself that way, I give myself a minute, then consciously pivot to something more positive, like karaoke or s.e.'s.

At times, my inner conversation resembles a conference call as I give all of my different aspects a voice, based on the Gestalt approach, originally developed by psychotherapist Fritz Perls. Not only did we practice this technique at USM, but it was an acting method I learned early in my career. J-R also taught me that Gestalt was a way to see the entire scene in a movie or to understand the whole form without picking it apart in my mind. Basically, we all have different parts of ourselves and each has its own agenda, so why not make it a board meeting? You can be the CEO. I'll start the meeting: "So what's going on?" "You're a jerk!" "True … next?" I only review those things that are critical, then say, "The board meeting is over in one minute." Often, I give all of those parts a voice, because they want to be heard. Sometimes I just tell them, "Clean up your act, I've noticed we've fallen short—so let's do better. I love you all, see you at the next meeting." Then I practice compassionate self-forgiveness and move on.

If someone in real life is ever criticizing you, you can simply leave—either walk out the door physically or retreat inwardly. You can sit there while you focus behind your eyes and between your ears, and maybe chant your tone or Ani-Hu. J-R said that when a baby is crying, don't worry about it, that's just energy. If someone is tripping or hating on me, I start drinking that in like a vampire and transmute it into love. I say inwardly, "I love you, God bless you, peace be still," or I chant my tone or HU. It's not wrong to lose it; you just need to go back and forgive yourself. In the Catholic Church, they label this "sinning" and call it evil. I've heard J-R say that sinning only means *missing the mark*.

As life goes on, it's easy to forget that we can reset things through forgiveness. So we just keep reminding ourselves and coming back to it again. Even when I'm trying to do things right, I can easily fall short. A few months ago, after I returned from Israel, nothing was flowing. I wondered, "What am I doing wrong?" My intuition is to take better care of myself. So I thought, maybe I just need to unplug. So I unplugged and the generator shut down. Nobody was home. Nothing got done that day or the next. After seven days, I still had accomplished absolutely nothing. Then I realized I had to take care of myself in a different way.

At that point, I went into direct knowing and heard that I needed to recharge. What did that mean? Spiritual exercises or walking, or both. We did a lot of walking—at least five miles a day—in London, when we were there last month. Movement is one of the best ways to get negativity out of your body. So if you're sitting at home and you've been down on yourself for over a half-hour, you need to get out. Either spiritually, which is to chant your tone or Hu/Ani Hu, or physically—get outside and take a walk. Otherwise, you may end up turning on the TV and wallowing in that negativity with CNN all night.

In one dream, I was watching a video game, but when I pulled back, I saw that it was actually my life. I said, "Oooh, cool! So it's all a game." But when karma hits, it looks so real. "No, I can't believe I'm in so much debt! It's real!" "I just got divorced! It's real!" Doing your s.e.'s assists you to pull back and realize that this is all shadows on the wall, nothing is real. This perspective can assist you in being more detached when things happen in your life. As I've heard J-R say, "This world is Maya (illusion). We want to be disillusioned. We want Manna."

He also talked about the triangle of thinking, feeling, and doing, which all need to be congruent. When we think something and feel it, but don't take the associated action, that leads to contraction and feeling stuck. If you think, "I'll go work out," but don't feel like putting your shoes on, your basic self registers the lack of action, not the intention. So the next time, you think about working out, your basic self says, "Naaaah…" and the cycle of inaction keeps going. So to set yourself up for success, the triangle needs to be: "I'm going to work out. I feel great about that; let's put my shoes on and get out the door." And then do it.

I used to get a lot more done with J-R, but I'm learning that there are seasons, or cycles, of activity—especially as initiates of the Traveler. We can be like a flashlight; it's On when we're doing stuff and Off when we're not. Those times that we are Off, we can feel very distracted, unmotivated, and non-productive for no apparent reason. That may be because we're not really here; we're Soul Traveling. Although we are always here and now, often we are simultaneously somewhere else in Spirit with a different part of our consciousness. Those of us who are initiated and being used by the Traveler might be learning in some *Mystery Schools* or Soul Traveling with John-Roger and John Morton—which means we're only 40 or 50 percent here in the world. Asking yourself, "How present am I today?" then intuiting or muscle-testing your percentage is a good way to gauge how present you are.

The problem is when we go into judgment of ourselves for not being more productive. Once I asked J-R, "What's going to be my ultimate issue?" and J-R responded, "Your judgments." I laughed then, but now that I'm much older, I realize what he meant. Speaking for myself, the slightest judgment can open up a Pandora's box of going nowhere. In my acting days, I used to be very judgmental. "That dude is not as good as me." I never went anywhere with that attitude. I only got roles when J-R would "fix" me. Many times I would hear from my agent about a role right after taking an Insight seminar or PTS workshop, because I had dissolved my blocks and judgments, at least temporarily. With a positive attitude, creativity expands and abundance comes in. J-R would say there is a warehouse up there with all the money and items that you have ever wished for, so you just have to know how to bring it down to this level.

J-R was spooky good at precipitating abundance; he only had to think of something and people gave it to him. For instance, when his phone stopped working, someone came up and gave him a new iPhone out of the blue. Another time, he lost his watch, then received a new one as a gift. When he didn't have money, someone would give him cash. I don't know how, but he never had to ask for anything. It was crazy; I've never seen that before or since. J-R didn't need anything or lack anything, because he was a living Master tapped into divine manifestation. His vow of poverty meant that he didn't own anything personally, but he could still use things as he needed to take care of himself. Although J-R had everything on the inner level, he came into and left the planet with zero materiality on the outer level. He had it all because he gave it all.

Q: I always have been motivated by seeing the actions of people vs. their words. There's a plethora of words that J-R said, but it's the things that he has done that have been an example for me to follow and do myself. You quote J-R a lot; so what are the actions he did that really influenced you going forward, especially after he left the planet?

A: His actions? Nothing. It was the best thing he ever did. Because he didn't tell me, "About two years after I die, you're going to feel horrible and lost. Hang in there." Although he did say, "Save your money." He didn't do anything out there, but he did it all here, inside of me, and I would never want an outer thing from him. In the beginning, he would show up in a dream. He knew, or somebody knew in there, that I loved his feet. J-R's feet were so tiny; for many years, he would let me lay on his feet and watch TV. In the dream, he asked, "Don't you want to lay on my feet?" I started crying. It was a crazy visitation. He did several things like that after he passed into the Realms of Spirit.

Recently, I've had some dream experiences where John Morton comes in. I love him like a brother, but I'd like J-R to be there as well. Gestalt dream interpreters presume that some aspect of yourself is represented by each person or item in your dreams. But from a spiritual standpoint, I've wondered if everybody took time from their lives to show up in my dreams. Whenever I dream about John, it's a good excuse to get together with him. So I'll call and say, "You were in my dream," and John writes back, "Maybe ... you were in mine." Then we have lunch, talk, and I realize that the inner matches the outer, so I can confirm that the John I saw in my dream wasn't a counterfeit Traveler. The authentic Traveler will never ask you to do anything in the inner that he doesn't on the outer and vice versa. That was cool, because I began using the same technique I learned from J-R with John.

J-R's love was off the hook. I witnessed him opening the car door many times for women, even when he was sick. He would even open up the door for his nurses, which I was always forgetting to do. That's love. I would often judge some of the couples who would come up for a hug. "Oh, come on! That girl drives me crazy. That dude is a bleep." But he would just hug them, because he didn't care about the personality level. He just loved everyone. I thought, "I need to do that." Trump winning the election changed my life, because it was a sign that I needed to get with it and start loving. I don't have to cooperate with him, I don't have to endorse

*"To sit in the company of a Saint
For even an hour is of more benefit than doing a
Hundred years of Meditation alone in your homes."*

– Maharaj Sawan Singh Ji

him. But I do have to love. I cannot watch the news and think, "I hate this dude," because then I am hating myself. If you want to hurt someone, then you are hurting yourself. That's what people don't understand, and it's not right. I can't do anything, so I just have to let it roll out the way it rolled out. If Jesus Christ and all the Travelers allowed him to be in office, then there must be something going on. Many of us just don't happen to like it. I watch the news and I am learning every day to love more.

How do we work that? How do we do that? When people are getting hurt, what's the level of our responsibility? When you are triggered by an upsetting situation you see on the news, yelling at the TV might signal that you are being over-responsible for something out of your control, as J-R pointed out. He did psychology on me all the time. I'd say, "I can't stand that dude, he's terrible!" J-R told me, "He is just like you. You do exactly what he does. What don't you like about him?" "I don't like this, this, this, and this." He'd ask, "Do you do that yourself?" "Well … yes." "Then you don't like YOU!" Back then, I was too young and ignorant to know what that meant. But since going through USM's Spiritual Psychology program and other courses, I'm now more aware of how projection works and can counsel myself through it.

Q: Can you speak more about feelings vs. thoughts?

A: Before I went to USM, I never really understood the difference. I would tell J-R, "I don't feel like this is fair," and he would say, "Those are just feelings." "I'm afraid you're going to leave me!" "Are your feelings always right? No. Then leave it alone!" "Yeah, but I think … "Are your thoughts always right? You've got to answer honestly. They're not right." The ego is made up of what you feel and what you think about. I'm going to guess that 40 percent of the time, you're wrong. And 40 percent of the time, I'm wrong.

Maybe a little bit more. But we have to sidestep it. And I became really good at thinking outside the box. The ego says, "I got this, I know what I'm talking about, I see it." If someone tells you, "I was thinking the other day … I feel you don't like me," that doesn't even make sense. But so often, we identify with our thoughts and feelings and allow them to control us. If you want to read up on this topic, I recommend *Emotional Intelligence* and related titles by Daniel Goleman, Travis Bradberry, and Jean Greaves.

When you find yourself over-identifying with the ego (as represented by inaccurate thoughts and feelings), it can help to have a journaling conversation, or "inner counseling" as USM calls it, with that younger part of yourself. Find out how old he or she was when they first felt that way; what was going on, who else was involved? If something comes up while I'm out, I will record notes into my iPhone and email them to myself so I can journal about the situation later. It's not always my own stuff, though. Maybe I picked up a thought form when that guy I ran into at the market told me about some terrible thing that happened. J-R used to call them "monkeys on your back," which need to be cleared. It can take a while to clear after four or five monkeys jumped on you when someone dumped their stuff on you. Practitioners that J-R went to, like Michael Hayes, Ed Wagner, and Bertrand Babinet, along with many other terrific holistic and energetic practitioners in MSIA, can really help to clear that sort of thing.

One key difference of J-R's approach was asking yourself, "How can I close the opening that I created?" This completely takes the blame off the other person and gives you 100 percent responsibility for your own response, even if it was unconscious. Rather than saying, "They attacked me," or "I feel judged by those three girls looking at me," you can do muscle testing and ask, "I went weak on that person, so what is that about and how do I close that opening?" Then you identify, "Oh! I wanted their approval! That's it! Clear." A more in-depth clearing process is used in Peace Theological Seminary's Master of Spiritual Science program.

The quickest way to release something as it happens is to say, "Clear, clear, clear" or "Deflect!" J-R said that you can say almost anything out loud, but within one minute, you need to deflect it before it sticks in your consciousness. So the guys on staff would play around with that, saying, "You're an idiot! Deflect!"

Muscle testing is a tool that can be used for or against you. Some people misuse it by rigging their responses to signal *yes* to choices that they know aren't really supportive: "Yeah, it's clear for me to have pizza, something is telling me to eat pizza." It would be more honest just to admit, "I think I'm going to get fat today and have a pizza." Otherwise, you're giving up your responsibility. That's why I won't say I'm going on a diet unless I truly mean it, because it can get ugly on vacation. We're going to Israel where they'll be serving hummus and pita bread every day. Before you know it, you're home and weigh 40 pounds more. But then I can get back on track with the celery juice cleansing and release those extra pounds. Now I try not to lie to myself.

As I said earlier, the basic self stops trusting you when you declare something and don't follow up. Then you become a rebel, because that part of you says, "No, I'm not doing that; I think I'll just sabotage it instead." J-R was well known for renegotiating his commitments. For example, if he made an appointment and needed to cancel it, he would call and communicate this in advance to reschedule, rather than flaking out at the last minute. I remember hearing J-R saying that each person has a dominant eye, right or left. Sometimes you might make an agreement with your dominant eye when you feel strong and capable. Yet when your non-dominant, or recessive, eye takes over another day, you feel completely different about that agreement. You may even feel smaller and unable to handle the commitment you had made.

In his life, J-R went to countless practitioners, kinesiologists, holistic doctors, and many other healers. He needed others to heal him; he couldn't do it alone, which is one of the 12 Signs of the Traveler laid out in the MSIA book, *The Path to Mastership*. However, he was an open book when someone was working on him. Sometimes he would say to the practitioner, "Ask me what I think." John-Roger contained universes inside of him. He was the totality of everything, the Preceptor consciousness, and connected to God; anyone working on him saw all of that because he remained open to them. I saw that with my own eyes and experienced that with myself.

I had dreams of J-R telling me to learn a technique known as muscle testing. For a long time, I resisted, but after taking the PTS Master's (M.S.S.) and Doctor of Spiritual Science (D.S.S.) programs, I love doing it now. They teach so many great tools like that one in the D.S.S. program, which is up to five years long. By the third year, you have the option to research and write your practical treatise (P.T.). I encourage anyone who is studying in the D.S.S. class to write your practical treatise. That goes for people who went through the program earlier without graduating. Your P.T. is the thing that will percolate eventually, if not at the time that you do it, and sets the course for your life and spiritual progression.

Q: I find myself sometimes saying, "I wonder if J-R said this to Zeus." I can't remember exactly what that would be right now but I was watching an alien TV show, and I thought to myself, "I wonder if J-R spoke to Jsu about these aliens, or whether Big Foot was real, or what's going to happen in the future?" Once I heard him say that the Loch Ness monster was a prehistoric snake, so I wondered if other stuff like that ever came up in your conversations.

A: One thing that comes to mind is, we used to watch *The X-Files*. J-R would say, "Yeah, that's pretty accurate" about things like shape shifters or the cancer-eating girl. I remember that he said invisible cloaks were a real thing; people can just disappear in plain sight. In fact, J-R did that numerous times himself. John Morton and Nat can probably confirm this, too. I would enter the living room and not see J-R, then walk through all the house calling, "J-R! J-R!" When I got back to the living room, he was sitting right there, asking, "What do you want?" I'm sure that he was shape shifting or putting on the cloak of invisibility so we couldn't see him.

Of course there are aliens, but he would always joke, "Did you see that?" "Yeah, I see it!" "That's an unidentified flying object." Because it was flying, it was an object, and we couldn't identify it. Most people couldn't take living in that house with J-R, with all the bizarre, invisible stuff that goes on late at night—all sorts of things visited J-R there while he was alive. Sometimes Phil and Brooke Danza, who lived downstairs, would hear footsteps up above when they realized that we were out of town. So I got used to that over 26 years, looking for something in my bedroom, I'd feel like everybody was there, crowding me. All the beings. I would say, "Dudes! Do you mind?" then call in the Light, and they would all go. Or I'd see something from the corner of my eye that I couldn't see straight on. J-R says you can only see them obliquely. Sometimes you can see the Light that way, too; purple is J-R, of course.

After J-R passed away, I was a bundle of nerves. He had often talked about being able to smell odors psychically, that didn't have a physical source. There was a weird psychic being who would appear at the Mandeville house that we called "Smoking-Man;" I could swear it was the same character as the "Cigarette Smoking Man" from *The X-Files* TV series. Because Mandeville Canyon is very lush and green, with clean, fresh air, Nicole liked to sleep with the door open to its screen. All of a sudden, we smelled cigarette smoke and Nicole said, "Smoking-Man is here again." Another time, as we were locking ourselves in for the night next to the kitchen, this presence came in; I can only describe it since I didn't see it. I felt the door open and said, "Who the hell? We locked it!" All I could imagine was the mothership above and the tentacles reaching out …

Nicole: The night J-R died, at two o'clock in the morning, the dogs started barking and then there was a sensation that something like an octopus was looking for J-R, to find out if this was real, is he really off the planet? They were in the house, going through all the rooms looking, and we just knew we couldn't go out.

Jsu: I didn't want to go out. I didn't want to see what was there. It was creepy and I didn't want to see spirits or anything. Later, I checked some of the audio recordings, because I could have sworn that J-R said aliens also need Travelers. I had also heard that from another guru. They're Travelers of universes, so I could see this mothership coming in with the aliens asking, "Where's J-R? Oh! He passed!" They didn't need an explanation; they just felt it in the house. It was the weirdest thing. The dogs barked like they had never barked before at deer or people. Afterwards, the house was never the same. Things left and that was the closest I ever got to really experiencing it. J-R kept a lot of that to himself. He never really told us, "Somebody's parent died and they're here right now."

People often asked J-R to check out individuals with various claims and phenomena. For instance, there was a Russian guy who could diagnose disease by just looking at someone. He wasn't a healer; he only identified the problem. He'd say, "Have that X-rayed, get out, pay me." Testing would confirm something was there. Someone said, "J-R, you've got to see this Israeli with electromagnetic energy coming out of his fingers." So he did. It was a therapist who had served in the Israeli Air Force, encountered UFOs, and was blessed with this healing gift. I laid down with my eyes closed, and no kidding, it felt like electromagnetic energy shooting out of his fingers into our muscles, and sounded like the light sabers in Star Wars. The sensation was as if he was running a sock with static electricity from the dryer on my hair. I opened my eyes and looked at the sides to see if he had a battery. But he was essentially just calming my aura with electromagnetic energy from his hands that had been randomly given to him by aliens. Perhaps in some invisible way we were healed, but I couldn't tell. It was a great experience anyways.

Q: I have studied and explored tuning the aura using sound with tuning forks. Did you ever experience healing through sound or tuning the body to the Sound Current with J-R?

A: In the early 2000s, we acquired a Rife Frequency machine, or something similar, from Dr. Ed Wagner's office. Royal Rife, the original developer of this technology, determined that every disease has its own unique healing frequency. J-R followed the manual that said things like, "If you have bladder problems, set the dial to 350–45," for example. We would be watching TV going "bzzzzzt." Were we healed? I don't know. But J-R tried everything, including some really crazy stuff.

Another thing I learned from J-R was ranging, which is like viewing a remote location in your consciousness. In several seminars that J-R did on this topic, he used the Eiffel Tower as an example. It's a powerful technique that shouldn't be used to inflict upon a person or invade their privacy, unless you are invited. In *The Love of a Master*, I share about how I inadvertently ranged into my manager's home, who was a substance abuser, while I was practicing. I saw her family, what she was depressed about, and everything. Although I came back with a deeper understanding and compassion for her, it was too intense. So I don't do that anymore.

As I understand it, empathy is a natural gift that is present in us with the purpose of seeing the divine in another—not to see their karma, disease, or heaviness. So, if I tune in empathically to someone and see something negative—such as illness, addiction, or depression—it goes into me, because I went somewhere I wasn't supposed to go. Then I'll need to see a doctor or practitioner for clearing.

Q: Do you put protections around yourself?

A: I hope so. I do. But most people don't know how to do that. There are a lot of sensitive people out there in the world. Many of the younger people, millennials and indigo or crystal children, are so empathetic that they feel the pain of the universe and want to kill themselves. That's not the way to do it.

One thing J-R taught me after so many years is to own my B.S. So I'll go home with my B.S.; I'm happy with it and learn to love it. When I get married, I'll share my B.S. with my wife, and vice versa. Then the kids come in with their own stuff. That's a lot of B.S.! The family unit says, "We chose this, we're all good. We are together as a family of B.S.!" And we understand each other. But when your mother-in-law comes over, for example, if you're not careful, you pick up her B.S., too. At some point, you have to learn how to keep other people's stuff from getting in.

Q: I do that! I tie in immediately to other people with the intention of only seeing their divine and wonderful parts.

A: Yes, the compassionate part. It's all you. You're the one leading it and saying, "I will look from this altitude. I will see the love, not their broken foot." Now this is also direct knowing. My experience of J-R is that he might see your karma and say, "No, I'm not touching that." Sometimes we want to save someone, which screws up the karma of an experience that they were supposed to have. Eventually, the smart people gain a higher understanding of karma being released that we don't want to be a part of. They sit it out and watch the salmon swimming upriver to spawn. "Oh, I see. I'd rather not be involved in that."

In USM, they explain the difference between throwing a rope down to someone who is stuck in a hole, or climbing into the hole with them. When both people are in the dark, they're both going to stay stuck. So unless you're a Traveler, I wouldn't go into the hole in the first place. I've experienced that many times and know how important it is not to drag the person who is trying to help into the hole with you. If you're helping, just tell them where the light switch is and show them the stairway to climb out. You can go away then and become the creator. Ultimately, we each made an agreement to experience our own karma, as Carolyn Myss says in her book, *Sacred Contracts*, and as J-R spoke about often. "He wins who endures to the end."

Unfortunately, women are often called names when they want to achieve something. But like Barbara Streisand said, "It's just determination." When a guy says, "No, I want to do this!" he's cool. It's sad that when a woman wants to do the same thing, she gets attacked.

Q: Can you talk about women and men? I know J-R said some interesting things about the female role.

A: The best explanation can be found in J-R's seminar and book, *Spiritual Warrior*. He describes the left and right sides of consciousness, which operate as polarities, where the left side is charged as negative/feminine and the right as positive/masculine—not meaning right or wrong, but correlating to the polarities of a battery that requires both sides to function. He also discussed this in an MSIA seminar, "What is Left-Sided and Right-Sided Energy?" In the soul realm, the divine masculine/feminine transcends duality, which is a trap set on this planet by the Luciferian deal to relate as opposites, male and female, for procreation as well as recreation. But at the end of the day, I don't buy that. Sure, while I'm in this existence, I need a partner who's a woman, but ultimately, it's still about two Souls. And of course, there are many people with non-dual gender identities and sexual preferences, who are also divine Souls.

J-R absolutely loved women. He didn't cater to the emotional part; he catered to the love. He knew how to hold women and love them. He adored his mom and his sister-in-law Elda. I even have a cool recording of J-R having a conversation with his mom. He was very ethical and fair-minded, especially when he counseled couples; his rule was that you could not speak about your spouse if they were not in the room. Often, the wife might walk up and say, "Bob doesn't treat me right!" J-R would ask, "Is Bob in the room?" "No." "I can't talk about him; let's talk about you." However, over the years, I noticed that he would side with women more often than men. In particular, when a couple broke up, he would tell the woman, "You have just as equal access to me as he does. Here's my number, call me." I never heard J-R split the difference for me.

Q: What do you mean?

A: I remember him saying that the way he treated a guy was different than a girl. He would never yell at a woman, such as Pauli Sanderson. To the staff, she was just one of us, like we're all one. Everyone on J-R staff was equal. It was never "Women sit in the back seat"—Pauli drove for J-R and was just as tough as any other dude. He could yell at the guys because we deserved it. We were a little bit harder, coarser, and thick-skinned. Sometimes, J-R had to figuratively stab me with a hot knife just so I noticed him. However, a woman is more sensitive, so he would never do the same thing to deliver the lesson.

In researching our last film, I discovered that, before he was given the keys to the Mystical Traveler Consciousness, J-R studied a system called "Personology" originally developed by Robert L. Whiteside, that was very popular in the '50s and '60s. Personology determined people's personalities by their eyes, face, and other physical features. He incorporated this approach into the Light Studies that he did in the '60s and '70s. J-R chose all of the staff according to our personalities. Because Personology also explains your strengths and limitations, he placed us in roles that corresponded to our innate talents. Each individual was chosen for a specific reason to do that job well. For instance, a close-tolerant (detail-oriented) person would be a bookkeeper. Someone wide-tolerant (creative) might be an artist or visionary who suggested big-picture ideas. Because I used to shift between both close- and wide-tolerant, J-R would say that I had all the talent in the world to do anything and I just wouldn't. I have often fallen short but was able to turn my failures into stepping stones and gifts, demonstrating that I can inspire and hold. Now, I find it fascinating to read the same books and study the same subjects that J-R did back then.

So it was my experience and point of view that before J-R even considered whether you were a man or woman, he would check the karma, confirm that you were a marked Soul for initiation, then he'd use the Personology method. That seemed to work pretty well.

*"The Traveler just shares himself with those
who are his beloveds, those who are the initiates.
The Traveler does not offer only an association;
the Traveler offers a relationship that abides
in the spiritual heart, nowhere else.
It is a relationship of living love.
And when the Traveler talks to you,
he talks to the Soul. The Traveler speaks loving.
It is love. It will lift you in love."*

– JOHN-ROGER, D.S.S.

"No one can put you on the pinnacle of masterhood. You anoint yourself, you crown yourself, you save yourself, and you become all things to yourself. All someone else is going to do is to reflect to you that you are there or not. It comes down to: 'to thine own Self be true.'"

– JOHN-ROGER, D.S.S.

Chapter 18

Superheroes and Soul Transcendence

The vision of a superhero that I got from J-R, mentioned in the previous chapter, reminded me of something I did recently. In my imagination, I had a conversation with all of my favorite childhood superheroes—Batman, Spiderman, and Superman. We talked about their stories, and I wanted to share my observations that came up.

First, I listened compassionately to Bruce Wayne, who became Batman to avenge his parents' murders. With all his inherited wealth, he has his Batmobile, costumes, advanced technology, and everything secreted in a bat-filled cave so he can dress up, combat evil, and overcome obstacles. Yet, he is afraid of bats and is a recluse who spends much of his life in hiding.

Then, I heard from Spiderman, who also dresses up and hides his identity, although he has the additional ability to climb and swing off buildings using his web. Originally, though, he was just Peter Parker, a high school kid in the lab, an ordinary guy who was accidentally mutated. Because he was orphaned when his parents died in an airplane crash, Peter struggles with often uncontrolled feelings of grief, loss, and abandonment.

Both Batman and Spiderman clearly have many unresolved issues. However, when I gave Superman a voice and talked with him, I didn't hear any problems. He has no psychological background, because he didn't come from Earth. He wasn't born here; he came from a planet where all the beings had superpowers. But down here, he's just ordinary Clark Kent, hiding his extraordinary abilities and greatness. Then, whenever a catastrophe or crime occurs, he runs into a phone booth, rips off his glasses and clothes, and he's already prepared to fly with his Superman suit on underneath.

As I was pondering all of this, I had the awareness that we, as humans (and especially for those of us initiated in MSIA), are quite similar to Superman. We don't belong here, either—we come from Soul and this world is not our home. We do normal things on Earth, yet have the secret ability to transcend and fly inwardly to higher realms in our Soul bodies. We chant the names of God and are connected to the Sound Current, which is like our phone booth.

In the inner levels, we can do so many supernatural things. But here on this planet, in this human body, we are Clark Kent. The Earth-based superheroes who started out human, like Peter Parker and Bruce Wayne, have a psychology that they identify with. We do the same thing, yet need to remember that we are not our psychology. As philosopher Pierre Teilhard de Chardin is credited with saying, "We are not human beings having a spiritual experience. We are spiritual beings immersed in a human experience."

At any time, we can go into that phone booth, rip off our clothes, and put on our Superman outfit, or the superhero ability suit, in the Sanctuary process taught by Insight Seminars.

Superman is here to serve and so are we. Truly, each one of us has the ability to be our very own superhero.

The Dreams of a Master

George Lucas Ranch with Yoda and J-R

"I am the presence of loving, living in total awareness in integrity and discernment, loving myself and others."

– Jesus Garcia, D.S.S.;
University of Santa Monica Master's Program
Affirmation, 2016

"I'm here to share your joy when you are experiencing that. And I'm here to share your sadness and your pain when you are experiencing that. I'm here to give you the keys to let go of the pain. I'm here to help you up when you've fallen. I'm here to be with you. And most of all, I'm here to love you."

– JOHN-ROGER, D.S.S.

Chapter 19

Loyal Forces of the Opposition

हू

Excerpted from a J-R Video Marathon event in Santa Barbara on March 23, 2019, with additional material.

When you attend a live John Morton MSIA seminar or a recorded J-R video seminar, you can either stick around for the information or take off and leave your body. It is possible to use the energy that is present to launch you into the higher realms, as many people do. This was very common whenever J-R spoke, and I traveled often during his sharings at Peace Awareness Trainings.

Most of the older videos I play during the Marathon events are from the time before I knew J-R in this lifetime. When I first started, I couldn't even believe some of the information he shared back then. I thought, "Are you kidding me? I lived with that guy?" But living with J-R, the man, was very different from seeing J-R, the Mystical Traveler, up on stage. He didn't sit around giving seminars to his staff at home. Rather, we clowned around, joked, ate, watched TV—it was very normal. He would turn "The Traveler" on during the seminars, then turn it off on the way home. Of course, he was still the Traveler, but he dimmed it down. Then he gave the keys to John, who is taking the teachings everywhere around the world now.

The two main reasons why I have also been traveling and sharing J-R these past few years are: 1) "For where two or more are gathered together in my name, there am I in the midst of them." We kick it off together—the seminar participants give me a lot by sitting in Satsang, sharing their experiences of J-R, and listening to mine, even if only one other person shows up. 2) "You too can do what I do, and even greater, because I go to the Father."

I can have the hardest day, get home, and put on a Soul Awareness Teaching audio, or often the Luxor Meditation. Playing J-R's voice throughout the house, whatever the recording is, calms me down instantly. Why? I don't know if this is accurate, but I'm convinced that his voice is like a carrier wave for the Sound Current. Have you ever noticed that some of the earlier recordings of J-R sound like a completely different guy? It's almost like they slowed down the speed and deepened his voice. At first, I wondered if it was even him, but now I say, "Please give me more of that."

Q: What do you have to say about the love that you received from J-R, the way you loved each other?

A: During the last six to eight months of J-R's life, I would look at him through the kitchen door and wonder, "Why can't I love other people the way I love him?" And the reason was, because I can't stand half the people I come across. But I realized, if he loves everybody, then that means I have it in me, too. Somehow, I needed to crank up the loving energy for myself and others.

After J-R passed, I felt like I was falling in consciousness; It appeared I was no longer traveling into Spirit during s.e.'s, which discouraged me. It's as if he said, "OK, I've trained you guys, now you all can have your own stuff back and deal with it on your own." And everything changed. You could feel that he physically left the planet. But his radiant form is still here, saying, "You can do it, because I trained you to do it." How did he train us? By doing spiritual exercises.

However, it took me a long time to figure this out for myself. You always have the choice and can go both ways at any time. You can feel the darkness, which just means you've turned away from what you know; it's not who you are. From what other ministers and initiates have told me, I wasn't the only one who temporarily lost my bearings those first few years after J-R transitioned.

I was never on MSIA staff; I was on John-Roger's personal staff. So when I lost him, I lost my job, too. Leaving the Mandeville house three years later, without knowing where I would live, was the latest in a series of devastating losses. Today, I know that it was all perfect for me, but at that time, I went into total victim mode because I couldn't stay there.

Without J-R on the planet, the Kal power was getting in my head, saying things like, "This is B.S. They don't care about you at all. Why do you bother showing up? The Movement is not the same as it used to be." This is how the Kal power influences us with its negativity over time; it's persistent and insidious.

One day in 2017, after I moved out from Mandeville, Nicole was out of the country with her ailing father and family in Australia, so

I was alone. I remember lying on the floor of my home with a bad fever from the flu—I could barely move, much less leave the apartment, and may even have been hallucinating. Feeling very sorry for myself, I said, "J-R, I'm done. I'm going to die here."

I just lay there, listening to one of my favorite J-R seminars, "Nuclear Radiation from Ground Zero," took two Tylenols, and was gone immediately. In my fever, I went out of my body, saw the Light, and was floating at a high place in the Spirit realms. I thought, "Oh, this must be like that Soul Awareness Teaching when J-R talked about the UFO." I was taken up to a vessel, where the aliens had an event like a Karmic Board meeting. I was given a ticket that was gold or very bright and returned back to my body, aka Earth. There was also an escalator that I couldn't ride up for some reason, which puzzled me.

I woke up feeling 100% better physically, with the awareness that I can't own that I love if I am in againstness. Love cannot enter a space that has negativity and againstness. Neither can the Traveler. If there's any againstness inside of me toward anyone or any situation, I'm not being loving and will be unable to transcend during my spiritual exercises (the escalator metaphor). Forgiveness is key to moving out of againstness.

So I started to experiment by loving everyone the way I loved J-R. J-R used to say that sometimes it's not a good experience to meet a living movie star you once admired and saw many times on the screen—feeling like you knew them—because it's going to screw up the image you have of them inside. So I hold great images of everyone I know inside, along with great images of John and J-R. I keep my temple clean so the Christ comes in, because loving is Christ.

Loyal Forces of the Opposition

J-R taught me that the "loyal forces of the opposition" (Kal power) can be very sneaky about getting into our consciousness any way possible, even through written communications like email. In a recent dream, J-R showed me to stay away from emails. Not long after, I was in Bogota, Colombia, when I was reading emails. In the physical level, I heard J-R's voice in my mind saying, "Don't touch that email." J-R came in, took me higher above the mind, and I saw the Kal power invading the letters of the email and in the Send button. It was right in there, like a listening device in the mind.

I also learned to be very mindful what I say out loud, to avoid testing from the loyal forces. For instance, once after taking J-R to Dr. Ed Wagner or Michael Hayes to get balanced, we asked, "How do you feel?" But J-R just said, "Fine." This was because, as soon as he said, "I feel great," he would be tested and get hit with some illness or extreme negativity. We figured, if that happens to the Traveler and Preceptor, then we need to watch what we say, too. I saw firsthand how often J-R took on the Karma of his initiates and wondered if the rest of us even had a chance. Then I realized that we do; because he was able to take it all, and now in the Movement, I feel like we're all taking it and holding steady.

I encourage you to reread your Soul Awareness Discourses, like J-R told us. They are our direct connection to what he did as the Traveler. But don't get hung up on the words, tune into the energy behind them. As J-R said many times, and I will paraphrase here, even if he just wrote "ham and eggs" over and over again, the true value of the Discourses and seminars was using the spiritual energy as a springboard into the higher realms. If you're having challenges with *Simran*, or spiritual exercises, go do them when you're out in world, like pre-chanting, so when you come home, you're ready. It's priming the pump, like taking a shower before you jump in the pool. Sometimes when I can't focus, I'll chant while having lunch with a friend, which pulls me more into the observer role to hear what he's saying, rather than my mind chatter. That also prepares me to do my s.e.'s later.

Before I met J-R and was new on Discourses, I went to a home seminar, where the host said, "J-R wants us to do s.e.'s kneeling, like in a church pew. He says it's the best way." Much later, when I moved into Mandeville to start working with him, J-R laid down with Cheerio, the cat, and Gort and Annie, J-R's top security Rottweilers, and started doing s.e.'s. I asked, "Don't we need to do them on our knees like in prayer?" He said, "No, just sit or lie down, it's fine. Try it … there's not a wrong way except not to do them."

During all those 26 years of driving J-R, he would mostly be out of his body in the passenger seat. My ego would want attention and a conversation, but he'd be off, snoring. That was life with the Master. It was part of his discipline, though. J-R would use any moment that he could to get out. In Discourses and SATs, I've heard J-R say to get good enough to leave the body any time you want. I asked myself, "why?" What I realized was that there is no better way to bring yourself back into harmony after an upsetting situation—for instance, an argument with your spouse, a fender bender in your car, or a negative meeting. Doing s.e.'s and Soul Traveling is a process of convergence and transformation of consciousness. When you come back, you may say, "God, I just love everybody."

Another concept I learned from J-R was, "Next!" This is about letting go of disturbance and moving on to the next thing without attachment. I had a disagreement with a close friend that didn't go well. The next day I said, "Hey buddy, could we just move on?" He said, "No, we need to talk about what happened." I responded,

"No, we don't; we've moved on." That's how it worked with J-R. When you bring something up later, you might be bringing the karma back with it, unless you can process the issue in complete neutrality. If one person is still holding onto the hurt and anger, that can backfire. At the University of Santa Monica (USM), they caution students not to avoid unresolved issues and emotions, but to process and heal them. And I do remember J-R saying, never go to bed angry. So it's important to handle that and keep from creating new karma. But in the morning, after traveling, it's all new again. In any relationship, it requires discipline from both partners to be able to say, "Let's be loving; it's done." But if you keep bringing stuff back a week later, that's the mind and ego, under the influence of the Kal power.

Once I told J-R, "I'm so disturbed about X person," and he responded, "So?" I said, "It was about such and such." He asked me, "How long ago did that happen?" "It was 1987." He said, "You're a fool—it's your karma now. I can't do anything. You've hung onto this for that long?" It's true, I was out of balance for holding onto my position years later, hoping to use it for some kind of revenge. That kind of thing is just going to bite you in the rear end. It can come in as a really bad disease or an accident. So the quicker you can let go, the faster you can move back to the loving. If you find yourself in the same circumstances, just forgive yourself. Let it go!

If you want to transcend, you can progress through the astral, causal, mental, and etheric levels, and you'll be tested all the way up. But if you want love and you stop the againstness inside of you, you can bypass that. In the book collection, *Fulfilling Your Spiritual Promise,* J-R says that everything not of Spirit will be pulled out of you, like with the talons of the eagle. He described this process during a talk he gave on February 14, 2000, at the Valentine Ladies Lunch:

"People are going to have special missions here, be taken to high places, high rocks, high peaks, high pinnacles, to high places, and be abandoned to the forces of negativity. *The forces of negativity come in like screeching birds with talons just ripping*, but the person who's there can't be hurt because there's nothing to hurt them. But what you do is you start to release all the fears, the impurities, and they just sort of drop away and you just come into the beingness of, 'Oh, OK, this is what's going on,' and it's very natural and very normal again."

I've had experiences like this, and it feels horrible. But as you transcend, all of that stuff will be ripped away from you, because as you go higher, those things can't be there. They are mutually exclusive; it's a natural law. So that inner 16-year-old girl or boy who got hurt and continues to influence you will be ripped out through the process of Soul transcendence. That is where USM comes in and can help you heal those memories at every age and grow them up. Then those parts of you cooperate in transcendence while we're living in the final one.

When you go into the Soul level and above, everything that we think we identify with disappears. We become the loving essence of Soul, and it is beautiful. However, we can still move around in consciousness. In a recent "Loving Each Day" email (which sends out daily quotes), J-R said: "It's nice to know there's a Kingdom of Heaven, but if you have to die to find it and know it as your home, it's too late. You may miss and go in the wrong door! Our goal in Movement of Spiritual Inner Awareness is to discover that Kingdom both within and outside of ourselves and to know it as our home while we are still living here in the physical body." I've also heard J-R say that you can dissolve stuff on the lower levels by pulling it up to the Soul.

Loyal Forces of the Opposition

The Love of a Master world tour,
Port Harcourt, Nigeria, 2019

In other words, practice doing your s.e.'s now and experience Soul Transcendence now, so that when you do die, you will be able to get through the right door. This is about staying awake, so when you need it, you can recognize the journey. "Oh, I've already seen that, I've been through there, let's go." That said, as his initiates, J-R's got us, so we don't have to worry about going through the wrong door.

In the past five years especially, I've been blown away by the melding of what I call J-R love and human love. I've learned that J-R love is unconditional and impersonal, but deep and abiding. So now, I encourage my spiritual counseling clients to meet people with J-R love; don't bring in the conditional, limited love that looks like, "You have to do this for me; scratch my back and I'll scratch yours." When we were with J-R, he would say, "Scratch my back," and we'd say, "OK." And we didn't expect anything in return, whether it was approval, validation, or a tradeoff.

Imagine approaching your relationship that same way, where you just love J-R for J-R, and he loves you for you. You and your partner can love each other for who you are without any expectations. There is no emotional bank account. You withdraw, I deposit. You did that, I did this to make things even. When I married in my early 20s, I did the conditional loving because I didn't know what real loving was. I still want to know more loving, because I was there with J-R and still have more to go. Taking care of J-R near the end was real love to me. I couldn't believe I was in it, and I loved it. Sometimes I can still tap into that. But I'd like to be able to tap into that for everyone.

That's true love. That's what J-R had for all of us. He would just look at you and love you; that gaze, the *Twaji*, could instantly heal tons of stuff. So go there.

"In this country the pilgrims take a dip in the waters of the Ganges and think that by so doing their sins are washed off. The river water may cleanse the body but not the mind. They do not know that the nectar that washes off sins is inside of themselves and the real place for pilgrimage is also inside of themselves. If they were to go inside and connect their souls with the Sound Current, their sins would be washed off."

– Maharaj Sawan Singh Ji's Letters

"Death is nothing but a gateway to birth. Nothing that lives ever dies, it only changes form. When a man's body is weary the soul leaves the body to receive newer and fresher garments. And so on goes this great play of God—from eternity to eternity."

– Guru Nanak

Chapter 20

Premonitions

घू

A big part of my personal experience in the Doctor of Spiritual Science program involved tracking various intentions and processes. For the purpose of this book, I found two excellent examples that provide evidence of premonitions in the dream state, both of which took place prior to John-Roger's passage into Spirit.

In January 2019, MSIA's spiritual director John Morton shared this dream memory (which occurred less than two months before J-R's transition) via email with me, Nathaniel Sharrat, Rick Ojeda, and his wife, Leigh Taylor-Young Morton. He gave me written permission to print it here verbatim, with his introductory comment:

"1/11/2019 Email – I was looking for a photo of when I was dancing with Brad Pie and the Black Eyed Peas on stage at the MSIA Conference in 2013 when we celebrated 50

Years/25 Years of Travelers and found this account of my dream with J-R in August 2014 just before the Israel trip.

"8/31/2014 Email – Subject: My Dream with J-R

"This was just before I awoke this morning.

"We were in some non-descript, resort-like hotel complex out on the first tee of the resort golf course. Jsu, Nat, myself, maybe Rick were about to tee off with some other MSIA people standing nearby watching us and some hotel guests around as well. We kept waiting and I was wondering what was going on to hold us up. Then a lovely woman by herself teed off ahead of us while we were still waiting and I knew we had lost our tee time. Then we just went back to the hotel which was a kind of modern complex of rooms that were like many small boxes that had been assembled by being connected in an up/down, left/right geometric configuration like something you might find in New Mexico. The hotel was bustling with MSIA people who had gathered for one of our trips plus other hotel guests. I went to Leigh's and my room which was kind of like a small niche room, small windows with no real views out, with access similar to the outer look of the hotel, up/down, left/right, kind of hard to locate or get to. We were packing up to leave with the group and I had a strong desire to go see J-R. Getting to his room was the same up/down, left/right and not easy to locate as the corridors were maze-like. When I arrived outside his thick wooden arched door, I could hear loud talking inside and Jsu's voice stood out. I did the secret knock in my regular way. No answer and the loud talking continued. Then I pounded out the secret knock, and Jsu opened the door and let me into the room. I don't remember who the 4 or 5 others were who were standing around as I was focused on J-R lying down on the all-white linen bed in the right corner of a small niche-like room like ours. When I walked in J-R appeared as he is today and was lying down on his right side on the right side of the bed. He did not move but warmly greeted me with 'Hello, John.' I went to him to lay down beside him with my head face down next to his chest and he put his arm around me. I began to vibrate powerfully with my love for him. Then I woke up.

"I'm going to call you today to check in and about coming to see J-R.

"John"

Two months earlier, on June 27, 2014, my now-fiancée Nicole had the following vivid dream about J-R, which she recorded upon wakening. This was before we embarked on our relationship, which was sparked during J-R's final Israel trip in September 2014:

"I dreamt that I was crying deeply, because I had this awareness of how much I missed John-Roger. There was a vision of a grassy hill and he was in a wheelchair. I realized that I think I needed to go to Israel because it may be the last time that I see him. I had this sense that afterwards, he was probably going to go. I don't know if I was making it up in the morning, but the explanation I heard inside was that going to Israel and the Middle East may take a lot of his Light, and after that he may need to leave the planet. But I was aware that there was something around, 'It's not long now,' and I was just mourning, crying so deeply. And even today, I feel like I've just been crying so very deeply; I feel a bit sensitive.

"In another part of the dream, I was aware that J-R didn't want to stay because of what was happening with the earth; we are trashing the earth with our consciousness. One of the worst things that was going to happen was poisoning the ocean, and the ones who were trying to save things more towards the end of the destruction of the world would be the dolphins. Because they were trying to clean up, then I remembered the Fukushima disaster this morning when I woke up."

Premonitions

Nicole and Jsu at their University of Santa Monica graduation, 2016

*"Whoever you are, I fear you are walking
the walks of dreams,*

*I fear these supposed realities are to melt from under
your feet and hands;*

*Even now, your features, joys, speech, house, trade,
manners, troubles,*

follies, costume, crimes, dissipate away from you,

Your true Soul and Body appear before me."

– Walt Whitman, "To You" (Leaves of Grass)

Chapter 21

My Needs Are Met

घू

In the five years since J-R passed, I recognize that my mind sometimes tries to take me to places of self-doubt and judgment. For instance, I could beat myself up over wasted time, worry, anxiety, and disappointment while I was still in the acting world, when J-R was supporting me to manifest film roles. There were so many dissatisfactions during that time—often I was rejected for a part I wanted and, even when I got hired, I would sometimes get edited out of the final cut.

Looking back, I can see that, ultimately, those negative experiences made me tremendously strong. I don't let myself go into the judgment, and I'm not even sore or resentful; I just feel strong inside. I never really think about that part of my life anymore, because somehow the acting karma shifted for me. Now I'm off doing something else that I feel very much pulled to do: sharing J-R all over the world.

Recently, a friend called me the Itinerant Preacher, which seems pretty accurate. At the drop of a hat, I'll toss a bunch of books in the car or in my luggage, and off I go! I get together in fellowship and Satsang with other ministers and initiates, speaking my truth about our Master, John-Roger. In particular, I remember J-R telling me how powerful it is to direct your mind toward a positive goal and allow it to come in, without letting negative thoughts get in the way. Seeding is a big part of that process. I recently seeded for my intention to have awareness of a stronger connection with J-R inwardly.

Being in the true place of manifestation, in the abundance, goes far beyond thought—it's higher and faster than a thought. Once it drops down into the mind, you need discipline to keep a positive focus. Instead, sit in the intuitive part, the direct knowing, the divine unknown, and know that whatever you put your eyes on, you can get, as long as it is more than 50 percent realistic and believable. Most of us wouldn't be able to say, "I want to be an astronaut" and have that come forward.

I learned from J-R that the instrument for manifestation is very strong in me. At that time, we were just using what I was most interested in, which was movies, television shows, getting the role, becoming famous—the lure of fame and fortune. That was my karma then, and in many ways, it was amazing. Even when I got stung, I would learn and keep adjusting my approach. These days, I have simply moved the target. Rather than getting a role in a movie and being adored by millions, my vision is now to travel the world, share about these beautiful things in groups, and work with people one-on-one.

Although both of those goals might seem ego-driven, since they are about being seen by others, they rest differently inside of me. Today, I want to be noticed for sharing J-R's teachings and the loving, instead of setting myself above people to be worshiped as a famous Hollywood celebrity. This feels much more inclusive to me. There is nothing wrong with the film industry—I still love my friends in the business, the other actors, and going to see movies—but it is no longer a trap for my ego. J-R used to tell me to "follow the money" when I went out for a movie role because it would keep me focused away from seeking fame. It was never a money issue for me; it was a fame issue; the constant lure and temptation to be famous. Following the money meant going from one job to another, working as a good actor.

Back then, whenever I went to a Hollywood party or trendy restaurant, I would ask myself, "What am I doing here? What's my point? What do I want?" It was like asking, "What's my intention in this scene?" as an actor. Often, after that, I would get the heck away from the party because with all the negativity around me, I didn't want to be attacked by entities or other lower influences. For instance, I'd ask, "Why do I need to go to this restaurant that's so hard to get into?"

"Well, I might run into so-and-so, the casting director." Back in the day, I often carried my demo reel tapes around with me to hand out in person. That seems very weird now, with all the technology we have.

But that's how I learned to hustle in the beginning; find out who would be at that party and irritate them enough to give me a shot. I even learned that from J-R, who encouraged me to approach Angela Lansbury when we were having lunch at Souplantation restaurant one day. He told me to go over and ask her for a job, and I did. I was actually cast in two different roles in her *Murder She Wrote* series. Once again, J-R proved the point, "You receive not because you ask not."

So if you think about what you want and let that higher part of your consciousness look at it, then God will supply it. You'll find a way to manifest it. That can apply to negative stuff, too, so be sure to keep your mind clear.

David Allen, author and developer of the *Getting Things Done* system, advocates having a "mind like water," which he describes as "A mental and emotional state in which your head is clear, able to create and respond freely, unencumbered with distractions and split focus." Following this guidance, and J-R's teachings over the years, I am able to experience mind like water and only put things that I need into my mind … and those needs are met, simply and gracefully.

The bottom line and theme of this book is that, more and more, my inner and outer dreams are matching each other and coming true, thanks to the continuing guidance of my master, John-Roger. They are indeed *The Dreams of a Master*. I wish the same for everyone who is inspired by the words in these pages.

It seems exceptionally fitting that after many months of writing and editing, on October 5, 2019—the day before my 56th birthday—John-Roger called the completion of this book by delivering copies to me in the dream state. He used to do that physically when we finished the movies that we produced together, so I interpreted this dream as saying, "We're done now."

I thank God, I thank the Lord, and I thank J-R for all of the gifts.

"The wind bloweth where it listeth, and thou hearest the sound thereof, but canst not tell whence it cometh, and whither it goeth: so is every one that is born of the Spirit."

– John 3:8 King James Version (KJV)

Q: I've been having a lot of bad dreams at night. When I wake up, I'm really frightened, and it can take hours to get myself back into balance and to sleep again. Can you suggest anything?

A: Your dreams could be all sorts of things: balancing past actions, working through unconscious or subconscious fears or blocks, etc., particularly when the traveler Consciousness is working with you. Whatever they are, don't give them a lot of power. If you wake up after a bad dream, just go to work with yourself. Chant your tone or the Hu or the Ani-hu. surround yourself with the Light. Ask for the Traveler to help you release the dream experience. Keep some water by your bed and drink a little of it to help break the intensity of the dream experience and to help you come back into the body.

There is also a tone of "e" that you can chant, which will help to bring you back into the physical focus. You just say, "EEEEEEEEE"—a long, drawn out sound. You start the sound low and imagine it down around your feet. Then you take it up as high as you can, and imagine it up at the top of the head. Then drop it back down as low as you can, back down to the feet. That will help to bring you back solidly into the physical level in a balanced way. Exercise can also break the unbalanced feeling from "bad dreams," so you might do whatever sort of exercise works for you. Doing a few sit-ups, dancing to a little music, or walking around are a few possibilities. Just do something to get the body energy moving and to help shift your focus.

- JOHN-ROGER, D.S.S., *DREAM VOYAGES*, REVISED AND EXPANDED EDITION

Epilogue:
Operation Beautify Mandeville

September 19, 2019

Yesterday, five years after John-Roger's transcendence into the Realms of Spirit, the house at 3375 Mandeville Canyon (called "Mandeville" by the staff)—where I lived for 29 years total, including 26 with J-R—was sold to another owner.

I am grateful that I kept my equanimity during the sale process and gracefully cooperated with the preparation that entailed. A few weeks before it was listed on the market, many of the items personally used by J-R were sold or auctioned off during MSIA's Conference of the Highest Good in Santa Monica, California. A request for the story behind a particular auction item inspired me to share some random remembrances about the house itself in this final chapter.

By the late 1980s, John Morton had become the Traveler and had gotten married. He moved out of the Mandeville house and lived down the road with his wife Laura and, soon, their baby daughter, Claire. So at that point, I was delighted to join J-R's personal staff and become the primary person who drove him. Others who lived at Mandeville included Jason Laskay, our resident carpenter, Liz Potts, who took great care of the dogs, and Phil and Brooke Danza, downstairs; Phil also ran the headquarters of NOW Productions out of Mandeville. In those days, NOW was booming with a full staff, including Nancy Carter, Cheryl Mathieu, Arissa Bright, and many other employees, nonstop daily activities, and efficient workflow. J-R would walk downstairs to record a new meditation and other materials. Phil would get the produced media back to J-R quickly so he could charge it all with the Mystical Traveler and Preceptor energy upon completion.

The winding canyon road from Sunset Boulevard to our driveway was nearly four miles in distance. Sometimes it seemed like it took forever to drive home, especially late at night, when it was quite dark. As J-R's chauffeur, in the early days, I primarily drove the brown "Mystical Traveler" Lincoln Continental. There was also a blue Lincoln with two fuel tanks, and over the years, we had a succession of vehicles on hand, including a Cadillac, Range Rover, brown 1990 Lexus, and eventually the blue Lexus that I am currently driving.

J-R preferred me to drive slowly while he meditated, so I would be exceptionally careful on that long, 3.8-mile drive up Mandeville Canyon. Sometimes I would allow the left tire to ride on top of the double-striped yellow lane divider, slowly and softly to avoid hitting the bumps. No matter what was going on in the city or the world, it was very important not to bring that energy into Mandeville. Therefore, my goal during those four miles was not to get J-R home quickly but to unwind and allow any negativity to disperse. In my imagination, I would visualize letting it all go, and by the time I rolled up to J-R's driveway, I was clear.

Epilogue: Operation Beautify Mandeville

I loved walking into Mandeville and looking up at its high, vaulted ceiling. Jason, the live-in handyman and carpenter, was our Michelangelo who uncovered and renovated the beautiful old woodwork in Mandeville's original ceiling, which the previous owners had plastered over. I fell in love with it then; today, Nicole's and my second-floor apartment in Santa Monica also has a high ceiling that reminds me of Mandeville's.

We had many green plants around the house, which were sometimes hard to keep alive when we traveled so often—up to six months out of the year at the height of J-R's traveling days. Fortunately, people like Jason, Gene Kaprelian, Paul Davidson, and Liz Potts would stay there during our trips to manage the house.

Years before I moved in, there were several serious fire and mudslide scares. J-R had the genius inspiration to install a sprinkler system on top of both the house and garage, with two pumps that dropped hoses into the pool and sucked up the water to keep the roofs wet in case of a fire. So every year, during the worst heat in July and August, we would water and keep everything wet to reduce the fire danger. J-R also covered part of the hill behind the house with a concrete and cement ditch to drain water during the rainy season and reduce the chance of mudslides from the upper orchard. As a result of these improvements, while we had a few fires and mudslides in the area, the house was never threatened again as it had been in the '70s.

On the other side of the property, there was originally a neglected volleyball court, which I called the "nothing court" after I moved into Mandeville. Eventually, at Phil's urging, J-R turned it into a basketball court, where the group of guys—mostly Phil, Mark Harradine, Erik Raleigh, Nat Sharratt, Rick Ojeda, and me—would play every Saturday and often during the week. Over the last 10 years, the players got younger and better: Tim, Zane, Jeff, Gabe, Marcus, and many more. Because J-R did so much incredible work in the world, at home we all needed a way to relax and play. We also had a ping-pong table and karaoke machine in the giant living room. Laurie Lerner gave us a huge LED TV that J-R had installed behind the kitchen wall to maximize the space; Jason helped with the configuration from an architectural standpoint.

When the Mortons' kids, Zane and Claire, were still young, Paulina Haddad assisted in cooking and caring for them. During family visits to the house, they would hang out in the back part with the guys. The living room was so spacious that J-R could get a massage or foot rub from his chair in the front, while everyone else was either playing ping-pong, doing karaoke, or watching TV, sometimes all at the same time. We would be watching the *24* or *Alias* television series on DVDs while Paulina prepared dinner in the kitchen. There was always delicious food and ice cream galore. Those were great times with crazy hours, including late-night Michael Hayes sessions and visits to Ed Wagner in between all the travel.

John-Roger was always thinking ahead to anticipate any circumstance. For instance, early on, he had acquired a state-of-the-art generator with a control panel installed next to his seat in the kitchen breakfast nook booth. As a result, many times over the years, whenever we lost city power, we were all able to continue our work without interruptions.

Eventually, as J-R got older and his activities tapered down, we focused more on the property, since he was spending more time there. It all started with a dream I had about a lamppost. For years, at the end of the driveway, there was an old, dim lamppost with a weathered address sign that wasn't visible to guests when driving

Epilogue: Operation Beautify Mandeville

up in the dark. I dreamt that Mandeville was super dark until a brightly lit lamppost appeared, illuminating the night with its diffused glow through frosted glass. Upon waking, I told J-R and thus began "Operation Beautify Mandeville." We installed a lamppost like the one in my dream, which was like a lighthouse for lost souls, and I also bought a backlit electric sign with bright numbers reading "3375."

As one of the Mandeville property managers, I fixed anything that was reported and oversaw all the improvements, together with our maintenance crew, Raul and Rudy. We also needed to maintain the landscaping and keep the property looking beautiful. I had disliked gardening in the past, but Operation Beautify Mandeville was delightful and easy. One day, while updating J-R on our daily projects, he said that I had once been a great landlord beloved by many people. Unfortunately, my life was cut short. J-R assisted me in completing the karma of this past life, which was a fantastic experience.

In our recent travels to France and Italy, the stately cypress trees we saw in various locations made a strong impression on me. My vision was to line J-R's driveway with a row of 12 cypresses, calling the disciples to mind. As a driver approached the property, the cypress trees would evoke a feeling of Tuscany, an Italian region that J-R really enjoyed. Along the right side of the driveway was the natural sagebrush that covered the canyon. These shrubs would dry up if they weren't watered regularly, which presented a fire danger, but the existing sprinkler system was inefficient. To avoid wasting water and keep everything wet, we installed drip lines for both the brush and the cypresses, inspired by Israeli farming methods. At the same time, we replaced the cracked PVC piping for the sprinklers above the house and garage with long-lasting copper pipes, and we put in new roof shingles, which needs to be done about every 30 years.

The Dreams of a Master

Mandeville, front entrance, 2019

Epilogue: Operation Beautify Mandeville

Mandeville, bird's eye view, 2019

J-R was always about maintenance, so we made sure to routinely test the two water pumps. They were old-fashioned mortar pumps with an internal combustion engine that required a pull-start ignition like a lawnmower or motorboat. We had to release enough gas into the combustible area so it could ignite and start the engine. Once it was idling, the hose could then suck up hundreds of gallons of water from the swimming pool to wet down the roof of the house and the garage. It was such a great invention by J-R. Whenever I say that I created stuff, it was usually because I was plugged into J-R; just being around him gave me ideas. I mistakenly thought that I was creating something, when it was usually his ideas I was picking up on. I quickly realized, "Oh, this is J-R's idea, not mine."

Operation Beautify Mandeville continued with additional property improvements. I wanted to attract more wild birds and hummingbirds to the house, as well as the flock of several dozen neighborhood parrots that flew over at 10 or 11 each morning. We removed the old double-deck fountain in the front and installed a new brass fountain with a statue of three spitting dolphins. This choice had special significance because J-R's walkie-talkie handle was always "Green Dolphin" (John Morton's was "16-Ton"), even after the technology was upgraded to iPhones and other communication systems.

At the base of the fountain, we placed a large brass tub for a koi pond with emerald-colored rocks. The few Japanese butterfly koi we started with eventually mated, expanding to nearly 40 of these beautiful, giant fish by the time J-R passed away. The koi pond environment is very sensitive—at one point, we sadly lost about 20 fish from oxygen deprivation when the pump broke. I always loved how magical the dolphin fountain and koi pond looked, both in the sunshine and at night, when the emerald rocks would glow

Epilogue: Operation Beautify Mandeville

with special lighting. For many years, Jason was the one who fed those fish and cared for J-R's dogs and other animals.

We installed a swing in the front yard near the fountain and koi pond. Due to the long, severe California drought, too many things were dying, so I decided on dry landscaping. We planted three beautiful olive trees to symbolize peace where the no-mow grass was. The basketball court looked great. There was also the box barn: four large, adjacent storage sheds in the back that J-R had the crew build, some time previously, to hold anything that he no longer wanted in the house or the NOW Productions office. When septic tank issues arose, Raul and Rudy helped to add a concrete slab with built-in drainage on the southwest side of the property, up on the hill by NOW's door, to eliminate the buildup of mud and dirt in that area.

As J-R's health issues became more apparent, we needed a faster way to get him out of the house and to the doctor (around seven miles away) than through the kitchen. So we built a back exit outside the sliding window of J-R's bedroom, by the spa, which we called "the J-R emergency staircase." I decided to build a cement staircase on a 45 percent grade dirt hill to support the weight of people and wheelchairs; this allowed us to leave the back way down NOW Productions' little alley, then get in the car and on the road. It was reassuring to have three or four exits if there was ever a problem, such as a brush fire or mudslide, which occur often in canyon areas.

During our many trips to the Holy Land, J-R had always liked the beautiful Israeli ceramic tiles. Each participant in his 2014 80th Birthday Israel Tour received one of these tiles. However, I had a set shipped to Mandeville a year earlier. While beautifying the NOW Productions side of the property, we installed the Israeli tiles with grout among the Spanish pavers in the west patio to honor his birthday.

As the beautification of Mandeville progressed, it became an amazing place to be. Honeybees were attracted to the koi pond, there were a lot of parrots, hummingbirds, crows, and the occasional hawk coming around, and at night, we even had several owls nearby. I loved discerning between different sounds that the birds made, particularly at night. Sometimes, very late, I was the only one awake and it was super quiet. I could hear the owls hooting gently when at rest; during their nocturnal hunts, they would communicate with loud screeching. For some reason, those sounds would lull me into my night sleep.

Many years ago, before J-R reconfigured the first floor, you could see from the living room through the kitchen to the backyard, where there was a beautiful fountain. One night in the '90s, we saw this huge owl with a six-foot wingspan land there and drink water from it. I believe this same owl and its mate may have bred offspring in subsequent years.

We had Raul and Rudy tear apart and rebuild the leaking pond in the backyard, keeping closely to its original design. The swimming pool area has always remained the same, other than replacing the PVC piping for an improved sprinkler system so the lawn wouldn't dry up. I've seen lots of photos with J-R laying in a little hammock back there where the spa is now.

Operation Beautify Mandeville continued with remodeling J-R's bathroom for enhanced functionality. As his health declined, we needed more room to maneuver while assisting him in the bathroom and shower, whether it was me, Nathaniel, or the nurses. With J-R's approval, we asked Jason to design a large, spa-like

Epilogue: Operation Beautify Mandeville

shower area with a wide entrance flush to the floor and plenty of room to roll in a wheelchair. There were double spigots, waterproof teak seating along the sides, similar to a sauna, so we could sit down while cleansing him, and a salon-style sink that had its own small showerhead so we could wash his hair. Safety rails were installed around the shower and entire bathroom perimeter.

Every elder should have a bathroom like this, if they can. In fact, one of our nurses, who also cared for a very wealthy celebrity, told us, "Everyone should copy the way you designed this bathroom. You guys take care of J-R better than anybody I've ever seen."

Raul and Rudy did most of the construction work, and they were brilliant at suggesting improvements for many of our ideas. While the official plans for this state-of-the-art remodel were drawn up by an architect recommended by Mark Lurie, Jason was the original designer, and Nat and I both added some bells and whistles. Jason—who passed into Spirit during the editing of this book in August 2019—saw firsthand what we faced at Mandeville and understood how we could best help take care of J-R in this situation. I want to express my appreciation for all of the great work he did for many years at Mandeville as well as at Miracielo in Santa Barbara.

In the final months, with J-R's approval and the Prez's support, we redecorated the living room. I strongly felt that aesthetics were very important for our peace of mind, to keep the environment positive and provide a soothing place for J-R to simply relax. So we visually transformed the room by concealing all of the medical equipment and pill bottles to prevent the sight of outer objects from triggering any thoughts of negative outcomes for J-R's healing. Whenever the nurses needed to give him medications or check his vitals, they would access those supplies from a drawer or bring a machine in from the other room. We hid them so everything visible to the eye was esthetically pleasing for J-R and for us, like the beautiful furniture, treasured photos, and MSIA artwork dating back to the '70s that I rescued from the box barn and preserved with museum framing.

Fortunately, J-R only had a single floor to navigate, other than the three or four steps at the side door of the kitchen, which led to the car. Ever since his bad fall down the back stairway in the middle of the night, I disliked the idea of steps. To avoid them, we had Raul and Rudy put in a gently inclined zig-zag ramp, with handrails and lighting, that was wide enough for a wheelchair.

Now that 3375 Mandeville Canyon Road has been sold, as of September 18, 2019, I hope the buyer enjoys these stories and appreciates all the love and care that was put into this house for its beloved occupant. Operation Beautify Mandeville was always intended to create a peaceful sanctuary for J-R so he could find peace whenever we brought him home after that 3.8-mile drive uphill. I encourage anyone reading this to find ways to beautify your own home and environment so you may esthetically enjoy your life in much the same way.

Epilogue: *Operation Beautify Mandeville*

J-R's living room

Mandeville, fountain rebuild

*"Dreams must be heeded and accepted.
For a great many of them come true."*

- PARACELSUS

*"Issue yourself a challenge,
And let that challenge manifest to you
All the time,
That from this moment on,
This moment of existence …*

*I will start to find
Happiness and peacefulness in me.
I will call upon the name of God
Morning, noon, and night.
And I will totally dedicate and devote myself
To the uplifting of every consciousness
Who comes by me.*

Therefore …

*I will smile inwardly and outwardly.
I will not be ashamed of my love.
I will demonstrate my love totally.
I will just be there and allow everyone else
The same space in which to unfold."*

– JOHN-ROGER, D.S.S.

Appendix A
Travel Journal

After the launch of my first book, *The Love of a Master*, I embarked on a global tour, journeying to various MSIA communities within the United States and around the world. As described in these pages, sitting in Satsang with other ministers and initiates of John-Roger is my soul's calling and heart's ministry. Most of my travels have been documented in a series of articles written for the *New Day Herald*, MSIA's online blog, which are reprinted here with minor updates and editing, along with previously unpublished journal entries.

October 10, 2017
From Russia (and London) With Love

"What the heck am I doing here in Siberia?" It is 5 a.m. on Saturday, September 30. My Aeroflot plane has just landed in Barnaul.

This is far from the first time I have asked myself such a question. In fact, it has become a common reaction at those times when my ego drops and I feel small. Filled with self-doubt, I ask the peanut gallery inside, "Why the heck am I [fill in the blank]?"

There is usually no answer. I have learned to just sit and observe until it shifts. Over the years, I watched John-Roger's ever-changing consciousness that agreed to do something on a Monday but canceled on a Friday because it was no longer in alignment. And he never questioned himself or his decisions. To me, that was a demonstration of trust, discernment, and faith.

My trip began two days earlier in Moscow, where I was greeted at the airport by Radislav and Katarina, who would be my "attached at the hip" interpreter.

Moscow was such a great light. The night of my arrival, I screened the *Mystical Traveler* film for seven souls in a journalist's office with a few seats and a projector. After introducing the movie and speaking about J-R, I took a nap in the back room. When I woke up about halfway through, Radi yelled, "Let's take a break!"

When the break was over, the group wanted me to talk. So I spontaneously had my first "Evening with Jsu Garcia" in Moscow, which is where the Satsang started in my travels. I did my own version of a Q&A, sharing about J-R and my new memoir, *The Love of a Master*. It was straightforward and very healing for some. Basically, I got out of the way and let the BUS (Boys Upstairs), GAS (Guardian Angels Society), and J-R handle it.

I spent my last day in Moscow in Red Square, drinking coffee at the Kremlin and staring at Lenin's tomb, wondering if he wanted to get out. The people in the Square seemed very happy. I remembered the first time I was there, with J-R and the PAT IV group in 1988. While planting Light Columns, I felt J-R's energy and sensed that the columns he had planted back then were still very present.

It was a moment of contrast for me, with the historic tomb on one side and directly across, the huge Gum Shopping Center in Moscow, the nearest store selling Cartier watches. Interesting. I'm aware of the work J-R participated in. The light and high vibration is very present in Red Square and Russia. Light and love to our countries sharing in the common good for all concerned.

Fourteen hours later, I was in Barnaul presenting the Volunteer of the Year award from MSIA's annual Conference in July to Lubov Zhikhareva. This woman is a powerhouse who is overseeing the effort to translate the Soul Awareness Discourses into Russian. Lubov is one of many ministers I have had the pleasure to collaborate with in the Movement who have become a rock in the wall of John-Roger's works and teachings.

The event room at the top floor of my hotel was filled with more than two dozen radiant souls beaming energized light from their faces after a full day of nonstop spiritual activities. Starting at 11 a.m. that morning had been a spectacular baptism with 25 participants, followed by Light Column planting at a park in the center of the city, and finally Barnaul's premiere screening of the *Mystical Traveler* film.

Running late for the premiere, I presented and started the film while wrapping up seven initiations and two ordinations that were scheduled for that evening. It was a full day of Light, Love, movie, and time. Except for two people, no one present spoke or understood English. Thank goodness an angel named Sofia showed up from Omsk who spoke perfect English and generously served as my translator the entire time.

Remarkably, the Omsk ladies, including Sofia, had taken a 13-hour train ride to Barnaul to be in the energy. After the screening and award presentation, they all raced back to the train station to head back home for another 13 hours!

"Where two or more are gathered, there he is," John-Roger has said. The pull of the Sound and Light in that room was hard to resist. I just wanted to lay down and fly. It was service from the heart—not much talking about it, just doing it. And I am so grateful that I can now walk to 2101 Wilshire Blvd. for events in Santa Monica.

I want to give a big shout-out to people like Marjorie Eaton, Betsy Alexander, Laren Bright, Paul Kaye, Angel Harper, and John Morton, who have supported the Russian community and kept it going. I know that Terry Tillman, Cleora Daily, Nathalie Franks, Leigh Taylor-Young Morton, and many others served the Loving call, planting and seeding the works of John-Roger in this region. It's great to experience the Spiritual work and also see it with my own eyes.

Between Barnaul and Moscow, more than 15 people took home *Mystical Traveler* DVDs to keep.

On October 1, I flew back to London to set up for *The Love of a Master* Book Launch and Signing at the Old Columbia Hotel, where J-R and John held many events over the years. The event would take place five days later, on my 54th birthday. I greatly appreciated the assistance of Nathalie Franks, who help me get everything set up and provided support during the launch.

Travel Journal

The book signing on October 6 turned out to be a sweet, successful event with 16 beautiful guests, including several dear friends. I felt J-R in the room with yet another gathering of "two or more." Simple and natural. I felt loved and supported in my ministry.

Thank you, U.K. Thank you, J-R.

❈ ❈ ❈

November 24, 2017

Jsu's Travel Journal – Fall 2017

My autumn European book tour was about turning up in person to do my ministry, share more about J-R, and distribute *The Love of a Master* books to friends and family.

I began by hand-delivering two copies to David and Kathryn Allen in Amsterdam. I didn't know what I'd get out of our meetings, but I knew I had to visit them. It was also a remembrance of the time I was with J-R in Amsterdam on a KLM overnight flight before heading to Russia after the PAT IV in 1988. The reference point I have from traveling with John-Roger in 1988 to now is staggering—I was astounded by this city.

The Light work that J-R did throughout Europe is in plain sight everywhere. I was told that the Netherlands has an egalitarian state. Yes, they care about their people for sure. Bicycle riders are king; cars are last in this food chain. It's true that you are more likely to be killed by a bike rider than a car or gunshot. Thanks, David and Kathryn, for your loving support.

The Dreams of a Master

I flew to Geneva to drop in on Veronique and Babadandan Ji and was once again shown the great parts of the city. In Geneva and other parts of Switzerland are numerous remains from the early Protestant refugees and settlements. We visited a church with many symbols on its walls; one in particular was a double-headed eagle similar to the design that J-R had printed for protection on T-shirts way back when. After our visit, Veronique served as my booking agent for high speed ICE trains to travel from Geneva to Essen, Germany.

In Germany, the first film I shot in 1984, *A Nightmare on Elm Street*, is a cult classic. The three-day House of Horrors convention in Oberhausen invited me for an autograph-signing extravaganza. I made new friends there, who all know about J-R now. I then boarded another ICE High Speed train to visit Arno Triebskorn in Karlsruhe, Germany, near Heidelberg—a great man all around, just beaming light. He picked me up at Mannheim and we drove down to Karlsruhe, hitting all the great spots: Speyer Cathedral, Heidelberg Castle, the bridge and Karlsruhe Castle. Karlsruhe translates to "Karl's sleep."

A bit of history: In 1988 before the Russia trip, J-R led a group of us through Germany to see Heidelberg and other cities, especially East Berlin where J-R planted the famous "Light worm in the wall." It was an amazing sight to see. I didn't need to know how J-R worked the Light, I just knew he could turn it on. One year later, the infamous Berlin Wall was finally demolished on November 9, 1989.

Arno hosted a *Mystical Traveler* movie screening and mini Q&A lunch in a friendly, intimate space. The *Love of the Master* book event went well, with Christine and Samaneh visiting from Strasbourg. Where two or more are gathered, there J-R is and he

244

was, even with just four of us. What a short but sweet magical time we had sharing in the spirit of love. Thank you, Arno and friends.

Following Spirit and J-R, I then jetted off to Malaga, Spain, and took a high-speed train to Barcelona. It's been 10 years since I had last set foot in Barcelona with J-R on the "Spiritual Warriors" movie tour in 2007. Every night I was having J-R dreams and Spirit dreams. I got the hit to call my friend Anne in Cannes and surprise her with copies of *The Love of a Master*. First, a high-speed train to Marseilles, then local trains to Cannes, France. Ha! I realized when I arrived at midnight, that Yes, the *Mystical Traveler* film has finally made it to Cannes, France.

I stayed across the street from where the festival takes place. Because it was off-season, it literally cost nothing to stay there. It was empty. I remembered when J-R took me to Monaco in 1990 to have a meal opposite the casino in Monte Carlo. The next day, I rented a car, a state-of-the-art 2008 Citroën. Man, I didn't know how to drive this spaceship. It basically drives for you!

Anne and I headed to have lunch where J-R took me in 1990. It was great to see her. The Light was with us doing our ministries. We kept running into friends, and lunch turned into dinner. We met Anne's friends who live in Monaco and insisted that we eat together. It was a late night of dining and being together with like-minded souls—a real blessing. Thank you. Anne. What a treat to just be spontaneous and right on track with Spirit!

The Dreams of a Master

February 15, 2018

The Love of a Master Southwest Tour 2018

After New Year's, I realized that I would have two weeks free later that month to take a road trip around the southwestern United States. With the support of my publicist, Teri Breier, the plan quickly came together with grace and ease—last-minute, spontaneous, and true to form! I threw a few boxes of books in the backseat, asked Amazon to print and ship copies of *The Love of a Master* to Boulder, Colorado, and off I went.

The Southwest tour began in Tucson, Arizona, on Friday, January 19. After an awesome nine-hour journey that felt like I was driving J-R, I met up with Don and Donna Cook, who hosted me at their beautiful new home. Not only did they put me up for several nights in the guest room, but we also held the events there. On Saturday, the local ministers and initiates showed up in fellowship, some from quite a distance—including people like Samuel Flagler and many other wonderful souls. We sat together in Satsang as I began with a talk about *The Love of a Master* book, detailing my experiences with J-R, then showed a 23-minute video clip from *The Mystical Traveler* movie focused on the gnostic parts: chanting of the tones, a discussion of the various realms, what is the Mystical Traveler and Preceptor. The following day, we spent seven hours together watching a J-R seminar marathon and screening the *Mystical Traveler* movie.

At one point, I flashed on a childhood memory when my mom had separated from my stepfather and ran off to Tucson from Orlando, Florida. My recollections of living there when I was quite young brought back memories of a wonderful time.

Next I was off to Phoenix, where Judi Goldfader, and Angie and Mike "the Colonel" Nicolucci hosted an evening event. I am the Godfather to Judi's daughter, Ella, which allowed me to play a temporary parent role. We shared a Dairy Queen experience together that she called "delicious quiet." It was a sweet, beautiful moment of peace with my spiritual daughter.

In Prescott, Arizona, Frankie Cardamone, his friend, and I gathered in Satsang, watching a seven-hour J-R Seminar Marathon and *Mystical Traveler* film screening. Our sacred time together was completed by Frankie juggling us to Spirit. On this trip, it seemed I was visiting my past—way back in 1986, I had volunteered for Frankie and Rinaldo Porcile in the Products Department at PRANA. We joyfully reminisced about pizza parties, shipping Discourses, and sharing fellowship in love, serving the Travelers.

Making my way to Santa Fe, New Mexico, I spent several days with Robert Waterman and Karey Thorne. If you have never visited or worked with Robert and Karey, give yourself the experience and check it out. While staying at their home, Spirit revealed to me the whole picture, the Gestalt, an inner knowing that there is an illusion ridden by the negative power out there that J-R is gone. For instance, my sentimental attachment to locations in L.A., such as PRANA, Mandeville, and the USM building, as reminders of John-Roger, creates an opening for a distorted perception of "it's not the same," "the energy is different," and so on. It's a reactive, reptilian-brain "fight or flight" process, where the negative power comes into play; it is the mind running this misperception. I follow my intuition, I am traveling all over the world; not to escape but to sit in Satsang with initiates and ministers, which then activates the Satsang inside of me with John-Roger.

This deep realization and strength-building inside of me happened far from the influence of L.A. J-R used to say it takes two years to see clearly regarding any relationship, business, or something new to realize if it's for you or not. The last three years since his transition have given me a perspective of newness because I don't have any set thought forms, patterns, or inner objects sending my reptilian brain into a negative spin. When I'm in the loop with new locations and meeting new people, it's God greeting me with a new birth.

Rebecca Skeele arranged for a wonderful *The Love of a Master* book signing event at a local hotel one afternoon, followed by a J-R marathon and *Mystical Traveler* screening hosted at her lovely home the next day. We had a fantastic turnout at both events. Continuing the theme of revisiting my past, I enjoyed flashbacks of Rebecca facilitating some of my PAT trainings in Lake Arrowhead.

I had a few days off, so I spent some time with my Sikh friends at Yogi Bhajan's Ranch in Española, New Mexico, known as the Hacienda de Guru Ram Das Ashram. During a tour of his retreat center, it really brought home the missing of J-R. I saw how they hold their guru in reverence and how we likewise hold our Wayshower, John-Roger, in reverence. I realized that I was seeing another group that suffers the same way and misses their teacher the same way that we do. I loved hearing about how modest and "ordinary" Yogi Bhajan was. He lived his final days on the Española property. God bless him, he was a good man. It brought back a lot of memories, such as when Yogi Bhajan insisted that all of his congregation read John-Roger's book, *You Can't Afford the Luxury of a Negative Thought*. I remembered that he, John-Roger, and I were all in Russia in 1990 to attend some religious forum. Pretty awesome.

Travel Journal

Capping off the Southwest book tour, I headed up to Catherine Corona's ranch home in Boulder, Colorado, the first weekend of February. It was a spectacular drive. The last time I'd been to Boulder was 20 or so years earlier, with John-Roger. Madonna and Tom Smyth supported this part of the trip; it was amazing to see them, as well as Bertrand Babinet and Tom Boyer—more flashbacks to early days. My USM Class of 2016 reader, Julie Klingel, also showed up to *The Love of a Master* book event, where I ended up selling over 25 books. Nice! Following the J-R Marathon and *Mystical Traveler* film screening the next day, I was invited by Mary Ann Downs to the ministers meeting and lunch on Sunday. It was amazing to once again experience the energy of "where two or more are gathered," there is the Christ … there is J-R … there is the Traveler and Preceptor …

On my way home to L.A., I stopped off in Helper, Utah, about two miles from where John-Roger was born. I rented an Airbnb and shared some meals with his brother and sister-in-law, Delile and Elda Hinkins. I ran into Louise and Charlie Hamilton, who had helped with *The Wayshower* movie, and Willie Ellington, a very good friend and local institution. It was great to see that this town is booming economically since we shot the film there in 2010.

Next stop on *The Love of a Master* 2018 book tour: the land Down Under. Thank you, Nicole and John-Roger. Love You!

❋❋❋

March 21, 2018
The Love of a Master Australia Tour

As my ANA Boeing 787 Dreamliner flight lands in Australia, I instantly flash back to my last time there with John-Roger, February 3, 2002.

A day or two after our arrival, J-R and I were sitting at a cafe in Sydney and I was down in the mouth. When he asked if I liked it there, I said that I wasn't feeling it. There was also an audition coming up that I might lose out on. J-R knew that I would always tell it like it was. The way he looked at me in return indicated that he wasn't feeling so well himself. So he said to call Brooke Danza to book our flights home to L.A. the next day. Since John Morton was the Traveler by then, running the Australian trip with staff, it wasn't really a big deal if we left.

I remembered what an amazing person J-R was in that way—he really cared about how I was feeling and always supported me in whatever I was involved in, whether it was acting, singing, or something else.

My recent visit to Australia was organized and supported by the local MSIA community, in particular the amazing Andrew Urbanski, as well as Susan Skelton and Ruth Commisso. More than 50 copies of *The Love of a Master* books were acquired by fellow ministers, extended family, and others at our three events.

The afternoon of Sunday, February 25, we held a book signing in Greenwich. John Hayson hosted a J-R Seminar Marathon and *Mystical Traveler* movie screening at his home in North Sydney all day on Tuesday, February 27. After the Ministers Meeting, I

Travel Journal

shared about J-R and the experiences with working with him that make up some of my stories in *The Love of a Master*.

Nicole's family, the Campbells, as well as many MSIA ministers, live in a quaint little town called Woy Woy, an hour north of Sydney. Surrounded by water, it is a magical place where schools of ducks cross the street and traffic must stop to let them by. We had a wonderful book signing and Q&A event at a beautiful, spiritual New Age store called Gnostic Forest, on Saturday afternoon, March 3, and even played a little bit of the *Mystical Traveler* film.

Spiritually, there's work being done with all of us, even if we are unaware. Coincidentally or not, one woman came in, noticed our event, and decided to check it out. It turns out that she had participated in Insight 25 years ago! Once she saw the cover of the book with J-R's face, she made the connection, then joined the audience of 15 or so guests. It was amazing how she was led there, right at that moment!

Thanks so much to the owner Mary, and all the great ministers who came: Chris Hat, Wendy Bennett, Dawn White, Irene Chlopicki, Judith, Peter, and many more. It was wonderful to see everyone! It's been years since I was last in Australia, and I hope to be back to share J-R through Jesus Garcia Ministries again soon.

On March 2, Nicole and I rented a car. First, we drove to visit the Jamberoo Retreat site in Kangaroo Valley, a powerful location where J-R did a Living in Grace training about 19 years ago. Then, following a dream I had in Woy Woy, with a message that I was to connect with John Morton in Bowral, Australia (where MSIA was holding the Pat 8), we headed there and ran into John and Leigh with perfect timing.

On the way back to L.A., I met Bodhi Kenyon for breakfast at Tokyo Palace Hotel during my seven-hour layover in Japan. It was really good to just take a train into Tokyo and enjoy the city, however briefly. This brought back memories of the 2016 Japan tour that John led. I've been having inner experiences where I really want to be in that area and take part in helping to develop the Asian region from China to India, including Singapore and Malaysia. Check out J-R's many Moments of Peace when he speaks of how amazing China is going to be (and has become as of now). There are many signals from the inner levels about being in China and bringing in the Light there. So I'm leaning in on this, following my ministry, and heading to China in April.

Thank you, John-Roger!

❋❋❋

May 30, 2018

Jsu's Travel Journal: China 2018

It was 1988 and the Russia tour was coming to an end. I asked John-Roger if I could move into Mandeville to work with him. He said, "Sure—finish your film in New York and then head to Mandeville." He added that first he had to go with John Morton to the Summer Olympics in Seoul, Korea, September 17 to October 2. So I began working with J-R after October 6, 1988. Now, 30 years later, the work that John-Roger and John Morton did in Korea has manifested with another Olympics—this time the Winter Olympics in PyeongChang, February 9-25, 2018.

In mid-April, I was invited to China to help a friend and I couldn't believe what I saw on television while I was there: the inter-Korean summit on April 27. North Korean leader Kim Jong Un crossed the line dividing the demilitarized zone (DMZ) to meet with South Korean President Moon Jae-in for what was described as a historic summit. The energy was thick with peace and possibilities.

This was my third time in China. My first time was with J-R on a group tour in 2000. In 2017, Nicole and I were invited by my good friend Ribal Al-Assad from the IMAN International Club to support worldwide peace leadership through the Belt and Road Initiative (BRI), a global development strategy adopted by the Chinese government involving infrastructure development and investments in 152 countries and international organizations in Asia, Europe, Africa, the Middle East, and the Americas. One year later, I returned on my own to assist IMAN again. This was perfect for me, because I remember J-R saying that China would someday be a great leader in world peace. I felt totally alone in that country and yet I loved it—one-billion-plus people and nobody knew who I was.

I met up with Sheldon Dorenfest there for the second time in two years. It's so amazing to connect with a fellow minister and initiate in such a vast land of strangers, or so it seems. David Clegg introduced me to Amy, a Chinese teacher for foreigners, an amazing person who taught me some basics of the language. In appreciation, I gave her the Chinese translation of John-Roger's book, *Living Love from the Spiritual Heart*, and she ended up translating *The Love of a Master* into Chinese.

When you cross the street in China, you'd better be aware! It's got a flow about it. I hired many three-wheeler taxis to navigate through traffic, which they accomplished with harmonious group consciousness. Amazing! I put the Light forward, trusted, and flowed through traffic like I was part of a giant school of fish.

After 18 years, I finally finished the Forbidden City by capping the top of Jingshan Park. I remembered that J-R and I took a photo in Tiananmen Square; what a trip to be back after so much time. I felt safe there, experiencing something like being watched and protected.

On April 22, I broadcast the *Mystical Traveler* film with Chinese subtitles and five Moments of Peace (MOP) about China by J-R and John. My favorite is the one called, "Peace with the Chinese people," where J-R says, "The karma of China is tied to Shambala, which was over the Gobi Desert. Their karma is now to flow so they can become a world power. Chinese/Japanese/Mongolian/Vietnamese, they will be playing a great part in the deliverance of the planet from a lot of negativity."

It's amazing what J-R predicted then. (I was also present in 1988, when he planted a "light worm" in the East Berlin wall and a year later it came down.) To hear my favorite excerpts directly, I invite you to view all five Moments of Peace from China. (See **Appendix C–Resources** for links.)

China has a fresh energy and sense of collective progress. Not taking political sides, it's important to be open in sharing the Love and Light. I strongly felt J-R with me. It's something I call on every day—the energy of John-Roger, the Preceptor, and the Christ.

As another Traveler, the prophet Muhammad, once said: "Seek knowledge even as far as China."

Thanks always to John-Roger.

❋❋❋

July 17, 2018

Jsu's Travel Journal: Latin America 2018

As soon as my book, *The Love of a Master*, was translated into Spanish, I scheduled the 2018 *El Amor de un Maestro* Jesus Garcia ministry tour to South America and Mexico, which took place in June.

Kicking things off in Bogotá, Colombia, I had the greatest time working with Alberto Arango. He and Diego Forero helped to set up the J-R Marathon, and my book event was also very cool. I did counseling sessions there and it was really good to see J-R's work continue on in Bogotá.

Next came Chile and it was amazing. I made a point of staying in the homes of people who wanted to host me. It was incredible to be one-on-one with some of these long-time ministers and initiates! Older but not aging, they're still very young at heart. They come packed with a lot of power, through the ministerial authority and being J-R's and John's initiates. It was really uplifting to sit in Satsang with these people.

Whether it's a J-R video marathon, *Mystical Traveler* movie screening, or *The Love of a Master* / *El Amor de un Maestro* book signing, the format doesn't really matter. These events are all just an excuse to get together, because where two or more are gathered, there's the Spirit. That's when J-R shows up.

The Dreams of a Master

My experiences were very, very clear on the inner and on the outer. In particular while traveling, every time I leave Los Angeles, I start to be aware of John-Roger being next to me and leading the way, as always. I don't carry anything special, we ALL do. So when we get together it begins the Satsang, a meeting of truth.

For an overnight side trip, I flew across the Andes from Chile to Mendoza, Argentina, where I was hosted by Eduardo Vera. The experiences I felt there were beyond words. Eduardo was able to gather many who came for the J-R marathon. John had approved some initiations, and it was incredible to be with the fire of Mendoza. The initiates and ministers there give that community an intense John-Roger energy that pulls people in— they're interested in MSIA and what we do.

I'll be returning to Argentina—this time, Buenos Aires—in November. In 2013, Nat, J-R, and a small crew participated in the Mar del Plata film festival with the *Mystical Traveler* movie, supported by Graciella Borges, Juan Cruz, and Kate Kirby. I look forward to seeing and working with them again.

Back in Chile, I was hosted by Remy and spent time with him, Verónica, Pilar, and so many people in Chile who I just love so much. I remember going to Chile in 1986 to do a film, then returned many times after that with John-Roger. I think our last visit was the last time I saw Alex Padilla; we were staying in the same hotel.

From there, I headed to Mexico City, where Graciella hosted me, and Marcos hosted the J-R marathons, *Mystical Traveler* film and *El Amor de un Maestro* book event. I spent quite a bit of time there, and it was really good to connect with that place. I walked around the many districts and got to know Mexico City very well. A group of us went to the Pyramid of the Sun—Graciella, Claudia,

Marta Soto, and some friends. Led by Claudia, we climbed the pyramid, called in the Light, and did a meditation early in the morning, which really set the tone for what was to come. I felt J-R very much present in Mexico City. Just trying to follow in the Master's path.

If you watch the *Mystical Traveler* film, there's a scene where we are obviously looking through the eye of a camera, and the person filming is John Morton, who says, "And here is the Pyramid of the Sun." Then you can see John-Roger walking up the Pyramid of the Sun with Edgar Veytia. It is very inspiring.

When I got home, my mother wasn't feeling well, so I flew to visit her in Homestead, Florida. Turns out that was simply the catalyst to get me down there. My mom immediately felt better, of course—J-R's got her back. She was out of the hospital, feeling great, and we were able to spend a couple of days together.

I want to take a moment to acknowledge my mother, Nicia Ferrer, for all the great things that she has done over the years. I never knew what exactly she did for MSIA when she worked on staff. But now, wherever I travel in Latin America or Miami, people regularly stop me and ask, "How's your mom?" "How is Nicia?" "Tell her we love her." And I'm just blown away by the impact she made in such a short time and how important it is for a Latin representative to be in the U.S. at PRANA, representing our community in MSIA. My mother was that person for a while, helping many folks in the Latin community. I saw her go to work, but now I've experienced the tremendous effects of it.

While in Miami, I was hosted by many MSIAers. I attended Luis Mario's home seminar and a fantastic MSIA meditation. It was incredible—the energy was on fire! Just recently, Skyler Patton and Debbie Roth had traveled there to support the community. I noticed that the attendees were primarily Latino, which was much different than I remember from the 1980s. Terilee Wunderman and a few others were there, too. I came away very impressed by the way that Luis, Teri, and others are keeping the Miami community going. I want to shout out—I love Miami!

I love my MSIA communities, and I'm here to ignite, promote, and share John-Roger within all of us. One of my primary tasks with Jesus Garcia Ministries is to travel to places and perform initiations and ordinations on behalf of John-Roger or John. Even if it's just one person in an isolated area, like when I took a four-hour side trip to Greece when I was recently in Europe. Generally, I travel at my own expense; sometimes people sponsor me to do that, and I'm open to receiving as much as possible. It's fantastic and I love it!

Finally, I made it to the Conference of Heaven on Earth, probably one of the best conferences since J-R passed. [At the time of this writing,] I'm a USM grad currently in the Consciousness, Health, and Healing program, and soon will get my 10-month Certificate of Completion after the lab in August. It was great to have Ron and Mary Hulnick facilitate the workshop and to hear John Morton share.

On Saturday of the two-day workshop, I raised my hand and had a cathartic moment. Thirty years ago, January 1988 at a relationship workshop at the Sheraton Universal, I shared with John-Roger. Earlier, he had come up to me and asked, "What's your name?" I responded, "Jesus Garcia" and he insisted, "No, what's your other name?" "Oh, Nick Corri, I'm an actor," and he said, "That's it. They know you as Corri," and I was like, "Who is 'they?'" J-R said, "The Karmic records." He was just a fisher of men. From that point, I was marked. And in my sharing that day, I said that

I wanted to work with him. I asked, "Can I do acting and still be spiritual? Can I work with you and do what John does?" This is before John Morton was a Traveler; he was sitting in the back. J-R goes, "Well, go talk to John about that" and I did. Long story short, 30 years later, 26 years with John-Roger was amazing.

The Conference of Heaven on Earth was incredible. Everything was on fire, mostly inside myself. Navigating through the passing of J-R has not been easy for me. Sure, it's challenging for a lot of his ministers and initiates. But, in particular, for me it's still daunting. It's hard. It's crazy. But when I travel, I get to connect with him inwardly and live in that. And it's so rewarding, especially if I have Sound Current experiences with John-Roger in the inner. When I hear him talk, I've got 26 years of John-Roger's voice in my head and it's like a jukebox. Every move I make I hear the advice. And so, onward.

Light ahead to my upcoming travels in Europe and leading a trip to Israel for the first time since J-R passed, celebrating John-Roger's 84th birthday. God bless.

October 19, 2018

Jsu's Travel Journal 2018:
The Love of a Master Tour to Israel and Europe

In August, Nicole and I traveled together to Europe a few weeks before starting *The Love of a Master* Israel Tour. I took last year's trip alone, because Nicole was helping to take care of her father, Owen Campbell, in Australia until he passed away in December.

God bless his Soul. So this time, it was really nice to have Nicole by my side on the road again to experience all the miracles and phenomena, just like on the J-R trips.

Our travels began in Amsterdam with David and Kathryn Allen. I cherished the fellowship and Satsang; it's always great to talk with them about the old days with J-R. Then we visited Claudie and Guillaume Botté in Toulouse, France, where the heat was scorching. We were struck by the distinctive architecture in that area, more similar to Spain than the rest of France, with its proximity to the Pyrenees mountain range. While we stayed with the Bottés, they were doing the Transcendent Leadership program, so the energy in their home was really powerful and we loved being there.

Next, we went to other parts of France for some fabulous private touring with Véronique Sandoz, until we left for Sofia, Bulgaria. This was quite an experience. It was really wonderful to be in fellowship with Hristina Kirimidchieva, Georgi Markov, and many of the MSIA ministers there. "Where two or more are gathered … " We did a book signing, took sharing, hosted a J-R video marathon, and screened the *Mystical Traveler* movie with Bulgarian subtitles. And I spoke a lot about my experiences of living and working with John-Roger.

Then Hristina and Georgi took Nicole and me on their incredible version of a Bulgarian tour and spoiled us the entire way. We went to tiny little villages where they make the authentic, natural, world-famous Bulgarian yogurt (which they call "sour milk") with their natively grown *Lactobacillus bulgaricus* probiotic. We also tasted fresh honey right from the bees and picked our wild berries and bought the unique Rose Oil, which has much healing properties.

This was near the Seven Lakes region, where the Universal White Brotherhood, a New Age religious movement, was founded in the early 20th century by Peter Deunov. Each of the Seven Lakes is a different metaphor or symbol, the last one representing SOUL. As we visited each lake in the sequence, it felt similar to our process walking the labyrinth or rising up through the chakra system. I experienced it as a very similar energy to Lake Titicaca in the Andes of South America.

I performed an initiation in Switzerland, then John Morton approved an ordination and initiation for a fellow MSIA-er in Greece. Hristina didn't hesitate to drive us to another country! We found ourselves in Larissa, Greece, close to Olympiaki Akti, or Olympic Beach. This really gave us the whole European flavor, like one giant pot with a variety of foods. At the beach were Greeks, Bulgarians, and Russians … all sorts of people from different countries, all mixed up, just bathing on a really beautiful beach together. We baptized each other in the Aegean Sea. First time for me.

And then we were off to an experience I've not had since J-R was still alive, on our last trip in September 2014, when a group of us celebrated his birthday in Israel, Jerusalem, and Palestine. I co-led this 12-day Israel trip with Benji Shavit of Regina Tours. It was a small, intimate group of only 15 people, mostly women—half U.S. citizens and almost half Latin Americans with one Australian. We kept the cost as affordable as possible for the participants. The evening the group landed in Tel Aviv on September 17, we held a group Welcome session where we all met each other, reviewed the itinerary, and handed out tour t-shirts, nametags, and luggage tags. It truly felt like J-R was present, just like the old days.

The Dreams of a Master

The tour officially began on September 18 which happened to be the sacred Jewish holy day of Yom Kippur, dedicated to atonement and forgiveness from the past year. We started with baptisms in the River Jordan to clear and align with the Spirit and our Inner Masters. On previous trips, John Morton was always the instructor who demonstrated how to perform and partake in the baptism process, so I really missed him being there. But this time, I found myself taking on that role!

MSIA-style baptism is for the remission of sins in this life and other lifetimes, and Spirit assigns you with a guardian angel. I do remember J-R officiating the guardian angel, which I wasn't able to do; but we simply assumed it. It's just like "mocking up" the Soul Realm, and you get it. It was an amazing experience. In the Moment of Peace called Guardian Angels and the Sea of Galilee, J-R explains this in his words.

We observed Yom Kippur that night at a local synagogue, then held a three-day meditation retreat in Kfar Kisch, a little village at the base of Mount Tabor, near the Galilee region. Participants walked back and forth from their different Airbnb housing in the village, and all our breakfasts and lunches were prepared organically by Benji, his son Gilad, daughter-in-law Mia, along with a woman named Karen. We were treated like royalty in his vineyard and took side trips to Mount of Beatitudes and finally Mount of Transfiguration. The workshop was beautiful, including the daily Luxor Meditation and nothing but J-R videos—an amazing experience of feeling him at every moment.

Next, we went into Jerusalem for three days, starting with the traditional Mount of Olives toast blessing. We went to Temple Mount, the Western Wall, and visited the different quarters of the Old City: Armenian, Jewish, Muslim, and Christian. We took a side trip to the Church of the Nativity in Bethlehem. On September

24 the group and some special guests enjoyed a celebratory John-Roger 84th Birthday Dinner at the Notre Dame Rooftop Cheese and Wine Restaurant overlooking the Old City.

One of my USM classmates who's Israeli, Helena Shoshana, and Barbara Schwarck from Pennsylvania also showed up for the dinner. We were in time to see the sun set over the Old City. It was beautiful. So I thank J-R for everything. Thank you.

Following our incredible time in Jerusalem, two days were spent in the Dead Sea area. Because we weren't allowed to climb Masada, we took the aerial trams up to the top. It felt like J-R was walking with us and was in the front of the bus with me and Benji. We also toured the Qumran caves, where the famous Dead Sea Scrolls were discovered in 1946/47, and many in our group did the mud packs and floated in the highly alkaline Dead Sea, which is considered to be the lowest place on earth.

Benji was amazing the entire time ... he even translated in both English and Spanish! We met Shraga and ended with a small Blessings Dinner close to Ben Yehuda Street near the Jaffa Gate outside the Old City. It was very nice to be back on the saddle leading a trip. So I do have in mind that there will be another trip for me. I'm trying to tap in to J-R inside of me and see what's clear in terms of the next destination, but it was an incredible experience. Stay tuned.

Then I flew off to London with Nicole to do more initiations for John, and I celebrated my 55th birthday with a J-R Marathon and *The Love of a Master* book signing event in Borde Hill, hosted by AJ and Eleni Clarke and Nathalie Franks. Nat Sharratt came over one day from France, where he had a fashion show for his business. We met at the Carlton Towers with our London MSIA family and friends to rekindled the memories of the times we were there with J-R, Delile and Elda Hinkins, and all the groups. A lot of MSIAers came out to the J-R marathon—it was awesome. Thanks to all of you guys for indulging me in my Jesus Garcia ministries, sharing, "Satsanging" with J-R energy, and sharing my experiences with J-R.

Nicole and I had some spiritual work to do up in Scotland, where we spent a night and two days. She headed off to Roslyn Chapel to plant more light columns, while I did an initiation for John Morton. I remember celebrating J-R's birthday in 2011, when John took a few people to Roslyn Chapel which is very cool. It's not far from Edinburgh, about 30 minutes, and then we took a train back to London. I really enjoyed sharing the trips that we did with J-R, with Nicole. It's beautiful to have someone to share those moments together, like I did with J-R.

In other news, I am excited to share that *The Love of a Master* book has been translated into Chinese! I'm off soon to do another *Love of a Master* tour in Mexico, Colombia, Chile, Argentina, and Brazil.

God bless you all!

✽✽✽

January 10, 2019

The Love of a Master Tour
Latin America & Asilomar, Fall 2018

In late October, I returned to Latin America with the Spanish translation of my book, *The Love of a Master*, revisiting many of the places I traveled to last summer. This time, I started off in Mexico City, staying again at the home of Graciella, one of my favorite places.

A new president had recently been elected, and there was a lot of construction at the airport. They shut down the entire water system of Mexico City, so a lot of people left. Some residences, like Graciella's, did have access to water, but many didn't. This was a good opportunity for me to just hold with ministers and enjoy Mexico.

Martha Soto and Marcos were also with me as we presented a John-Roger Video Marathon and my new *The Love of the Master Workshop*—a one-day immersion in J-R videos and sharing, based on my book and experiences. I think about six or ten people showed up because we were there just holding the Light.

My next stop was Colombia. I stopped in Bogotá long enough to connect with Ilse and Alberto Arango and Juliana and Diego Forero and then traveled with them to La Calera, a beautiful mountain town about 11 miles (18km) away. At nearly 9,000 feet (2,718 meters) elevation, I had a hard time breathing, since I am prone to altitude sickness.

Thanks to Pablo Lipnizky, who works at the Ekirayá Montessori School of Education, we were able to set up in a large classroom on the campus. It was a fantastic experience. We showed some great J-R videos that the locals hadn't seen, because they were newly subtitled in Spanish; I also subtitled *Journey to the East*. Participants enjoyed a very full couple of days in the workshop format watching J-R videos and doing some sharing.

Melba Alhonte in New York had sent several new people to us, who got a huge dose of the love that was in the room. One new lady shared that the videos and information about John-Roger were great, but what really got her going was the love she felt in the room for J-R. I guess J-R did his job from the other side, because everybody in the room shared about J-R, their Master and teacher, as well as John Morton, which is what the new people wanted to hear. That was very good feedback to learn how important it is to talk and do some sharing, along with the J-R Videos, because when two or more are gathered in that way, it really gets the energy going.

And then we were off to perform initiations in various places—starting with Chile! I stayed at Remy Urrich's place in Santiago. Vania Grimalt flew out from Los Angeles, and Isabella and Pedro also helped. We all went down to the coast, spending time with Ana Maria and about 10 new folks who were interested in the Movement of Spiritual Inner Awareness. As usual, we did a marathon of J-R videos and sold copies of my book. And really, it becomes a fantastic setting to just do Satsang and share about J-R and talk about this teacher. It's almost like some dream, some other life that we're talking about, but bringing it present in this moment, not as a memory but right now, and really basking in that energy.

We went to Viña del Mar, which is a casino that J-R took me to in the late '90s … I believe that John was also on that trip. It was a great experience to walk through and get reignited by the energy of the Light columns that J-R left behind. Then we visited Nora Valenzuela's home in Viña del Mar, which is really beautiful.

Next, on the itinerary was Mendoza with Eduardo Vera, who holds MSIA seminars three times a week. It was amazing to jump into that structure and discipline! We had two awesome nights of sharing back to back. I think we did three-hour sharings, really cool. Some people were new, some were in the Movement, some were Soul Awareness Discourse subscribers. We also did several initiations there for John. So much Light and love to all of them.

Staying at people's homes gives me more and more of the sense that J-R is everywhere in everyone. And it's so beautiful. The Traveler works in mysterious ways. John had recently completed his South America trip, so I got a taste of visiting several communities soon after John had left and there's a LOT of energy.

By the time I arrived in Buenos Aires, the G-20 Summit had started, so many world leaders, including Putin, Trump, and President Xi from China, were there. It was perfect timing for me. Even though not many people came to my J-R Marathon or the workshop, I got to hang out with Diana Berengue, as well as Vania and Isabella, who came to support me from Santiago. So there we were in Buenos Aires holding the Light for the G-20. Very cool—loved it.

One night I was invited to hang out with the Insight community, which is really big there. The feeling there brought back the time in Buenos Aires in 2013 with J-R when we brought the *Mystical Traveler* movie to the Mar del Plata Film Festival.

Before that—possibly 1997 or so—was the last time I saw Alex Padilla, who was a longtime Insight facilitator and Spanish translator for J-R's MSIA seminars. As the lights went up in the audience, J-R told the participants, "Everyone say goodbye to Alex," as he was leaving. Soon after that, Alex transitioned suddenly.

And then I went to São Paulo, Brazil, where I ran into Wagner, who had hosted me in 2007. This time, I stayed at Adi Ribeiro's house, which was really beautiful, and I sold 48 *The Love of a Master* books in Portuguese—big shout-out to Adi, thank you so much! I was also able to initiate someone there for John.

I really enjoyed my time in South America, especially because of the gorgeous weather. As the Northern Hemisphere was heading into winter, it was bursting out in spring down there. I'd never seen Santiago de Chile look so lovely, or Mendoza, or Buenos Aires, that name is perfect for the city. It *was* "beautiful air." And, of course, all those reps for MSIA, who are good friends of both J-R and John Morton, were simply fantastic and treated me very well.

From my point of view, the state of MSIA is doing very well all over the world. The Traveler is connected everywhere—there is no border, and there is no limit except what's in the mind and what people want to believe. But in my experience, the Traveler as J-R is powerful everywhere, and this line has continuity with John, the current Traveler, who is working everywhere. He's beloved and I support him and MSIA, and I'm just really glad that I get to see J-R everywhere.

That's been my ministry, too. After 26 years with J-R, it's been very important for me to seek him out and to learn another language, similar to learning Greek. It's like a completely different inner language, a spiritual language of connecting with that loved one, in particular my master, my teacher, my Traveler John-Roger. And where do I go for that? Chant my tone.

When two or more are gathered, there he is, and I can see his presence and feel his presence as I did when I finally flew back to LAX on December 9. I got a good night's sleep at home, packed, and hit the road the next day to join up with the start of "The Royal Road" retreat in Asilomar, to be of assistance to John Morton and Sheri Wylie. Four years earlier, in December 2014, we had spread the ashes of J-R from a boat in the ocean right off the Asilomar beach, which you can see when you take a peek from the conference hall where we do the PAT processes.

The end of 2018 marked 30 years since I raised my hand at the Sheraton Universal Hotel, during the relationship workshop with Drs. Ron and Mary Hulnick. It was the day that I raised my hand and said I wanted to be like John and serve J-R—and I was blessed to have gotten that wish.

I want to continue having another 30 years if J-R gives it to me, and I'm here to seek my master, to seek the kingdom of heaven. I remember J-R quoting the Bible verse to me: "Seek the kingdom of heaven and all else will come unto you." And then he added his commentary: "It doesn't say you have to find it, just keep seeking."

Baruch Bashan and New Year's Blessings

❋❋❋

March 7, 2019

The Love of a Master Tour: U.S., Winter 2019

This trip started in mid-January with a drive from Los Angeles to Tucson, Arizona, one of my favorite places to hang out. Once again, I stayed at Donna and Don Cook's home, where they hosted a beautiful *The Love of a Master* Q&A, and we played a few John-Roger seminars. The following day happened to be a local ministers meeting; it was very nice to spend time with the Tucson folks, including Barbara Wieland, Joyce Evans, Samuel Flagler, and others.

Proceeding on my "itinerant preacher" tour for *The Love of a Master*, the next stop was Phoenix, where I saw Judi Goldfader and her daughter, and stayed with Angie and Mike Nicolucci. We had a private VIP J-R video marathon with two new guests: one Discourse subscriber and someone who knows me from Facebook. I flew to Denver for an initiation, came back and spent the night in Las Vegas, Nevada. In memory of the tragic October 2017 mass shooting, someone put me up at the Mandalay Bay hotel, where I took the opportunity to plant Light columns. A J-R marathon brought out the locals, David Wilkinson, Elaine Baran, and Will Porter. It evoked vivid memories of my third aura balance in Las Vegas at Lucretia's house more than 30 years ago, the time that J-R touched the tips of my feet. From that point on, I was hooked, and would go on to participate in my first of many PAT IV trips in 1988.

I made a quick side visit to Helper, Utah, to spend the night with J-R's brother and sister-in-law, Delile and Elda Hinkins, and also saw his nephew, Dave Hinkins. I enjoyed seeing them all. Utah was quite cold, yet beautiful. My itinerary then brought me to Robert Waterman and Karey Thorne in Santa Fe, New Mexico, for four days, including their weekend workshop that was attended by my friends Robert Zack, Denise Lumiere, Wendy Kunkel, Doreen Dietsche, and David Sand. We all got an Airbnb together. It was great to be on the road doing work and learning, taking a course from Robert Waterman, who began his work with J-R all the way back in 1966, making him one of the Movement's "founding fathers." My conclusion is that it doesn't really matter what we do, but only that J-R's initiates and ministers come together in Satsang. The way we create this magic is truly amazing, and I appreciate experiencing this over and over during my travels.

After a quick return home to L.A., I repacked and took off to the East Coast on January 31 for my *The Love of a Master* talks and J-R marathons. A huge blizzard hit the Northeast when I arrived, so it was icy, bone-chillingly cold. Nevertheless, I really enjoyed my time in Satsang with Kathy Kienke, Paula Beldengreen, Caryn Kanzer, Bill Blanding, David Clegg, Jim and Christine Lynch, and my Latinos, Melba and Marc Alhonte.

I took the train to Philadelphia where I was delightfully hosted by Stephanie Kozak. Her assistant R.C. and I were invited to attend the local ministers meeting, where we saw Lou and Lenny Tenaglia, Peter Bort, and so many others, just really solid folks. I loved it. I felt the love and the way that everybody is taking care of everybody else.

Then I flew to Miami for a visit with my mother, Nicia, who is going through recovery from cancer. I was grateful to be able to support my mom, her healing journey, and her life. On the way home, I pondered interesting thoughts and feelings about how we're all at some stage of aging and getting ready to transcend and see the Lord.

On my flight to New York, I had a fantastic experience where I fell off the plane. I just went right through with the Sound Current, then came back. When I opened my eyes, it felt like I had no idea where I went, but it was an incredible occurrence that reminded me of a similar experience I had with J-R. My whole life with J-R was planes, trains, hotels, automobiles. And on one particular flight, I remember being quite irritated. I had the window seat, and

J-R told me to lean on the window and chant my tone, which I did. Then I started falling through the jet plane's fuselage and caught myself. I snapped awake—I was scared to death. J-R looked over me and said, "You like that, huh?"

Half of my life has been those kinds of experiences with J-R. Now, they're somehow even more tangible and solid. Although I didn't have him physically there on that flight to NYC, I was aware of the radiant form, the energy of him next to me. This time I just went with it, let myself fall through the plane into some other dimension, and I was flying. When I came back, things were different—and they have been different ever since. It was all set up perfectly for me, for my travels to New York, Philadelphia, and Miami.

Now I am back in L.A., getting ready for the Easter events at the 2101 Wilshire building. Sending my love and Light to all MSIAers everywhere. Light to the world, to my mother´s recovery, to Nicole, and to all our friends and family.

July 1, 2019

Spring Travels in the U.S. and Spain

Everything that I do in my travels—touring for *The Love of the Master*, J-R video marathons, seminars, and Q&A's in communities around the world—falls under my ministry, which is sharing the teachings of J-R and MSIA. I learn so much that it feels like I'm a student again. Revisiting all of J-R's and John's ministers and initiates in MSIA fulfills the New Testament to me; when two or more gather in his name, it is truly incredible.

In April, I was invited to Austin, Texas, by Grace Meyer, where I was graciously hosted by Candy Spitzer and Rosie VonZurmuehlen. My last visit there would have been in the '90s with John-Roger and John Morton. I recall that it was quite humid. We stayed near downtown, and I drove J-R along the side of the river. That's when I was first introduced to chicken-fried steak, which J-R absolutely loved. There is no chicken, just a thinly sliced, battered and fried steak, usually served with mashed potatoes and collard greens. In the morning, we had good, old-fashioned, homemade grits.

On Saturday, April 27, many treasured friends showed up to the seven-hour J-R Video Marathon, *The Love of a Master* book talk, and Q&A at the Integrity Academy at Casa de Luz. It was wonderful to see Richard Powell, Liesl Schott, Jennifer Halet, and others who came out to support me and do Satsang together. To me, Satsang is sitting around, talking about our spiritual teacher, J-R. I shared about my experiences of living and working with him, doing the Master and Doctor of Spiritual Science programs, and my three years at the University of Santa Monica, including the Consciousness, Health, and Healing class.

This is really about connecting and sharing from that place that we all have access to. My experience of being with J-R is that two Souls are better than one; you need another person who can reflect it back in a conversation, in the being-ness. As J-R has said, "We are all Travelers, and John holds the key to the door."

Once back in Los Angeles, I was soon invited up to Denise Lumiere's home in Santa Barbara (I call it, "North by Northwest PRANA") on May 11. It was great to sit in Satsang there, and play a J-R Marathon at her house with ministers like Beverly Terrill, Rama Fox, Connie Stomper, Jack Reed, Karen Avalon, Ellie Gantt, and Connemara. Santa Barbara is where it all started. I had a lot of experiences with J-R at Windermere Ranch and Miracielo—the barbecues, pool parties, fundraisers, and J-R birthday celebrations.

The annual Founders Dinner, which was started by Jan Shepherd, also took place at Miracielo. Jason Laskay constructed the large round tables (inspired by the King Arthur's knights version), where dozens would gather and listen to John-Roger share for hours, sometimes into the early morning. Many friends were involved in catering the food, valet parking the cars, and providing entertainment during the event, which was always a lot of fun.

In *The Love of a Master*, I wrote about evacuating from a fire at Miracielo when I accidentally locked the keys in the trunk of the Lincoln Continental while packing up our stuff. The fire was advancing up the hill from the ocean as J-R monitored its progress, using the walkie talkie and a police scanner. He remained calm and relaxed while everyone else ran around in panic mode. I told him, "I locked the keys in the trunk" and he said, "OK, no problem. Go down with Jack Espey and see if he can pop the trunk from the glove compartment." The moment we did that and got the keys, J-R said, "No need to leave, the winds have shifted." That was a magical time with J-R. The beauty of those memories never go away and the best is still yet to come.

My next venture was returning to New York City in early June, hosted by good friends, including Paula Beldengreen, Kathy Kienke, Melba and Marc Alhonte, and Janet Ellis. We had fun and did a lot of good work in the community. I remember J-R saying once that ministering is schmoozing and networking, so these are the things that I try to do in my life today. It's unconventional, but that's OK, I love it. When I see another minister, it's fantastic. We had a seminar at Michael Weinberger's on Tuesday, Kathy's on Wednesday, and in between I saw clients. Melba and I visited with Maxine and Howard White, Joan Witkowski, and Bill Blanding. We did our J-R Marathon and *The Love of a Master* Satsang at Paula's. Then we worked with Sheila Steckel, who opened up her apartment for the first event, and thanks to her, it really ignited something in the community. Since J-R passed away, navigating has been really hard for many people, especially me and perhaps the others who worked one-on-one with him. But I can assure you that when we get together, it's like J-R is there, because he is still present in all of us.

Then I was off to Spain! I was invited by a client to go to Spain and had the opportunity to mix personal stuff with spiritual stuff. There happened to be work to do there for MSIA, and I got together with several ministers in Marbella, such as Katja Rusanen, George Monday, and Cecilie Beck Kronborg. One of the things that I've experienced is that it's one thing to email folks and another to text people and get an immediate response. On top of that, there's a mobile app called "What's App?" where you can group people in conversations; mine are called "J-R Marathon" and "Mystical Traveler Movie." That mutated and converted into a kind of ministerial phone tree, which J-R started years ago before the Internet. The idea is that when someone needs help, they tell the phone tree administrator, then each person calls ten, who then call another ten, and before long, it could be hundreds of people hearing, "So-and-so is in the hospital; please put her in the Light." It evolved into a beautiful process for different communities, in different countries. Facebook is another format where people can share with one another instantly and request prayers.

I think it's very important, from my experience, that we all share with one another, even if you are in isolation. Granted, there is a thing called karma, so it may be that person doesn't want any contact. J-R told me that sometimes the best thing you can do for someone is to leave them alone. So you have to use your discretion and check inside to see intuitively, not as an ego thing where you must save someone, but "Hey, how are you doing? Just checking in." That kind of outreach really helps your community. I love Skyler's Heartreach emails about who needs the Light, who needs service. That's great! I'm not a socialist, but my parents left a communist country.

Then again, I believe that in some ways we can privatize outside of MSIA through friends, through resources. "You don't have any money for Discourses, no problem. There's a fund to help you with Discourses." I know my mom couldn't afford SATs and a good friend of hers is helping her renew them for the rest of her life. These kinds of things people can help one another with. I love that. I'm always feeling that I need to do more. I enjoy myself and I enjoy serving; in some ways on my terms. Working closely with J-R means I will never forget the part inside that's to be obedient to the Spirit, to do what's next. It could be going to a certain place that was initially clear spiritually, but within a week it's canceled because I'm obedient to that.

Everybody has their own connection with J-R, and I'm well aware of that. The Traveler is beyond the understanding of the mind. So I'm very grateful that people host me, that I'm able to participate in the world out there, promoting myself and the community. Like J-R said, as one of our foundational ground rules in MSIA: "Take care of yourself first, so you can help take care of others." There's another more recent J-R quote that applies as well, which MSIA ministers will recognize: "We're to be out in the world ministering to all regardless of race, creed, color, situation, circumstance, or environment."

I returned home from Spain and went straight into the "Conference of the Highest Good". It was a blast, and I enjoyed having it at the 2101 Wilshire building. I live 18 blocks away, so I scootered to the building. I was assisting at the Workshop and was the MC for Saturday night. Leading the Anthem Road Band, Valerie Ojeda rocked our socks off late into the night. On Sunday, I accompanied my mother to the Ministers and Initiates Meetings. It felt like I was back in the 1980s when Insight Seminars seemed to be taking place in every room. Baraka Center, once operated by Marcy Goldstein, was open for a health check-up, and the Insight/MSIA store was in the lobby selling T-shirts and tapes for $10. John-Roger spent many years in that building, in his office, and all the seminar rooms. His energy is anchored all over 2101. Let's bathe in it—great job to all that worked Conference. Nice work! Love to Nancy Carter, who has retired from NOW Productions.

Love you all. God bless.

[Ed. note: Marcy Goldstein passed into Spirit in Jacksonville, FL, October 23, 2019. God bless his Soul.]

❈❈❈

August 18-27, 2019

My First Visit to Nigeria

During my s.e's one morning in the December 2018 PAT 8 retreat at Asilomar Conference Grounds, I received an inner message clear as day that I was meant to go serve and see our spiritual Nigerian family with my own eyes.

Eight months later, in August 2019, I paid for my trip and flew to Nigeria carrying a suitcase full of John-Roger books. I held a J-R Video Marathon and *Mystical Traveler* movie screening in Lagos, then presented the *The Love of a Master* Workshop in Port Harcourt. I had the most amazing experience of Grace-filled protection. When traveling, I can feel J-R with me every time, guiding me and holding me up.

I felt fully supported and encouraged by Spirit to do this work. In my s.e's, I saw hundreds of Nigerians come up to me and look at my face; then I heard J-R say, "They are God's children."

On the day I flew to Europe, the Great Rev. Madus T. Weleonu passed into Spirit; God bless his Soul. Just the previous night, he had been part of the chieftain group that made me an Honorary Chief of the Igbo tribe. I am called Owah of Africa, meaning: "The great moon of Africa."

The people of Nigeria are truly God's children, and I'm blessed that I was allowed to share Light, Love, and J-R with them.

Travel Journal

Jesus Garcia, John-Roger, and John Morton

"Those who sit very quietly in the silence that roars the name of the Light and do the most mundane jobs in love and devotion are performing a beautiful service that God sees as very great, indeed."

– John-Roger, D.S.S.

Appendix B

Glossary of Terms

हू

*W*hile many of the following terms were used in both *The Love of a Master* and *The Dreams of a Master*, other phrases not specifically mentioned have been included as common references by John-Roger or used often within the MSIA community. Most of these definitions are excerpted from the three-book set, *Fulfilling Your Spiritual Promise* by John-Roger, D.S.S. Other defined terms are taken from *Spiritual Gems* by the Great Master Hazur Baba Sawan Singh.

Affirmation – A positive statement that is repeated to oneself in order to generate an uplifted mindset and positive results.

Akashic Records – The vast spiritual records in which every Soul's entire experiences are recorded.

Ani-Hu – A chant, or spiritual tone, used in MSIA. "Hu" is an ancient Sanskrit name for God, and "Ani" adds the quality of empathy and unity. See also *Spiritual Exercises* and *Tone*.

Ascended Masters – Nonphysical beings of high spiritual development who are part of the spiritual hierarchy. May work out of any realm above the physical realm. See also *Spiritual Hierarchy*.

Astral Realm – The psychic, material realm above the physical realm. The realm of the imagination. Intertwines with the physical as a vibratory rate. See also *Inner Levels/Realms* and *Psychic, Material Realms*.

Astral Travel – Occurs when the consciousness leaves the physical body to travel in the astral realm.

Aura – The electromagnetic energy field that surrounds the human body. Has color and movement.

Aura Balance – A service offered by specially trained MSIA staff members that helps to balance the aura and dispel negativity using a crystal pendulum.

Baruch Bashan (bay-roosh´ bay-shan´) – Hebrew words meaning "the blessings already are." The blessings of Spirit exist in the here and now.

Basic Self – A part of the consciousness that has responsibility for bodily functions; maintains habits and the psychic centers of the physical body. Also known as the *lower self*. Handles prayers from the physical to the high self. See also *Conscious Self* and *High Self*.

Beloved – The Soul; the God within.

Glossary of Terms

Causal Realm – The psychic, material realm above the astral realm and below the mental realm. Intertwines somewhat with the physical realm as a vibratory rate. See also *Inner Levels/Realms* and *Psychic, Material Realms*.

Christ, Office of the – The Christ is a spiritual office, much like the presidency of the United States. Many people have filled that office, Jesus the Christ having filled it more fully than any other being. One of the highest offices in the realms of Light.

Cosmic Mirror – The mirror at the top of the void, which is at the top of the etheric realm, just below the Soul realm. Everything that has not been cleared in the physical, astral, causal, and mental levels is projected onto the cosmic mirror.

Crown Chakra – The psychic center at the top of the head.

Devas – Nonphysical beings from the Devic kingdom that serve humankind by caring for the elements of nature. They support the proper functioning of all natural things on the planet.

Discourses – See *Soul Awareness Discourses*.

Doctor of Spiritual Science (D.S.S.) – a degree program from Peace Theological Seminary & College of Philosophy.

Dream Master – A spiritual master with whom the Mystical Traveler works and who assists one in balancing past actions while dreaming.

Etheric Realm – The psychic, material realm above the mental realm and below the Soul realm. Equated with the unconscious or subconscious level. Sometimes known as the esoteric realm. See also *Inner Levels/Realms* and *Psychic, Material Realms*.

False Self – Can be thought of as the ego, the individualized personality that incorrectly perceives itself to be fundamentally separated from others and God.

Great White Brotherhood – Nonphysical spiritual beings working in service to mankind in the spiritual line of the Christ and Mystical Traveler. They can assist with spiritual clearing and upliftment.

High Self – The self that functions as one's spiritual guardian, directing the conscious self towards those experiences that are for one's greatest spiritual progression. Has knowledge of the destiny pattern agreed upon before embodiment. See also *Basic Self*, *Conscious Self*, and *Karmic Board*.

Holy Spirit – The positive energy of Light and Sound that comes from the Supreme God. The life force that sustains everything in all creation. Often uses the magnetic Light through which to work on the psychic, material realms. Works only for the highest good. Is the third part of the Trinity or Godhead.

Hu – A tone, or sound, that is an ancient name of the Supreme God in Sanskrit. See also *Spiritual Exercises* and *Tone*.

Initiation – In MSIA, the process of being connected to the Sound Current of God, known as Shabd or Shabda. See also *Initiation Tone*, *Shabd*, and *Sound Current*.

Initiation Tone – In MSIA, spiritually charged words given to an initiate in a Sound Current initiation. The name of the Lord of the realm into which the person is being initiated. See also *Initiation*.

Inner Levels/Realms – The astral, causal, mental, etheric, and Soul realms that exist within a person's consciousness. See also *Outer Levels/Realms*.

Inner Master – The inner expression of the Mystical Traveler, existing within a person's consciousness.

Insight Seminars – A series of experiential, transformational seminars designed by John-Roger and Russell Bishop in 1978 to provide people with practical and accessible tools for living a successful life, based on universal truths of loving, acceptance, and personal responsibility.

Institute for Individual and World Peace (IIWP) – A non-profit organization formed in 1982 to study, identify, and present the processes that lead to peace.

John-Roger Foundation – An organization that established an annual global Integrity Day on September 24. Presented International Integrity Awards to such luminaries as Mother Teresa, Bishop Desmond Tutu, Solidarity leader Lech Walesa, Dr. Jonas Salk, and others between 1983 and 1987.

Karma – The law of cause and effect: as you sow, so shall you reap. The responsibility of each person for his or her actions. The law that directs and sometimes dominates a being's physical existence. See also *Reincarnation* and *Wheel of 84*.

Karmic Board – A group of nonphysical spiritual masters who meet with a being before embodiment to assist in the planning of that being's spiritual journey on Earth. The Mystical Traveler has a function in this group.

Light – The energy of Spirit that pervades all realms of existence. Also refers to the Light of the Holy Spirit.

Light, Magnetic – The Light of God that functions in the psychic, material realms. Not as high as the Light of the Holy Spirit, and does not necessarily function for the highest good. See also *Light* and *Holy Spirit*.

Light Masters – Nonphysical spiritual teachers who work on the psychic, material realms to assist people in their spiritual progression.

Line of the Travelers – The line of spiritual energy extending from the Mystical Traveler Consciousness, in which the Mystical Traveler's students function.

Lords of Karma – See *Karmic Board*.

Master of Spiritual Science (M.S.S.) – a degree program from Peace Theological Seminary & College of Philosophy.

Masters of Light – See *Light Masters*.

Melchizedek Priesthood/Order – Spiritual authority emanating from the Christ that originated with the Biblical high priest who met Abraham. The line of energy into which MSIA ordains its ministers. See also *Minister, Ministry,* and *Ordination*.

Mental Realm – The psychic, material realm above the causal realm and below the etheric realm. Relates to the universal mind. See *also Inner Levels/Realms* and *Psychic, Material Realms*.

Midnight Train – See *Soul Travel*.

Minister – A person in MSIA who has been ordained into the Melchizedek priesthood. *Melchizedek Priesthood/Order, Ministry,* and *Ordination*.

Ministry – The spiritually charged focus on service to self, others, community, and the world by an ordained MSIA minister. See also *Melchizedek Priesthood/Order, Minister,* and *Ordination*.

Movement of Spiritual Inner Awareness (MSIA) – An organization founded by John-Roger whose major focus is to bring people into an awareness of Soul Transcendence.

Muscle Testing – An alternative medicine practice, also known as applied kinesiology, May be used to access the unconscious, gives direction to identify issues, and clear karma.

Mystery Schools – Schools in Spirit, in which initiates receive training and instruction. Initiates of the Traveler Consciousness study in mystery schools that are under the Traveler's auspices.

Mystical Traveler Consciousness – An energy from the highest source of Light and Sound whose spiritual directive on Earth is awakening people to the awareness of the Soul. This consciousness always exists on the planet through a physical form.

Negative Realms – See *Psychic, Material Realms*.

New Day Herald – MSIA's bimonthly printed newspaper for many years. Now available only online, except for special issues.

90-Percent Level – That part of a person's existence beyond the physical level; that is, one's existence on the astral, causal, mental, etheric, and Soul realms. See also *10-Percent Level*.

Ocean of Love and Mercy – Another term for Spirit on the Soul level and above. See also *Soul Realm* and *Spirit*.

Ordination – A sacred ceremony to ordain a new minister into the Melchizedek Priesthood with a universal charge to minister to all, regardless of race, creed, color, situation, circumstances, or environment. In the MSIA Ministerial Handbook, John-Roger says, "Once a person is [approved to be] an ordained minister, there are two levels of ordination that take place. One is the fulfilling of the law; the laying on of hands ... those that hold the keys to the Melchizedek Order then communicate to other people a direct line of electric, magnetic spiritual energy. The other is the gift of Spirit through the Order of Melchizedek; the Spiritual Blessing. Almost every [minister] has the same wording [at the beginning of their] ministerial ordination. Then the Melchizedek Order stands in and says, 'And Spirit brings its blessings.' AS YOU FULFILL YOUR MINISTRY IT IS THEN THAT SPIRIT DROPS THE BLESSING IN UPON YOU." See also *Melchizedek Priesthood/ Order*, *Minister*, and *Ministry*.

Outer Levels/Realms – The astral, causal, mental, etheric, and Soul realms above the Soul realm also exist outside a person's consciousness, but in a greater way. See also *Inner Levels/Realms*.

PATs – See *Peace Awareness Trainings*.

Peace Awareness Labyrinth & Gardens (PAL&G) – The official name for PRANA since 2002; its grounds feature an embedded stone labyrinth and terraced meditation gardens that are open to the public. See also *PRANA*.

Peace Awareness Trainings *(PATs)* – A series of week-long spiritual retreats offered by Peace Theological Seminary & College of Philosophy in various locations around the world.

Peace Theological Seminary & College of Philosophy (PTS) – A private, nondenominational school founded by John-Roger as the educational arm of MSIA to present his teachings of practical spirituality that integrate the physical and spiritual worlds.

Physical Realm – The earth. The psychic, material realm in which a being lives with a physical body. See also *Inner Levels/Realms* and *Psychic, Material Realms*.

Positive Realms – The Soul realm and the 27 levels above the Soul realm. See also *Psychic, Material Realms*.

PRANA – An acronym for "Purple Rose Ashram of the New Age," a group residence and the headquarters of MSIA and PTS since 1974, located in the heart of Los Angeles near downtown. The property was renovated and renamed Peace Awareness Labyrinth & Gardens in 2002. See also *Peace Awareness Labyrinth & Gardens*.

Preceptor Consciousness – A spiritual energy of the highest source, which exists outside creation. It has manifested on the planet in a physical embodiment (such as John-Roger) once every 25,000 to 28,000 years.

Psychic, Material Realms – The five lower, negative realms; namely, the physical, astral, causal, mental, and etheric realms. See also *Positive Realms*.

Reincarnation – the repeated embodiment of a Soul onto the physical realm to clear its debts, right any wrongs, and bring balance and harmony. See also *Karma* and *Wheel of 84*.

Sant Mat – (Sanskrit) "Teachings of the Saints" or "Path of Truth," distinguished by inward, loving devotion by the individual Soul to the Divine God.

SATs – See *Soul Awareness Tape* (SAT series).

Satsang – (Sanskrit) A spiritual discourse or sacred gathering, such as when a congregation is addressed by a Master; to contemplate the Master's teachings and engage in the prescribed meditation; association of one's Soul with the Shabd or Sound Current inwardly. See also *Seminar, Shabd, and Sound Current*.

Seeding – A form of prayer to God for something that one wants to manifest in the world. It is done by placing a "seed" (donating an amount of money) for the highest good with the source of one's spiritual teachings.

Seminar – Refers to a type of Satsang (sacred discourse) to an assembly of students by John-Roger or John Morton; also, an audiotape, CD, videotape, DVD, or download of a talk either of them has given. See also Satsang.

s.e.'s – See Spiritual Exercises.

Shabd (or Shabda) – Sanskrit name for the Sound Current; the Word of God that manifests itself as Inner Spiritual Sound, as the Soul manifests in the body as consciousness. Also known as the Audible Life Stream. There are five forms of the Shabd within every human being, the secret of which can only be imparted by a True Master. See also Sound Current and Spiritual Exercises.

Simran – A Sanskrit term for Spiritual Exercises. See also Initiation Tone, Shabd, Sound Current, and Spiritual Exercises.

Soul – The extension of God individualized within each human being. The basic element of human existence, forever connected to God. The indwelling Christ, the God within.

Soul Awareness Discourses – Booklets that students in MSIA read monthly as their spiritual study, for individual private and personal use only. They are an important part of the Traveler's teachings on the physical level.

Soul Awareness Tapes (SAT series) – Audiotapes, CDs, or mp3s of seminars given by John-Roger, for individual and private study only. They are an important part of the Traveler's teachings on the physical level.

Soul Consciousness – A positive state of being. Once a person is established in Soul consciousness, he or she need no longer be bound or influenced by the lower levels of Light.

Soul Realm – The realm above the etheric realm. The first of the positive realms and the true home of the Soul. The first level where the Soul is consciously aware of its true nature, its pure beingness, its oneness with God.

Soul Transcendence – The process of moving the consciousness beyond the psychic, material realms and into the Soul realm and beyond.

Soul Travel – Traveling in Spirit to realms of consciousness other than the physical realm. Sometimes known as out-of-body experiences. This can be done in one's own inner realms or in the outer realms, the higher spiritual realms. See also *Inner Levels/Realms* and *Outer Levels/Realms*.

Sound Current – The audible energy that flows from God through all realms. The spiritual energy upon which a person rides to return to the heart of God, also known as *Shabd* or *Shabda*. See also *Shabd* and *Spiritual Exercises*.

Spirit – The essence of creation. Infinite and eternal.

Spiritual Exercises (s.e.'s) – The active practice of the Sound Current; the union of the soul with Shabd; applying the current of consciousness to hearing the Sound within; joining the mind and attention to the Sound Current through chanting a spiritual tone such as "Hu," "Ani-Hu," or one's initiation tone. Assists a person in breaking through the illusions of the lower levels and eventually moving into Soul consciousness. See also *Initiation Tone, Shabd, Simran,* and *Sound Current.*

Spiritual Eye – The area in the center of the head, back from the center of the forehead. Used to see inwardly. Also called the *Third Eye.*

Spiritual Hierarchy – The nonphysical spiritual forces that oversee this planet and the other psychic, material realms.

Spiritual Warrior – A spiritually focused person who expresses with impeccable honesty using the "sword of truth" from their heart and lives a life of health, wealth, happiness, abundance, prosperity, riches, loving, caring, sharing, and touching to others. From a John-Roger audio seminar and book of the same name.

10-Percent Level – The physical level of existence, as contrasted with the 90 percent of a person's existence that is beyond the physical realm. See also 90-Percent Level.

Third Ear – The unseen spiritual ear by which we listen inwardly and hear the Sound Current of God.

Third Eye – See Spiritual Eye.

Tisra Til – The area in the center of the head, back from the forehead and between the two eyebrows. It is here that the Soul energy has its seat and the Soul energy gathers. Because the first nine doors (eyes, ears, nose, mouth, and two lower apertures) lead outward, this is also known as the Tenth Door or Gate—the only one that leads within.

Tithing – The spiritual practice of giving 10 percent of one's increase to God by giving it to the source of one's spiritual teachings.

Tone – A spiritual sound such as "Hu," "Ani-Hu," or other specially charged word that is chanted inwardly (and sometimes aloud).

Twaji – Gaze of grace from the Spiritual Master; the gaze of God.

Universal Mind – Located at the highest part of the etheric realm, at the division between the negative and positive realms. Gets its energy from the mental realm. The source of the individual mind.

University of Santa Monica (USM) - A private, non-profit institution that pioneered a Master's in Spiritual Psychology program from 1981 to 2016, and continues to offer Soul-Centered educational courses worldwide. John-Roger was the Founder and Chancellor; John Morton serves as the current Chancellor; Drs. Ron and Mary Hulnick are USM's Co-Directors.

Wheel of 84 – The reincarnation, re-embodiment cycle. See also *Karma* and *Reincarnation*.

Windermere Ranch – MSIA's 142 acres of land in the Santa Ynez mountains overlooking Santa Barbara, California, originally established by the Institute for Individual and World Peace, which was founded by John-Roger, D.S.S.

"Contemplation for an hour is better than formal worship for sixty years."

– MOHAMMED

Appendix C

Resources

Cited MSIA Materials

Browse and order at the MSIA online store: msia.org/shop

Books

Dream Voyages (Mandeville Press, Stock #931-9)

Fulfilling Your Spiritual Promise (Mandeville Press, Stock #017-7, 3-volume set)

Inner Worlds of Meditation (Mandeville Press, Stock #977-7)

Journey of the Soul (Free download at bit.ly/journeyofasoul)

The Master Chohans of the Color Rays (Mandeville Press, out of print)

The Path to Mastership (Mandeville Press, Stock #957-2)

Psychic Protection (Mandeville Press, Stock #969-6)

Spiritual Warrior: The Art of Spiritual Living (Mandeville Press, Stock #048-1)

The Way Out Book (Mandeville Press, Stock #998-X)

Also available on Amazon; search for author "John-Roger D.S.S." or use link: bit.ly/jrdssbooks

John-Roger Seminars

Are You Listening to the Sound Current (Stock #7793)
How to Transform Yourself (Stock #7305)
Inner Voices: Diabolical or Heavenly? (Stock #8208).
Journey to the East: Israel and Egypt (Stock #3924)
Luxor Meditation for Peace and Harmony (Stock #7303)
Passages to the Realms of Spirit (Stock #7037)
Re-Creation: Conducting Divine Energy (Stock #8071)
What is Left-Sided and Right-Sided Energy? (Stock #8103)
Which Voice Do You Follow? (August '84 SAT, Stock #7082, for SAT Subscribers Only)

Moments of Peace Videos

What is Twaji?
John-Roger, D.S.S. (MOP, December 1998)
youtube.com/watch?v=wLDSseC0QhE

Resources

Windermere Peace Retreat
John-Roger, D.S.S. (MOP about the Tisra Til)
youtube.com/watch?v=aWolFtiltZg

Guardian Angels and the Sea of Galilee
John-Roger, D.S.S.
youtube.com/watch?v=UZDl9lKHDI0

From China:

Moment of Peace (MOP) in Guilin China
by John-Roger, D.S.S.
youtube.com/watch?v=WLetZWPS_us

MOP in Suzhou, China, 2000 by John-Roger, D.S.S., and John Morton, D.S.S.
youtube.com/watch?v=ru7iLKSsA0s

MOP with the Chinese people by John-Roger, D.S.S.
youtube.com/watch?v=HzrYrZOFYWI

MOP from the Li River China by John-Roger, D.S.S., and John Morton, D.S.S.
youtube.com/watch?v=Vc3AugMKf44

MOP at the Great Wall of China by John-Roger, D.S.S., and John Morton, D.S.S.
youtube.com/watch?v=qWbYcBSJpZI

Additional Moments of Peace:

Scott J-R Productions, Inc., YouTube Channel
youtube.com/channel/UCuunille3Gfg5um70WCoy8A

Full-length interviews for Mystical Traveler films:

youtube.com/channel/UCrVnsIWp6gQebAb7ha56kVA

Love of a Master 2019 Virtual Tour to Israel:

www.soultranscendence.com/new-products

"The question is, are we able to hear 'the still small voice'… and respond, 'Hineini—here I am'?"

– George Gittleman, Rabbi, Shomrei Torah Congregation

(from a sermon delivered September 1, 2011; full text at shomreitorah.org/hineini-here-i-am)

"There are dreams that we have while we're sleeping, and there are waking dreams. With waking dreams, it's important to dream positively. It makes a difference how we focus our dreams. So focus positively and dream about what you want more of."

-John Morton, D.S.S.

Ithaka

*As you set out for Ithaka
hope the voyage is a long one,
full of adventure, full of discovery.
Laistrygonians, Cyclops,
angry Poseidon—don't be afraid of them:
you'll never find things like that on your way
as long as you keep your thoughts raised high,
as long as a rare excitement
stirs your spirit and your body.
Laistrygonians, Cyclops,
wild Poseidon—you won't encounter them
unless you bring them along inside your soul,
unless your soul sets them up in front of you.*

*Hope the voyage is a long one.
May there be many a summer morning when,
with what pleasure, what joy,
you come into harbors seen for the first time;
may you stop at Phoenician trading stations
to buy fine things,
mother of pearl and coral, amber and ebony,
sensual perfume of every kind—
as many sensual perfumes as you can;
and may you visit many Egyptian cities
to gather stores of knowledge from their scholars.*

Keep Ithaka always in your mind.
Arriving there is what you are destined for.
But do not hurry the journey at all.
Better if it lasts for years,
so you are old by the time you reach the island,
wealthy with all you have gained on the way,
not expecting Ithaka to make you rich.

Ithaka gave you the marvelous journey.
Without her you would not have set out.
She has nothing left to give you now.

And if you find her poor, Ithaka won't have fooled you.
Wise as you will have become, so full of experience,
you will have understood by then what these Ithakas
mean.

(C.P. Cavafy, Collected Poems. Translated by
Edmund Keeley and Philip Sherrard.
Edited by George Savidis. Revised Edition.
Princeton University Press, 1992)

[Author's note: Recently, I met a Greek man in France who spoke this poem to me over dinner. I wept and thought of this as a metaphor for Mandeville and the Soul Realm.]

J-R and Jsu at the Conference
of the Spiritual Family, 1991

"Seek ye first the Kingdom of God, and all else shall be added unto you."

- JESUS THE CHRIST

Acknowledgments

ॐ

I'd like to acknowledge my global spiritual family who supported me through *The Love of a Master* world tour over the past three years, every person who contributed in some way to this second book, *The Dreams of a Master*, and anyone who has loved me and held me in the Light while we all healed from the physical loss of our Master.

Always first is John-Roger, for reasons way too numerous to mention, but I'll try. J-R, I so appreciate your letting me be with you this lifetime. I'd do it again in a heartbeat. Wherever you go, I'll go. You taught me so much and I'm indebted to you. I always asked you before going to sleep and I'll continue to ask: "Wanna do s.e.'s, J-R?" J-R: "Sure, you first." Jsu: "Take me with you?" J-R: "Okay." I ask to continue to walk and work with you forever, John-Roger. I love you.

Nicole Campbell, thank you, my sweet love, for your loving and holding for me during the really difficult times. You are my heart and J-R's got us always!

Elda and Delile Hinkins, I met you both years back and we became family immediately. Thank you for your love and kindness over the years and especially after Roger Hinkins, AKA John-Roger, passed. I'm forever grateful to the Hinkins' DNA instilled in my blood. Love you always.

John Morton, thank you for serving as my example of devotion to our Traveler John-Roger and continuing to show up and hold for the things he stood for. And for being my older brother. Love you.

Leigh Taylor-Young Morton, thank you for your caring and your examples of devotion. Keep smiling and shining.

Nat Sharratt, thank you to my dear brother. Love you.

David Sand, thank you for the many trips together with J-R. I appreciate all of the great images and graphics you captured to document the life of a Great Master and your friendship. Love you.

Nicia Ferrer, my mother, who gave me my strength of heart. I am grateful that you made it through your healing journey and came to Conference. I've prayed for you and Granny Rosa Rey to be taken home by J-R, and I'm so glad he's got you, Granny.

LDM, you supported John-Roger and his personal staff for many years. Personal trips, etc. I won't forget. Thank you so much for your endless and bountiful Christmas days with you and your family. I love you.

Zoe Golightly Lumiere, thanks for your endless devotion to J-R, your loyalty and the amazing ride we had. You are a true soldier and Spiritual Warrior. The mission was "Get J-R out." You never failed. Thank you. Love you.

Keith Malinsky, my friend since 1982. You lovingly did a massive job of transcribing and preserving for NOW Productions.

Acknowledgments

I really thank you for your friendship. We've come a long way. I love you, my friend.

Ron Hulnick, thanks for your support days after John-Roger passed. The lunch with the scorpion was a learning. USM was a lab that helped make my broken pieces stronger. Love you.

Mary Hulnick, I will always love your reading of the USM handouts; it truly was a beautiful reminder that it was how I loved learning from grade-school days. USM truly comes from John-Roger's teachings and he chose two masters to run it and demonstrate its love into the world.

Howard Lazar, my dear friend. Thank you for holding and encouraging me to be strong. You helped me through many tough times. Thanks for playing J-R in *The Wayshower*. Love you.

Heide Banks, thank you for your love and support to me and J-R. Thanks for your help.

Marilyn and Irwin Carasso, thank you forever for your love and support. Thanks for being there. I love you.

Laurie Lerner, appreciate your support to J-R and staff and your continued support to me. Love you forever. RJ, too.

Zane Morton, thanks for letting me be your second father. I love you. Thanks for ministering to me, son.

Clare Morton, it's so wonderful to see you grow into the real you. Love you.

Teri Breier, thank you for your patience. I'm truly grateful for your editing and ideas for *Dreams of a Master*.

Ana Arango, I listened to your father and learned that you are a unique, awesome, amazing, artist, designer angel for both *The Love of a Master* and *The Dreams of a Master*. Love to you always.

Betsy Alexander, we've worked together and I truly learned from you. Thanks for letting me borrow parts of your Glossary from FYSP. I really appreciate it. Thanks for being with John-Roger to the end. You're a warrior. I love you.

Laren Bright and Penelope Bright, you were there for me in the beginning as my J-R home seminar leaders back in 1986. You are here now, supporting my Ministry. God bless you and I love you.

Nathalie Franks, thank you for your support and I love you. You are my Lighthouse when London calls me to visit.

Barbara Wieland, you are amazing and so resourceful, and I'll always treasure the work you did for me and J-R on *Mystical Traveler*. Love you!

Phil Danza, 29 years in the same home with J-R. Thank you for being there for me at Mandeville after John-Roger's passing. I love you always.

Brooke Danza, 29 years living together ... amazing. Living with J-R was amazing. Living with the Danzas was easy. I appreciate your excellent travel agent skills that have assisted me over the years for the work. Love you.

Prez (Paul, Mark, and Vincent), thanks for holding for MSIA and John-Roger and supporting my ministry. Love you.

Jason Laskay, love you always. You served the Boss for many years, Don Jason. J-R's dogs love you forever. You are a good man; it was awesome to have known you. May God bless your passage to the Spirit realms and beyond ...

Jan Shepherd, thank you for being there when times were tough. Thanks for serving J-R and for being my Jewish mom. I love you.

Rick Ojeda, thanks for being there for J-R and me. Great times and I appreciate your devotion and dedication to the Master, love you, my brother the auxiliary staff member.

Erik Raleigh and Mark Harradine, my brothers, thank you for being there for J-R and me. Only a J-R staff member knows what that is, and I wanted to say I love you guys.

Ishwar Puri-ji, you were there and brought understanding on the inner. You also lost your master physically and allowed me to

Acknowledgments

lean on you for comfort; thanks so much for that. We are friends always. I love you.

Toshi Puri, once I saw you, we were connected. I truly appreciate how you loved and supported Ishwar in this lifetime. May God bless your inner journey to the realms above Soul. I love you.

Akash Maharaj, thank you for inspiring me and igniting my devotion to my master every time we are together, talking about the love for our masters. Love you, brother.

Nicholas Brown, thanks, brother, for all you've done for me and John-Roger and the trips we led together. Love you very much.

Marc Alhonte, thanks to you for helping, supporting and creating the freedom I needed for my ministry. Love you

Melba Alhonte, you have been the light for J-R trips to NYC. Thank you for all the continued support for *The Love of a Master* and *The Dreams of a Master*. I love you. Gracias.

Christine and Jim Lynch, thank you for the continued love and support. Love you.

Katherine and Frank Price, thank you for being there months after J-R's passing. You've always hosted J-R with love, and I felt the fellowship and love from the Prices.

Hollie and Robert Holden, thank you for your dinners and welcoming me to your warm home with your wonderful kids. I love you.

Carrie Doubts, my Project Reader, thanks to your commitment and encouragement during and outside of USM. You are Light. Love you.

Howard and Jeeni Lawrence, thank you for your love and support.

Pauli and Peter Sanderson, thank you for your Light and love. I love you.

Nancy O'Leary, thank you for your impeccable proofreading. Ana and I improve our English writing skills and grammar with you every day. You rock it!

Veronique and Babadandan, thank you for being my friends. The creative trips we have taken over the years have been a great part of my spiritual growth. Love you guys.

Wayne Alexander, thanks for being there for me.

Jesus Garcia, Dad, I love you. Thanks for being there.

Terry Garcia, my stepmother—I love you and my brothers always.

Lana Barreira, you nurtured me and took care of me. Your heart is Brazil.

Paulina Haddad, thanks for your friendship and all you've done for J-R and the kids. I see you.

Juliana Rose, thanks for letting me be me.

Rinaldo and Maritza Porchile, thank you and I love you guys.

UK Ministers, thank you for all your support and love for John-Roger and our trips.

Reymi Urrich, thanks for supporting my *Satsangs*, *The Love of a Master*, and *The Dreams of a Master*.

Yoci Touche and Mavi Lopez, thank you for your support and love.

Ozzie, Maravilla, and the rest of the Delgadillo family. I still feel Ozzie's presence every time I visit South America and see the amazing work he's helped to build. I love you and so appreciate your support of John-Roger and my ministry.

Myles and Olga Abrams, thank you both for your friendship. Myles, you are my hero; much love and Light for your Soul's journey Home.

Angel Harper, thanks for your Light and Love. I love you and appreciate your watching over me.

Timothea Stewart, love you and appreciate your artist's eye. Always my love is with you.

Steve Small, you were there in the beginning, working with J-R. I love you and appreciate your many years of supporting us.

Acknowledgments

Thank you to all the practitioners that I've witnessed over the years assisting J-R and staff. I appreciate all the teachings I observed. God bless Baraka Clinic.

Roberta and Bertrand Babinet, thank you for the many memories with J-R.

Michael and Alisha Hayes, thanks for your support to J-R and staff. Love you always.

Ed Wagner, thanks for your love and support to J-R and many in MSIA. Love you.

David and Serene Denton, I remember the love and support of J-R and me. Thank you and I love you. God bless.

Bryan McMullen, thank you for all your help and support of me.

J-R's Nurse Angels: Rodi, Trish, Joan, Nancy, Christina, Shannon, Annie, and Terri.

Lin and Larry Whittaker, thank you both for the artwork that has been my inspiration for many years. Much love and Light to you both.

Sally Kirkland, thank you for all those Hollywood events you invited J-R and me to throughout the years and for giving me a lead role opposite you. Love you.

Cate Kirby, thank you. Over the years you've made it easy for J-R and staff to travel down south. Thank you for the dedication and love for *The Love of a Master*.

Rosemarie Jeangros, thank you for supporting Cate; we needed your eyes and Light on TLOAM. Love you.

Adi de Lima Ribeiro, thank you so much for supporting *The Love of a Master* and *The Dreams of a Master;* much love to you.

Nir Livni, my Israeli brother from another mother, it was 2005 when I met you during the *Spiritual Warriors* movie. I recognize and appreciate your love for J-R in the work you do for MSIA and NOW Productions. I love you.

Sat Hari, thanks for your Light and support of J-R and staff. Love you.

Claudia Flores, Raw Warrior, you have supported J-R and me over the years. I thank you and send blessings to you and your family. Love you.

Marjorie Eaton, thank you for your continued love and support for my work. God bless you. Love you.

Alberto Arango Hurtado and Ilse Arango, my life changed when I spent a summer with you both. I so appreciate you hosting my ministry. Thanks and I love you always.

Juliana and Diego Forero, my friends, thank you for your caring and loving. Love you.

Nora Valenzuela, thank you for your love, support, and Light. Love you.

Juan Cruz, I love you, my brother from another mother.

Graciela Bordes, thank you for loving and supporting J-R in the *Mystical Traveler* film during our last trip to South America. Love you.

Susanlinn Gibson, thank you for your love and support of J-R and me.

Amy Huang, you are the Light of Beijing, China. Thank you for being my friend and translating *The Love of a Master*. This means so much to me to share the stories of John-Roger. I look forward to sharing *The Dreams of a Master* and more J-R with you in China FTHGOAC.

David and Kathryn Allen, thank you for your love and support. I enjoy meeting with you guys every year. Love you.

Martha Soto, thank you for your support in sharing J-R through *The Love of a Master*. Love you.

Marco Mejia, my brother, thank you so much! You are my hero. Love you.

Jorge Garcia, thank you for supporting me. Love you.

Acknowledgments

Mavi Sroor. Love you and thanks for the fun times in 1988 with Yoci in Egypt.

Monica Mestre, God bless you and thanks for supporting me and J-R. Love you.

Gaby Grigorescu, thank you for opening up Venezuela to the *Spiritual Warriors* and *Mystical Traveler* films and *The Love of a Master* book event. Love you.

Kaiser Petzoldt, brother, thank you for being my friend and family. Love you.

Romina Gonzalez and Gazu Mendoza, thanks for the support and love. Love you.

Wayne and Julia Pepper, thank you for your support and love for my ministry.

Andra Carasso, you have been there holding for me and supporting me in all that you are. Love you.

MJ, thank you—I really appreciate your supporting J-R and staff. Love you.

Hristina Kirimidchieva and Georgi Markov, thank you for your devotion to J-R and John and MSIA. I am grateful for all the times you hosted us, invited us to exotic locations, and gave us the freedom to be ourselves.

MSIA ministers and initiates, I love you, bless you, and ask the Travelers, Jesus Christ, John-Roger, and John Morton to walk by your side and love you through it all. I'm here to serve and continue the work. Love to each and every one of you.

*"And in that day ye shall ask me nothing.
Verily, verily, I say unto you,
Whatsoever ye shall ask the Father in my name,
he will give it you."*

– JOHN 16:23 KING JAMES VERSION (KJV)

"The Traveler is freedom, expresses freedom, and gives freedom. Because it is free, it defies definition, but we can say that its nature is love, joy, and upliftment. It brings health, wealth, and happiness on the physical level, calm to the emotional level, peace to the mental level, ability to the unconscious level, and the fulfillment of all the dreams to the spiritual level."

– JOHN-ROGER, D.S.S.
(*FULFILLING YOUR SPIRITUAL PROMISE*, VOL. 1)

About the Author

हूँ

Rev. Jesus Garcia, D.S.S., spent 26 years working for and learning from his spiritual teacher and Mystical Traveler, John-Roger, D.S.S. (known as "J-R"), founder of the Los Angeles-based Church of the Movement of Spiritual Inner Awareness (MSIA). Garcia was initiated into the Sound Current of God by John-Roger and ordained as a minister into the order of Melchizedek Priesthood by John Morton, who currently holds the keys to the Mystical Traveler Consciousness.

Garcia's first book, *The Love of a Master*—which detailed his nearly three decades as J-R's personal assistant, driver, and bodyguard—reached #1 Amazon Best-Selling status for the New Age Mysticism category in September 2017. In his second book, *The Dreams of a Master*, published in 2019, Garcia continues to take us on his journey of awakening after the passing of his beloved Traveler and friend, J-R, sharing his experiences and those of other initiates of even purer inner connection to Spirit and the Traveler than was ever realized on the physical level.

In creative collaboration, John-Roger and Garcia, a respected Hollywood cinema veteran, co-produced three feature movies: *Spiritual Warriors, The Wayshower,* and *Mystical Traveler*; and four short films, as "Scott J-R Productions." Since John-Roger's transition in 2014, Garcia has continued his ministry of sharing the spiritual teachings of J-R through movie screenings, Practical Spirituality workshops, and spiritual counseling to students and initiates of the Traveler all around the globe.

Previously, as a recognized actor, Garcia appeared on-screen in such popular films as *A Nightmare on Elm Street*, *Along Came Polly*, *We Were Soldiers*, *Spiritual Warriors*, *Collateral Damage*, and *Atlas Shrugged*. He currently resides in Santa Monica, California.

www.ingramcontent.com/pod-product-compliance
Lightning Source LLC
Chambersburg PA
CBHW031133160426
43193CB00008B/122